RESILIENCE

RESILIENCE

RESILIENCE

Queer Professors from the Working Class

Edited by
Kenneth Oldfield
and Richard Greggory Johnson III

cover photograph: *KOnfrontation* by Tina Mutschler

Published by
STATE UNIVERSITY OF NEW YORK PRESS
ALBANY

For information, contact
State University of New York Press, Albany, NY
www.sunypress.edu

Production and book design, Laurie Searl
Marketing, Anne M. Valentine

Library of Congress Cataloging-in-Publication Data

Resilience : queer professors from the working class / edited by Kenneth Oldfield and Richard Greggory Johnson, III
     p. cm.
  Includes bibliographical references and index.
  ISBN 978-0-7914-7637-6 (hardcover : alk. paper)
  ISBN 978-0-7914-7638-3 (pbk. : alk. paper)
1. Working class—Education (Higher)—United States. 2. Gay college teachers—United States—Social conditions. I. Oldfield, Kenneth. II. Johnson, Richard Greggory. III. Title: Queer professors from the working class.

LC5051.R47 2008
378.1'208664—dc22
                                 2007052317

10 9 8 7 6 5 4 3 2 1

This book is dedicated to the memories of Ms. Elsie Bilderback,

Ms. Madolyn Kimberly, and Ms. Jeanette Johnson.

Their resilience continues to inspire us.

Contents

ACKNOWLEDGMENTS

The editors thank Larin McLaughlin, Laurie Searl, and Lisa Chesnel (State University of New York Press) for their considerable support of this project. We also thank Angela Oldfield, Sandra Dahlberg, Fayneese Miller, Jackie Weinstock, Lawrence Brewster, Richard McKee, Susan Hasazi, and Kathryn Friedman for their encouragement along the way. Finally, we send a heartfelt "Thanks" to the authors for sharing their amazing stories with the world.

ONE

Introduction

KENNETH OLDFIELD,

RICHARD GREGGORY JOHNSON III

This collection of narratives has its roots in an American Society for Public Administration (ASPA) National Conference held in Washington, D.C. We were both invited panelists speaking about how our discipline, academic public administration, mostly ignores social class concerns when examining policy formation and execution. In our separate discussions, we described how public administration students receive little or no instruction about the role of socioeconomic status in the development and implementation of government programs. (For stylistic convenience, we will use "social class" and "socioeconomic status" interchangeably.) To call attention to the group's focus, the chair invited only speakers who were, like him, "working-class academics," meaning college professors whose parents were high school graduates or less and who held, at best, blue- or pink-collar jobs.

Although having never met, following our session we, the editors of this text, immediately struck up a warm and animated conversation based on our shared socioeconomic origins and common experiences as working-class academics. Almost instinctively, we started by discussing *Strangers in Paradise* (Ryan and Sackrey 1984) and *This Fine Place So Far from Home* (Dews and Law 1995), two must-read collections of essays authored almost exclusively by working-class academics.

As these books and other research show, people of poverty and working-class (hereafter simply "working-class") origins are significantly underrepresented within the professoriate. We discussed the countless published studies showing the strong relationship between social class origins and one's chances of completing an advanced degree or even finishing high school. We traded stories of how higher education abides an environment that allows professors to say things about working-class people they would never say about practically any other group. We had both heard nonchalant references to people who are "poor but honest." Certainly, if any professors offering papers at our national conference (or most other conferences) were to describe someone as "Hispanic but honest," or "African American but honest," they would have been roundly condemned, and rightly so.

We were pleased that over the last several years, higher education has become a more representative enterprise, at least on a few fronts. Many universities have been actively recruiting more women professors and faculty of color. Unfortunately, and not surprisingly, no college or university includes social class origins among its faculty diversity concerns, despite the well-established constitutionality of such plans (see Kahlenberg 1996; Oldfield 2007a; Oldfield and Conant 2001; and Taylor 1991). We found this omission especially revealing given higher education's popular image as a place of innovation and a willing opponent of the status quo. However, when it comes to social class background, most people within the university are unaware of its import, notwithstanding a substantial body of literature showing its profound effects.

Our conversation about social class flowed seamlessly. After finishing our coffee, we went for a walk and continued talking. As we traveled along the boulevard, we shared personal stories of colleagues raised in middle- and upper-class homes who tautologically and dismissively insist that once people of humble origins receive an advanced degree, they are no longer working class. The underlying assumption is that, upon finishing their studies, these individuals somehow abandon all memories of their youth, an expectation applied to no other demographic group we knew.

As various authors in *Strangers in Paradise* and *This Fine Place So Far from Home* show, instead of abandoning their pre-graduation recollections of being of humble origins, these faculty often see themselves as becoming "bicultural" as they move between their noncollege-going family and friends and their university students and colleagues. These professors evidence mind expansion, not memory loss.

The lasting effects of social class origins should be evident to anyone who knows us, for certainly most would consider us an odd pair. One (Oldfield) is a white, straight, emeritus professor of public administration at the University of Illinois at Springfield, who has been happily married to his first wife for over thirty years. The other (Johnson) is in his early forties, African American, openly gay, an assistant professor in the Educational Leadership and Policy Studies program at the University of Vermont, with dreadlocks to die for. But social class origins are a strong force, and they quickly united us in friendship.

Near the end of our walk, we started trading stories about the academy's prevalent classism versus the progress it has made on other fronts, including how openly gay students, administrators, and professors are insisting that college campuses recognize and respect them, and grant them the same rights other groups enjoy. Not surprisingly, this movement has been spawned and accompanied by a growing body of literature ranging from, for example, the unique challenges lesbian faculty members face (see Mintz and Rothblum 1997), to general writings that are finding an audience on college campuses nationwide (see, e.g., Allison 1995; Heron 1994; Kumashiro 2004; and Pratt 1991).

One story we shared was of a colleague one of us had met at a national conference. She had recently come out as both a lesbian and a working-class academic. To her surprise, she said she encountered perhaps more prejudice from colleagues because of her socioeconomic origins than her sexual orientation. Although she faced considerable homophobia, she spoke of her ongoing battle against classist comments from professors and students of higher socioeconomic origins. She said these insults were leveled against her and the working class in general. She explained that coming out as a lesbian and a working-class academic forced her to reflect more on how both her sexual orientation and her socioeconomic origins affect the way she approaches life inside and outside the academy.

This last story led us to question whether there were other professors like her who were still deeply conscious of how their socioeconomic origins and sexual orientation affect their academic relationships and their off-campus lives. We wondered whether we could attract enough contributors to compile an anthology of autobiographical narratives wherein the authors use the joint criteria of social class origins and sexual orientation to interpret their lives before and after entering the academy. (For more on the educational value of personal narratives, see Nash 2004.) We agreed the best way to answer our question was to issue a Call for Manuscripts.

The immediacy and number of responses we received surprised us. We quickly hit our target figure for contributors, and the demographic diversity of the authors was striking. They ranged in age from retirees to people still early in their careers. Some were raised in big cities while others grew up in small towns or on farms, and, as we would learn later, their religious affiliations, family situations, and sexual proclivities varied in many interesting ways. The authors taught assorted subjects and at many levels, going from English to earth science and from doctoral seminars to community college classes. There were scholars of color among the contributors, including Richard Greggory Johnson III, the volume's coeditor.[1] There was a roughly even split between male and female contributors. We were also happy to receive a proposal from a higher education administrator, who had done some college-level teaching and wanted to submit a manuscript for consideration. We encouraged her to do so.

Except for Angelia R. Wilson, all the authors included in this anthology are native born and live in the United States. We found Dr. Wilson's narrative invitingly insightful and because she was raised in Texas but eventually became a professor at a British university, we thought her "overseas" perspective would add yet another dimension to our work. As you will see, Wilson's chapter raises many provocative questions about differences in attitudes between the British and American cultures regarding sexual orientation. We agreed that perhaps others would take Wilson's writings as an incentive to produce still more texts like ours, but with an international cast of authors.

In corresponding with the contributors as they completed their narratives, it was intriguing to see how many said they found the assignment painful but therapeutic. A few mentioned they had always hoped someday they would have the opportunity to tell their story in a scholarly context, and our proposed anthology gave them that chance.

After reading all the chapters, we noticed a leitmotif running through them. While each author faced countless prejudices and setbacks, all of them, in their own distinct ways, found solace in books, school, work, family, or friends. When the going got especially difficult, they used these support systems to gain the sustenance necessary to continue. All these scholars triumphed over incredible odds to become academics. They survived because of their *resilience*, a term, interestingly, just one author mentioned, and only in passing, when describing his mettle. By then, we knew this word had to be in the book's title.

Not long ago, "queer" was a derogatory descriptor used to insult certain people. Today, a growing number of authors and commentators use this term with pride, much as African Americans began reclaiming "black" as a dignified label. James Brown's 1968 hit record "Say It Loud—I'm Black and I'm Proud" contributed mightily to this campaign for racial self-respect. Although not everyone in the "gay" community embraces "queer," the term has become so widespread that Johnson insisted we use it in the title, so we did. Perhaps our book will give the word still further credence as a statement about strength and pride.

We arranged the chapters into four categories based on either the author's teaching specialty or role as an administrator. Applying these criteria, we grouped the manuscripts as follows: physical science, language arts, social science, and governance. Even with this arrangement, we were impressed that authors writing under the same rubric had such different stories to tell, which was yet another lesson they taught us.

CONCLUSION

Ideally, this anthology will contribute to knowledge in at least two ways. First, these writings should help people in the majority comprehend how certain minority group members deal with dominant power structures. Personal narratives can help majority group members empathize with the "other" and the challenges that accompany being outside what might be called "the taken-for-granted view of what or who *should* be." In short, the writings of these authors can help readers appreciate the components of subjectivity and oppression.

Second, these narratives have a symbiotic link to quantitative studies, and vice versa. Consider, for example, that when survey research shows only one percent of the population falls in some category, this information can prompt subsequent qualitative analyses designed to improve our understanding of the lives of people in the subset. Inevitably, information gleaned from this research can stimulate still other follow-up quantitative hypotheses. This cycle repeats endlessly. Another way to appreciate this interpretation of symbiosis is to recall physicist Richard Feynman's story of how one day while eating in his college dorm's cafeteria, he watched as a student threw a plate into the air. Feynman thought he noticed a pattern in the plate's spin and later applied this insight in some of his own research. His analysis eventually earned him a Nobel Prize (Feynman 1985).

Consequential intellectual growth—the proclaimed hallmark of higher education—involves exposure to ideas and people we might rarely encounter otherwise, or at least not on their terms. These first steps into the unknown can be unsettling. There is solace in the familiar. However, comfort is seldom conducive to meaningful learning. It has been said, "Sailing ships are safe in their harbor, but that's not what sailing ships were built for." This anthology was built to carry those new to the subject to places far beyond their safe harbors and into a sea of ideas only authors like these can offer. At the end of this voyage lies the promise of an enhanced appreciation for the lives of those who have rarely been credited for the extraordinarily long race they have had to run in pursuing and maintaining their current, and well-deserved, academic stations. Perhaps the paramount lesson they teach us is how, despite the myriad hardships they faced along the way, all recount their journeys without lingering bitterness, thereby evidencing the restorative power of resilience.

NOTE

1. The other coauthor describes his working-class origins in Oldfield (2007b).

REFERENCES

Allison, Dorothy (1995). *Two or Three Things I Know for Sure*. New York: Plume.
Dews, C. L. Barney, and Carolyn Leste Law, eds. (1995). *This Fine Place So Far from Home: Voices of Academics from the Working Class*. Philadelphia: Temple University Press.

Feynman, Richard P. (1985). *Surely You're Joking, Mr. Feynman!* New York: Bantam. http://www.gorgorat.com/ (Accessed June 26, 2007.)

Heron, Ann, ed. (1994). *Two Teenagers in Twenty: Writings by Gay and Lesbian Youth.* Boston: Alyson.

Kahlenberg, Richard D. (1996). *The Remedy.* New York: Basic Books.

Kumashiro, Kevin K., ed. (2004). *Restoried Selves: Autobiographies of Queer Asian-Pacific-American Activists.* New York: Harrington Park Press.

Mintz, Beth, and Esther Rothblum, eds. (1997). *Lesbians in Academia: Degrees of Freedom.* New York: Routledge.

Nash, Robert J. (2004). *Liberating Scholarly Writing: The Power of Personal Narrative.* New York: Teachers College Press.

Oldfield, Kenneth (2007a, July). "Expanding Economic Democracy in American Higher Education: A Two-Step Approach to Hiring More Teachers from Poverty- and Working-Class Backgrounds." *Journal of Higher Education Policy and Management,* 29 (2): 217–230.

Oldfield, Kenneth (2007b, January 18). "Humble and Hopeful: Welcoming First-Generation Poor and Working-Class Students to College." *About Campus,* 11 (6): 2–12.

Oldfield, Kenneth, and Conant, Richard F. (2001). "Professors, Social Class, and Affirmative Action." *Journal of Public Affairs Edcuation,* 7(3): 171–185.

Pratt, Minnie Bruce (1991). *Rebellion: Essays, 1980–1991.* Ithaca: Firebrand Books.

Ryan, Jake, and Charles Sackrey, eds. (1984). *Strangers in Paradise: Academics from the Working Class.* Boston: South End Press.

Taylor, Stuart (1991, September 30). "A Case for Class-Based Affirmative Action." *Connecticut Law Tribune:* 18.

TWO

Class, Sexuality, and Academia

ANDREA R. LEHRERMEIER

"Andrea R. Lehrermeier" is a pseudonym. Certain names, locations, and references have also been changed to assure "Lehrermeier's" confidentiality. This
author's request for anonymity suggests that our culture is still scary enough
to force some professors to seek protection through obscurity, at least from
a wider audience.

*Sometimes I can almost convince myself I am an intellectual; other times I am a
farmer, plain and simple.* (undated entry from my personal journal, probably
from the mid- to late 1980s)

As a teacher, scientist, butch dyke, poor farm girl, and person living with
mental illness, it hasn't been easy being me. I didn't come with instructions, I
didn't see anyone before me walk this path. I didn't know what I was doing
and I didn't know where I was going. I wanted to get off; I wanted another
planet, one where things made more sense. An angry and resistant childhood
and adolescence gave way to a young adulthood of believing I could move
from poor white trash to professional, from masculine to feminine, from queer[1]
to straight, from rural to urban, from psychological torment to comfort and
privilege. It didn't work out that way.

This is my story of trying to make something work, of trying to figure
it out.

I grew up on a small dairy farm in northeastern Minnesota, the eldest of
five children. My great-grandparents on all sides of my family emigrated from
Germany in the late nineteenth century to settle and farm in the Midwest.
My dad worked the quarter-section farm owned by his mother, whose parents
gave it to her. We milked about thirty cows and grew corn, oats, and alfalfa

7

on the parts of our hilly farm that weren't too steep to till. Most income from the milk went to pay rent for the farm, so my parents worked other jobs, too. At times, we were on food stamps and received free or reduced price school lunches and free government-surplus cheese.

I helped work the farm, doing what chores I could as soon as I could be more help than hindrance in the barn. Scraping manure off the barn floor into the gutters, carrying milk buckets to the strainer and changing the filters, washing the milking machines, and later, heavier work, like making fence and bailing hay. I did housework, too—laundry, especially, and lots of peeling potatoes, washing dishes, and helping look after the younger kids.

I imagine my parents laughing reading this. I was not an enthusiastic worker. I especially hated drying dishes, whining as I slid down the cabinets, "I'm going to die!" Mom would chuckle and ask what kind of flowers I wanted on my grave, and I would shout back, "Thistles!" I would much rather read a book or, better yet, play out in the woods and fields. I was an introvert, a sensitive kid who saw beauty and mystery all around me in the natural world. I loved being outside, being a tomboy who ran and jumped and climbed and fell and got dirty, bloody, and sweaty. I loved my body moving through open space, feeling the stretch in my legs as I hurtled over creeks or rows of corn in the fields. In the fall, I would don one of my dad's John Deere caps and use one of his flannel shirts as a jacket, rolling up the sleeves so my hands could stick out at the elbows. I remember the smell of his sweat mixed with the odors of manure, sour milk, hay chaff, and tractor grease. It was the smell of strength and determination, and I wanted to cloak myself in it.

I was quite male-identified as a child. I didn't want to be physiologically male, but neither did I want to be culturally female. I wanted to inhabit my body with confidence, move freely in my clothes, and interact physically with the world around me. Although I got the message all over the place that girls were supposed to be soft and sweet and weren't expected to excel at math or science, I never believed that applied to *me*. I internalized sexism; I didn't think of myself as a real girl, and I dismissed other girls as silly and weak. With sexism, I could trick myself into believing there was escape in associating with masculinity in my community. But there was no analogous trick to escape the restraints of socioeconomic status. It was clear how poverty damaged me and *all* my kin. I couldn't just imagine my way into more material resources.

I developed my class consciousness at a very young age. I always knew that my folk were the workers, not the people in charge. From my family I learned that rich people and bosses were idiots, and life wasn't fair, but that the meek would inherit the earth. I identified with the underdog, and I saw

Jesus as a social-justice activist, sticking up for the downtrodden. A powerful historical figure who emphasized community and the life of the spirit over material gain was someone I could believe in. I wasn't especially religious; I didn't read the Bible and I didn't enjoy attending mass. But the line, "it is easier for a camel to pass through a needle's eye than for a rich man to enter the kingdom of God" gave me a special hope that, in the end, justice would be done.

When I first learned the term "social class" in grade school, the lessons weren't like those I learned at home. "Us" and "them" meant different things. I remember a teacher telling us, very solemnly, we should be grateful for what we have, that some people don't have much, that some kids have only one pair of shoes or maybe no shoes, that sometimes they don't have enough to eat. She went on, and I looked down at my red sneakers, at the faint green stain texturing the rubber of the soles, where that morning, as most mornings, I stood over the brown paper trash bag in our kitchen closet with an old butter knife, scraping off dried mud and cow shit. There was a pile of rubber boots at the bottom of the basement stairs, the pile we kids sorted through before going outside for chores, trying to find two that kind of fit, two without too many holes. But there were nearly always holes, and mud and shit would get through to my only pair of shoes, the ones I wore to church and school. I looked down at my red canvas sneakers and thought it suspicious I was being taught about myself in the same way I was taught about other strange and different things, like sea turtles.

From then on, it seemed the subject of social class kept coming up in school. We'd talk about poor people as if they were "those people" somewhere "out there." Students from middle-class homes would pipe up and volunteer that poor people were poor because they wanted to be, they deserved their fate because they were stupid and too lazy to work hard. I'd think of my parents, running a farm, working as "unskilled" labor and cleaning houses, taking care of other people's children and elderly parents. I'd think of my mom, who wanted to go to high school but at fourteen years of age was forced by her father to work as a domestic and sign her paycheck over to him each week to help support her siblings, a dozen and counting. I'd think of my dad's ingenuity, fixing things with spit and bailing wire, the men at his job calling him MacGyver.[2] I'd fume inside and imagine the soft bodies of my classmates collapsing in a trembling heap after half an hour doing chores on my farm. Insult was added to injury when I learned that many of them received a weekly cash allowance for cleaning their rooms and taking out the trash. I thought they were morons.

It was also difficult for me when we were given homework that required resources beyond the classroom. The first time we were assigned to bring in a current interest article from a newspaper or magazine, I made the mistake of asking the teacher what to do if you didn't have any newspapers or magazines at home. She told me I needed to find a better excuse for not doing the assignment because everyone has newspapers and magazines. Other projects had me swearing in frustration, trying to make something out of nothing. My parents read children's books to us when we were little, but we didn't have many other books in our house. We had *Good News for Modern Man* (1966) and a coverless paperback dictionary with most of the a's and all of the z's missing. I checked out a lot of books from the bookmobile in the summer and the school library during the rest of the year. I remember especially lusting after the reference books, the large hard-covered dictionaries and the rows of gilded encyclopedias. When I was a bit older, my parents splurged on a *World Book Encyclopedia*, bought on time. I had never bought a book, so I had no idea back then how expensive this purchase was and how much of a sacrifice it was for my parents to make that investment in our educations. Many family photos after that show me with an open volume on my lap, looking up and scowling into the camera at the interruption. Mom swears I took the thickest one to a drive-in theater once, just in case I got bored with the movie.

Sometimes I think I might never have gone into academics if I had been straight. When I was a kid, I didn't know I was a lesbian, but I knew for certain I would never get married and never have kids. What followed was the realization I would need to support myself financially. The only single women I knew were widows, nuns, and teachers, and the only thing I knew I was good at was getting good grades in school. I wasn't sure at all what the future held for me, but if I were to avoid marrying the boy next door, it looked like education was my best bet out.

Although I eventually focused on science, my earliest aspirations were to be a writer. At ages nine and ten, I wrote adventure stories of a self-sufficient young boy who went off exploring the world on his own. I was further inspired by my fourth grade teacher, Ms. Smith, who read us stories and encouraged us to write our own. I didn't realize it then, but, looking back, I think she was my first crush. She had smiled at me the first day of school; I was a tomboy in a beige 1970s girl's polyester pantsuit, my arm in a cast from rough-and-tumble play that summer, waiting in line with all the other kids before classes began. The way she looked at me was scary, not because it was creepy, but because I was used to being invisible, and it seemed she really *saw* me. Her gaze didn't just bounce off my surface; the smile in her eyes went right into me and said hello. Shocked at something getting through my defensive shield, I gasped and looked away, flushing red.

Many other rural kids attended my elementary school, located at the edge of town. I had a few friends, and most people in my classes knew me to some extent. The most aggressive of the bullies refrained from physical attack, perhaps because they observed my rough play with boy buddies at recess. But things got worse when I moved to a very large junior high school in Mc-Carrierville to start seventh grade. My friends from grade school went to the other public junior high in town, so I started off alone, without social support. Extreme shyness, my inherent distrust of middle-class kids, and working-class kids' apparent distrust of my intellectualism made it hard to connect with others in my classes. I was a loner, and a target. Bullies stole my notebooks and pens, pushed me, elbowed books out of my arms in stairwells, stepped on the backs of my shoes, threw spitballs at me, and sometimes threw much larger objects. On the school bus, icy snowballs broke my glasses, and I was knocked unconscious from a blow on the back of the head from a full can of pop.

I used to sneak out of the bedroom I shared with my sisters and sit on the stairs in the middle of the night, and, illuminated by the hallway light, I'd write. Muffling my sobs, I'd pour my confusion into my diary, hot tears dripping on the pages as I wondered, "Why?" Why were they hurting me when I did nothing to them? Was it because I was a tomboy, because I was a poor dumb farmer, because I wore worn clothing, because I was a science geek, because I was Catholic and taught to turn the other cheek?

I am reminded of my adolescent fantasies of being the six million dollar man and picking up my tormentors with one arm and flinging them across the room. They would hit the wall and slide to the floor in a heap and know firsthand my might and power and never bother me or anyone else again. (journal entry, December 5, 1991)

But I never fought back, I rarely even spoke up. I felt like I was from another planet, alienated even in my own family. Many of my lesbian friends say, "I always knew I was different" when they speak of their childhood. No doubt, part of my feelings of difference was due to my sexual orientation and gender rebellion, but there were other roots to that feeling. I loved my family and felt fiercely loyal to them, but I ached with loneliness. Somehow, I learned at a very young age that I was utterly on my own; I could not expect help or comfort from adults in issues that mattered most, concerns that seemed life or death to me at the time. I don't remember details of the circumstances that may have triggered that response, but I do remember shutting myself off, retreating deep inside where I hoped pain could not reach me. I remember practicing playing dead, breathing shallowly, and trying not to move much when I lay down to sleep. I remember alternately giving into and retreating in shame from the violent images that arose with sexual feelings. I built up a thick shell, practiced not feeling being hit by the things other kids threw at me just as I practiced not feeling cold when my coat was too thin for the winter. Just as I practiced not feeling my own feelings of longing and loss.

I was solid as a rock, stubborn to the core.

When I was a senior in high school, I was invited to a Chamber of Commerce banquet to honor top students who would be the future leaders of the community. I declined. I was not going to get dressed up in nice clothes I did not have, didn't even want, and couldn't afford anyway, be picked up by some well-to-do white businessman and his charming wife who would likely arrive ticked off that they were the ones picked to drive thirty miles out of their way to our small muddy farm, go to a dinner where I would not know the rules of which fork when, and be praised for my excellent scholarship when I was certain that they would have no clue about what learning and intellectual inquiry meant to me. It certainly did not mean that I was aspiring to become like them; I resented like hell that implicit assumption. (undated journal entry, probably from the late 1980s)

One theme persisted throughout my adolescence: I would not become "them." I would not "dress up and smile more"—my football-coaching history teacher's only advice during an academic conference. I would not play down my intelligence to be less intimidating to boys, as another male teacher suggested. If being me meant I'd have no friends, so be it. I was not about to pretend to have the same interests as my middle-class schoolmates, just to get them to try to like me (at the time I viewed it in terms of class, but in retrospect it's clear much of it was related to gender and sexual orientation, too). I was angry I had to live in their world during the schoolday, but they had no idea what my life was like.

I'd overhear other honors students talking about me: "Of course she can get straight As—all she does is study! She doesn't participate in any after-school activities, and she doesn't have a part-time job." As far as I could tell, they weren't working to help support their families—they were working to put gas in cars their parents gave them.[3] They had no idea of the hard work I did on our family farm, no idea our family had one car, no idea my working a few hours at McDonald's would have cost my family the time and money of shuttling me back and forth to town.

I used to fantasize that one of my clueless classmates would be out for a drive in the country with his family when their car would break down in front of our lane. We'd be milking, but Dad would stop to help them. I'd amble out of the barn and head up the hill. Me in my tank top, my tan muscled arms gleaming with sweat and faintly coated with chaff and dust, the smell of manure about me. I'd entertain the kid while dad went off to fix the car. I'd offer him a drink of water, go over to the pump, take the upside-down mason jar off the top of the post, pull the pipe leading to the cistern aside, and let one or two big splashes fill the jar. I'd hand it to him and watch his face. Watch his eyes grow wide as he decided whether to drink it. I'd hock up a loogey and spit to the side, clearing the dirt and chaff from my nose and throat. I'd be in my element, and he'd be trapped on unfamiliar turf with different rules.

Enjoying the beauty of the natural world provided one means of escape for me. Even on the bus on the morning ride to school, I would sit, forehead pressed to the window glass, smiling at the sunrise, the way the mist lifted off the streams, or the patterns of the dew on the grass. Other kids taunted me, "Whatcha staring at, huh? You in love with the window or something?" This was just another way I was not like my peers. I didn't even know any adults who felt the way I did until I took an earth science class in ninth grade and heard the teacher talk about how the closest things he had to religious experiences were out in the wilderness. I didn't know at the time that was almost a cliché. I thought it profound. I thought I had found a kindred spirit.

He was an environmentalist, a backpacker who liked a lot of other outdoor activities, too, like canoeing and caving. He encouraged my interest in geology, looking at the rocks and fossils I brought in from my collection at home. He paid attention to me, seemed to really listen to what I was saying. With him, I felt I could really connect, something I didn't seem to be able to do with my classmates. I started to think of him as a mentor and even a friend.

"Educator sexual misconduct," I later heard it called. I wanted his attention, his affection; I sought it out. I did not seek out sex, though. He started fondling me at night around the campfire on school camping trips. I froze, feeling both pleasure and revulsion, knowing it was wrong, but thinking perhaps it was a sign he really did care for me. "Maybe he loves me," I thought, and I told myself I loved him. Shortly after I graduated from high school, while on a hike on his property by the river, he kissed me, pushed himself up against me, and when I hung my head he lifted my chin with his hand, saying, "Chin up, kiddo; people do this kind of thing all the time, all the time." I think he meant, "Commit adultery," which was bad enough, but it was so sad and so true that male teachers do this with teenage female students, all the time, all the time.

After having sex with me the first time, he rolled off and said he couldn't believe I had never done that before.

School was hell in so many ways, but I loved learning. When I began talking about going to college, my parents started to think of ways to tell me I couldn't go. "People like us" just didn't do that. But I applied and got financial aid, so off I went to Minnesota State University, less than two hundred miles away from the farm. My parents thought it might as well be the moon.

Although I had scholarships, grants, loans, and work-study, I still struggled financially. My budget for things beyond tuition and room and board was a fraction of my classmates.' In a spiral notebook, I kept track of every penny spent. My calculus teacher was flabbergasted by my refusal to apply to Pi Mu Epsilon, a mathematics honor society. How could I not want to be recognized and honored for my talents? The fee was seemingly insignificant to her, but to me it was a hefty percentage of my spending money for the semester. The dorms didn't serve supper on Sunday night, so if my projections showed money going out too fast, I'd eat a big lunch and stuff some extra rolls in my backpack. I know when I repeatedly declined invitations to go out for pizza with other students they must have wondered if I was stuck up, but it was easier to let them think me aloof than try to explain.

But in college, even with the class differences, I began to feel like I almost belonged somewhere. I was enjoying the intellectual stimulation, and I was finally meeting people more like myself, making friends with other science geeks in the honors program. I started to feel more normal. But then I'd get thick envelopes in the mail from my high school teacher, long letters stuffed with newspaper clippings annotated with sexual innuendo and jokes. He'd come visit me on my college campus, take me to a cheap motel on Saturdays when my roommate was out of town and not around to miss me, and drop me back at my dorm the next morning where I would go stand in the shower and cry for a long time.

While this was going on in college, I realized, for the first time, I was not straight. Giving a backrub to a female friend, I noticed my hands wanted to go other places, that something was springing to life in me. It was desire, sexual desire; not just sexual stimulation, but a longing and a fire and something that felt very, very good and resonated in my core.

Which, of course, freaked me out to no end. Here I was just starting to feel "normal," starting to feel like, maybe, I could even do something to get myself out of the situation with my teacher, and then that happened. I ran away. It wasn't a conscious or calculated decision, but I convinced myself I was bisexual and decided the young man I was interested in becoming good friends with could be more than that to me.

"Andrea's got a boyfriend! Andrea's got a boyfriend!" I hate being teased. And it sounds so strange, anyway—"boyfriend." David is my friend. He is like me in many ways—mainly in that he doesn't like to play "games" and doesn't like getting too involved with superficial things. But he is different than me, too, which is good. We can learn a lot from each other. I think it would be neat if this relationship works and lasts. (journal entry, March 20, 1984)

A few weeks and a few pages later, I scribbled, *"Dreams and restless thoughts . . . I am in a period of questioning—I am left without a framework upon which to stand for I know not what it is I believe."* I drew a bold line beneath it, and, in more legible writing, later that same day noted, *"I think this summer I'll write lots of letters to David— 'love letters' of a sort but not really."* One more entry after that, and the rest of my college journal is left blank.

David and I coordinated our search for graduate school, applying to the same places, or at least to places in the same city. When David, who was now my roommate, met me at my P-Chem class and handed me an acceptance letter from my top choice, Prestigious Private University (PPU), it felt like the happiest day of my life. We both were awarded National Science Foundation Graduate Research Fellowships, and we both accepted our offers to study at PPU. We loaded up a moving van, drove to Boston, rented an apartment together, and a year later tied the knot in the chapel on campus and moved into married student housing.

For a shy Minnesota farm girl, the move from small midwestern college town to large East Coast city was, needless to say, a bit of a culture shock. As a kid, I couldn't even handle riding the city buses in McCarrierville—when I stayed with my grandma after school, I'd rather walk for an hour than try to negotiate public transportation—and suddenly I found myself riding subways. Sometimes, emerging into an urban canyon, I'd poke fun at myself. I'd put one hand on top of my head, pretending to keep my feedstore cap from falling off as I looked up and exclaimed, "Golly! We ain't even got *silos* 'at high in Minne-soo-tee!" Once, at a party on the roof of a brick apartment building on Rudolph Hill, I called the cows. Opened up, just like I was facing west up into the pasture at 4:30 in the afternoon, and let it out, strong and loud: Kaah Baahsss, Kaah Baahsss, Kah Baaaaahsss![4]

With my fellowship stipend, I was making more money than my parents' combined income. I even had a credit card before my folks got one. Shortly after getting married, I decided I'd like to buy a nice silk robe for my husband. I didn't think I'd be able to find one in the kind of store I usually shopped, so I headed across the river to Barr's. The sales associates in the gleaming store weren't at all helpful. Harsh eyes burned into my back, following me, waiting for me to make my move and confirm their suspicions. A security guard showed up a few minutes after I arrived. I couldn't decide what to do. Why would I want to give my money to a place like that? But I didn't want to be run off, either. I bought the robe, maintaining stony eye contact during the transaction, even when asked to show my identification with my credit card.

There wasn't much escape within the walls of the ivory tower. The classist comments that seemed to have let up in college came back with a vengeance at that elite institution. When one of the geology professors heard I was from a farm in Minnesota, he groaned, "Oh, god! I hope she doesn't bring her pig!" A fellow student, leisurely strolling through the hallway, late to class, gestured with his coffee cup to a group of physical plant workers sitting down on break, exclaiming, "Look; *that's* where our tuition money goes!" Friday afternoons the students in my program were invited to tea in one of the lounges. I tried to attend a few times, but I was too uncomfortable. Listening in on an amusing anecdote of how some oaf confused two different kinds of cheese, I didn't know how to respond. Should I pipe up and share that the free government-surplus cheese I had eaten a few years before didn't come as Brie or Boursin? It was easier to spend that time working in the lab.

Although I did feel privileged to be studying at one of the most prestigious universities in the world, grad school wasn't turning out to be the enriching intellectual experience I had expected. I was idealistic and had many interests, but as I finished my coursework and spent more time in the lab, my training felt more like drudgery. Another student described working in our research group to be a cross between working in a factory and memorizing a phone book. I had been hoping to escape that kind of life. In my journal a few months before defending my dissertation, I wrote, *"In a world of extremes, where long hours of exhausting effort with little time for outside interests is both the price of success and the cost of failure, where am I to turn?"*

I came to see high-powered scientific research as more about ego trips than curiosity-driven quests for knowledge and exploration. It seemed that for many people I was meeting, asking new and interesting questions wasn't the point as much as publishing a paper that would prove you were smarter than the other guy. And it was mostly guys. Up to then, I had thought of myself as an exceptional woman, ignoring or not even noticing the sexism around me. But in graduate school, something finally snapped. I couldn't pretend anymore that nothing was wrong. Some male advisors slept with their female students. Other male advisors belittled their female students' intelligence and questioned their suitability for science, only to turn around and go out for beers with male students who got lower grades in courses and screwed up experiments in the lab.

I was in turmoil. I was disillusioned with science, but I had so much invested in the goal of getting a PhD. My attraction to women kept growing stronger, even though I tried to push it away so I could stay with my husband, so that together we could have a nice middle-class life after finishing school. I wanted to *pass*. I was a dykey poor white-trash German-American Catholic woman who wanted all the goodies of straight white middle-class Anglo-Saxon Protestant men. I was so conflicted. I started to slip into a major depressive episode. On scraps of paper stuck into one of my journals from the late 1980s, I found

Sometimes I wish I could give my conscious a lobotomy. Recently I fantasized about voting for Pat Buchanan for president, joining the Young Republicans, and making as much money as possible. I see people who seem so confident, so assured of their rightful place in the world, and at times I feel I would give anything to feel that way, too. If I could only, snip snip, sever those connections in my mind, cut away those parts of my heart, if only I could sit back and enjoy my privileges in peace. I am existing in middle ground between working class and middle class, blue collar and professional, gay and straight, rural and urban.

And,

I think it must be harder to kill a part of yourself than to kill your whole body. You can't decide to murder part of your personality and then just have it instantaneously cease to exist. You have to find a way to kill it, then do it, and then it takes time for it to die. And, even worse, a part of you remains alive, not only to wait for it to die, but to feel that sense of "Uh, oh . . . why did I do that?" which you feel at the moment just after you've done something really stupid and irreversible, like jumping off a cliff. That feeling would be frozen in time and then stretched out to last your entire life.

I felt if I were to be successful, I would have to become someone else, do the very thing I had resisted so strongly in high school. I tried to go through with it. I tried to take a deep breath, steel myself, square my shoulders, and cross over into that brave new world. But it didn't work. About a quarter of the way through a clothbound journal from 1988, this is the last entry:

I feel like no one believes the seriousness of my condition. I go from thing to thing in my daily life, and even the smallest seems a struggle. But I am expected to be able to do them with no problem. I have tremendous willpower. If this were only a matter of will I could do it. But something is seriously wrong with me and I'm scared and I need help. (journal entry, February 22, 1988)

I didn't know where to ask for help, but luckily help found me. When I went in to the student health center that semester for my annual pelvic exam, the doctor walked into the room and asked how I was doing. I burst into tears. She told me to get dressed; we would do the exam another time, and she would make an immediate appointment for me with one of the therapists on staff.

That was the first time I had any help dealing with my dysthymic disorder. I took a leave of absence, went back to Minnesota for a time, and lived with my parents. They didn't know what to do with me, how to help. All I wanted to do was sleep. One day my dad practically dressed me in winter clothes and dragged me over to the ski area where my mom worked. He rented skis for me, put my boots on, helped me step into the bindings. He practically pushed me toward the slope, stayed with me, helped me up when I fell. I cried and wailed and he said, "Get up! Ski!" I hated it, didn't want to be there, but I knew he was loving me the only way he knew how at the time; he was trying to get me back into the world, he was trying to keep me moving. He didn't want me to lie down and give up and die.

I didn't want to die either, but I was so tired, and I couldn't see what there would be for me on the other side of this. I knew grad school was hard on a lot of people; even my straight, white, middle-class husband remarked that in getting into PPU, "We lived our dream, and our dream was hell." But I think a lot of my peers had a sense of entitlement that enabled them to picture their rightful place in the world after school. I had no idea what lay ahead for me. I couldn't imagine myself as a lesbian, alone, supporting myself. What kind of work could I get if I couldn't be a professor? How could I hold down a job of any kind living with depression? Where would I go? Where would I ever feel I belonged? I never had much of a clear idea of what my life would be, but this was turning out much worse than I had expected.

I feel like I have come to a screeching halt, a dead end. I feel I had so much promise, that I came screaming out of Minnesota like a locomotive and slammed with great force into a brick wall. PPU was not the type of learning and growing experience I had expected. It schooled me in cynicism. I came to hate academic science. I came to fantasies of blowing my brains out with a gun because I imagined my intelligence was causing me so much pain. I wanted to destroy myself because I thought I was the problem. (journal entry, December 6, 1991)

After several months off, I managed to recover enough to go back and finish my dissertation. I wanted that damn degree, that piece of paper with prestige attached, and I had come too far to give up. I put my head down and plowed forward, working long hours. But sometimes, usually in the middle of the night as I sat in the computer room on the sixth floor of the White Building, the feeling would come over me: I wish I were baling hay. I hated bailing hay when I lived at home. I hated going down into the basement to the box on top of the dryer and sorting through the pile of Dad's leftover, mostly left-handed, holey cotton gloves, putting two on each hand, trying to pick them so the holes were in different places. Emerging from the cool basement into the bright July or August heat in tennis shoes, jeans, and tank top, my hair tied back in a ponytail. My sister Angela wanted to make a game of it, putting the bales on the elevator, but I liked using anger better. Anger produced adrenaline and gave me strength. I'd think of something that pissed me off, growl and grab the twine, jerking the bale up and bouncing it against my right leg as I hobbled it to the ramp leaning against the wagon. Sharp edges of the cut alfalfa pricked the skin on the inside of my forearms, irritating them polka dot red. Hay chaff stuck to whatever was wet and filtered into every crevice of my body. Rivers of sweat ran between my breasts and down the small of my back. I hated it, I absolutely hated it, but in the middle of the night, working on my dissertation, I wanted to be baling hay. At least hay baling is real work. At least you sweat. At least you can see the reason behind it. It's hard, but it has a point. What was the point of my dissertation, anyway?

I had a hard time finding a job after that; I wanted a job where teaching was emphasized, but since my degree was from a high-powered research institution, none of the search committees at liberal arts institutions believed me enough to give my applications a second look. My lack of teaching experience beyond a few semesters as a T.A. wasn't helping much, either. I was unemployed for a while, volunteering as a science and math tutor at a community college while my husband supported us on his post-doc salary at the Lewton Lab. I had a lot of time to run, ride my bike, cry, read, write, think. I took women's studies courses at the University of Texas, making the three-hour drive twice a week. I continued to try to figure out what to do with my life.

I've been reading a book called Strangers in Paradise: Academics *from the Working Class* [Ryan and Sackrey 1984]. *I also went to the UT library today and read some of Vivian Gornick's* Women in Science [Gornick 1983]. *Both depress the hell out of me. All the troubles that people from the working class have in academia; all the troubles women have in science. I'm screwed. The academic environment seems hostile to my values (not that government or industry would be any better). The life stories in both books are often angry, telling of the process of their disillusionment. I can relate to that. I, too, am disillusioned. But, do I want to chuck it? Do I want to concede science to assholes, academics to middle- and upper-class folks who have little interest in really changing the world? Am I too much of a feminist to be a scientist? Am I too much of a scientist to be anything else? Am I too much of an intellectual to do any actual, concrete work?* (journal entry, October 1, 1991)

Eventually I found a two-year post-doctoral position in another city, and, separated from my husband by distance, I finally had the courage to come out. It wasn't an easy decision. My husband grieved the loss of the life he thought we were going to have together, but he turned out to be amazingly supportive. Still, I knew that ultimately I would lose his friendship. And I had no idea what would happen with my family back home.

Home. Standing on the limestone ledge in the pasture, wearing my leather jacket, the same style I bought for my husband for his thirtieth birthday the year before. Thinking about this last Christmas together, thinking about how the shit is going to hit the fan soon, thinking about my new girlfriend, standing, thinking about growing my dyke feet into the earth, into this place, soaking my queer identity into this ground, absorbing as much of this place into myself as I can, just in case . . . just in case I am not welcome back for a while. (journal entry, December 1993)

When I finally did come out to my parents, I came to visit in person, to tell them I was getting divorced, and explain why. My car was packed and pointed out of the driveway, the key in the ignition. I had a reservation for a motel room in town, in case I needed it. I went so far as to make sure the guns weren't loaded; I really had no idea what would happen. But, when I told them, they just cried and hugged me and said they loved me. A few years later, my mom even helped start a P-FLAG chapter in McCarrierville.

Coming out was a turning point in unexpected ways. I was still struggling with my identity and with depression. I was still afraid of trying to make it in the world on my own. But eventually I realized that if my life were to be struggle, I might as well be fighting *for* myself rather than against myself. At one point, when I was wrestling with the decision, I imagined myself ninety years old, sitting on a rocker on my porch, looking out at the sunset and looking back at my life. What did I want to look back on? There was no debating myself after that; my choice was clear. And I found that in embracing my sexual identity, I could more easily embrace my class identity as well. In my social circle, I didn't know any other academics from working-class backgrounds who were "out and proud" about that, but I was finding plenty of role models in the lesbian community who were showing me how to be out and proud as a dyke. I took a deep breath, squared my shoulders, and stepped across, not with dread into a living death, but with a smile and a swagger out into the open. I felt taller, more solid. I claimed my space. I was still plenty angry at social injustices, but eventually I noticed amusement replacing self-anger and shame when I found myself on unfamiliar turf or confronted with classist comments.

My friends and our hosts, friends of my friends, are talking about Berkeley and some Ivy League school out East and the wine and wine-tasting. . . . The wine is very good, I agree, a Chardonnay from some vineyard in California, but I don't care about the terms "dry" or "fruity." I can't help thinking about a big glass jug of Mogen David in the refrigerator "back home," or of the white and red Old Milwaukee beer cans Dad used to toss down the basement steps when he was done. I drift away from the conversation and lean back and try not to grin too much. There's only so much I can take of speaking this second language of my nonnative culture. I daydream in my first language. I'm grinning because I am thinking of resting my delicately stemmed wine glass on my belly and enjoying the vibrations of a well-delivered belch in my chest and throat. (undated journal entry from the early 1990s)

Nowadays, with both class and sexual orientation, it would be *possible* for me to pass as a member of the dominant group. In neither do I want to pass, but I find it's easier being obvious about being lesbian. I can wear lesbian symbols on buttons, T-shirts, jewelry. I can talk about my partner. Straight academics can usually figure out I'm not straight, and either they turn out to be tolerant or accepting of homosexuality or they just decide not to express their homophobic opinions in front of me. But I don't know what symbol to wear to signify that I come from a poor and working-class background. People from the middle and upper classes repeatedly assume I must be "one of them," that I couldn't possibly be or come from "those people" because I don't immediately look or act like they think "those people" do. Or maybe they think I have lived the American Dream, that, even if I came from the lower class, I "applied myself," worked hard, and moved up and out and left all that happily behind.

At my first post-doc, when one of the graduate students learned where I earned my PhD, the conversation shifted to how he had been accepted at an Ivy League institution, but chose to come to Bucolic University, even though it was in the hick Midwest, because it was better for his area of study. I told him I was a midwesterner myself, and I took exception to his comment. He tried to back off by clarifying, "You know, I mean the *rural* people are hicks." I told him I was from a rural area. He tried again, "Well, you know, the uneducated ones, the rednecks." I maintained eye contact and smiled and said, "You realize I come from rednecks, that my folks have eighth grade educations." He gave up and excused himself.

When I came out as lesbian, I discovered I was more able to own my class background with pride. Ceasing to hide one aspect of myself made it easier to come out in all kinds of ways, including being open about my struggles with mental illness. But I think that coming from a working-class background in the first place was what made it relatively easy for me to come out in academia. Some gay and lesbian academics from middle-class backgrounds are extremely closeted at work. I haven't talked to them in depth about it, but I'm guessing they're afraid of losing something. Losing their jobs, or not being able to get a job, being looked over for grants and awards. Afraid of losing their rightful place in the academy. I never had a rightful place to lose, so why be shy about it?

What I *did* have to lose was my sense of self. When we were growing up, my sister Angela would ask me, "Andrea, why are you so angry?" I realize now that it was not only my differences but my anger that kept me so isolated. There were a few who tried to reach out to me, but I would have had to reach out pretty far to meet them, too, and I was afraid of losing my balance and losing myself. My siblings didn't have as rough a time in school as I did. I know at least some of them think I helped pave the way for them: "If Andrea can go to college, we can too." And they all did, with eight degrees among the four of them. But I suspect also that their straightness may have given them a foothold into their sense of place in the rest of the world, when, for me, there was nothing like that on which to stand.

Now I'm a tenured associate professor at a diverse urban university. There aren't a lot of other butchy, geeky, white-trashy, half-crazy ex-Catholic Minnesota farm girls running around, but there aren't a lot of any one type of person running around, either. Within this diverse environment, I feel more at home than I have in any other academic setting.

I don't want this to be a happily ever after story—all you have to do is persevere and things will turn out okay in the end. Mine is not the story of an exceptional individual who overcame great obstacles to emerge victorious. Like this is a race? Like this is over? Thinking like that is all part of the same myth that has the privileged among us sitting back, self-satisfied in the belief they've earned what they inherited, while those among us who know better, those whose efforts would change the world, use too much energy for survival, for resisting the message that maybe *our* dreams really do deserve to die.

How many people with similar stories aren't here anymore to tell theirs? I didn't even want to tell mine. It's been hard on me, going back and revisiting my history, sorting through that box I keep in my closet, all those words of anguish poured out in pain and desperation onto anything I could find—spiral notebooks, napkins, the backs of envelopes.

I'm finding it hard to write, almost impossible. I have a pile of scraps; I conceive brilliant ideas and abort my scribblings halfway down a page of dull nonsense. It's slippery. I can't get a handle on it . . . It may be easier just to chuck it—not write at all. But I'm filled with restless energy—some physical thing is trying to erupt from my body, and it's work keeping it in. (journal entry from 1988)

I didn't want to write this. A half dozen times I decided to quit. But Dorothy Allison wrote, and Gloria Anzaldúa. And Audre Lorde and Adrianne Rich. Ferron wrote songs and sang them. These women and others put their stories, their ideas, their words into the world, and somehow I found them, and they helped keep me alive.

NOTES

1. I don't use "queer" to describe myself now, but it's the closest word to express how I thought at that time in my life.

2. MacGyver was the main character from a television show broadcast on ABC in the late 1980s to early 1990s.

3. To be fair, many were probably saving some money so their parents wouldn't have to pay their entire college cost.

4. Contraction of "Come (here), bossy." Bossy is a nickname for cows.

REFERENCES

Good News for Modern Man (1966). New York: American Bible Society.

Gornick, Vivian (1983). *Women in Science: Portraits from a World in Transition*. New York: Simon and Schuster.

Ryan, Jake, and Charles Sackrey, eds. (1984). *Strangers in Paradise: Academics from the Working Class*. Boston: South End Press.

THREE

Middle-Class Drag

RENNY CHRISTOPHER

Prior: She has . . . well, she has eight vaginas.

Angel: Regina Vagina! Hermaphroditically equipped as well with a Bouquet of Phalli . . .

Prior: God split the World in Two

Angel: And made YOU:

Prior and Angel: Human Beings. Uni-Genitaled: Female. Male.

— Tony Kushner, *Angels in America: Perestroika*

A WORKING-CLASS BOY

I grew up a working-class boy, dressing in cowboy clothes, playing with my toy Winchester rifle (later a BB gun, later still a .22 rifle), my bow and arrow, my GI Joe. I played with toy tools my dad gave me until he taught me to use the real ones, and then I worked construction with him from the time I was eleven or twelve until I left for college at seventeen.

There were only two problems with this working-class boy's childhood: first, I wasn't actually a boy, anatomically speaking, and, second, for every hour I spent playing with guns and tools, I spent three or four hours with my nose "stuck in a book," as my mother called it, working on becoming a nerdy intellectual, which was not an appropriate activity for a good working-class boy (or girl, for that matter). Thus, I always felt divided and different, and my internal feeling was reinforced by how people responded to me.

My mother was the first to tell me I was gay, long before I had any idea, and she was also the first person to tell me I should go to college, long before I had any idea of going. She had known many gay people, including her cousin and several aunts, and if I were gay, that was no big problem for her. But she'd never known a college graduate, and she had no idea what a problem that would be, as I became more and more of an alien to my family through my pursuit of higher education.

My mother was an only child, daughter of a father who was a mechanic and a mother who worked factory jobs and ironed shirts in a laundry. Both were alcoholics and lived on the wild side, partying, hanging out in bars, sleeping around. My mother's cousin, Elaine, two years older than she, was more like a sister to her than a cousin. I don't remember the first time I heard my mother talk about Elaine, who died before I was born; it feels like I've always heard about her, from my earliest childhood. The story goes like this: Elaine was brilliant, far smarter than anyone else my mother ever knew. She could draw and play the piano by ear; she was athletic and unhappy. She put the stock of a shotgun on the floor, put her head on the end of the barrel, and pulled the trigger with her toe when she was thirty-four years old. There's another element to the story and, again, I don't remember a time when I didn't know this part, so I don't know how old I was when my mother started including this piece: Elaine was a lesbian. My mother's explanation for Elaine's lesbianism was that she could never find a man smart enough for her. That explanation made perfect sense to my mother. It wasn't until I was in my forties that I ever thought to question it, and realized what a low opinion my heterosexual mother had of men.

When I was maybe twelve or thirteen, my mother added another element to the story. When she'd talk about Elaine, she'd look directly at me and say, "And you're just like her." What I heard her saying was that I was really smart and that she was afraid I'd kill myself. Now I realize that what she was saying was, "You're really smart, I'm afraid you'll kill yourself, and I think you're a lesbian." My family never spoke directly about anything abstract, anything involving emotions or ways of being or how we thought about issues or ideas. We talked about sports and work, concrete things. We told stories. When we did try to speak about anything abstract, we did it through indirection. So I now understand that my mother telling me that I was just like Elaine meant that she was trying to tell me that she already knew I was gay and that she wasn't going to have a fit about it.

I was thirteen the first time my mother said anything to me about going to college. It was May 4, 1970, the day the National Guard shot protesting students at Kent State University. We were watching the news and my mother said, "I hope this trouble's over before you go to college." That was the moment I knew I was going to college, although I didn't know how, or what college really was.

That indirect manner of talking was all my family ever did. I was shocked when I visited a middle-class friend's family while I was in college and they talked to each other as though they were psychologists or something. "What's your plan? And how do you feel about that?" I'd never heard people talk to each other like that around a dinner table. For all the troubles I had in my youth, I never thought about talking to anyone about them. I held them inside and never felt a need to name or a classify anything—all I felt a need for was a story. Until I was in graduate school, I never had a name for my gender identity. I was just a girl who acted like a boy and never worried about what that was called or what it meant. I didn't need a name for my sexual orientation, either. I wasn't exactly a lesbian, as my mom thought, nor was I exactly straight, either. And I certainly didn't have a name for my social class background. I thought everybody was like us until I started meeting middle-class people, who were so different they seemed to come from a foreign country.

BEGINNING AT THE BEGINNING

So let's wait on the names and classifications, and start with the story. I was born in 1957 in southern California. My mother was thirty-seven years old when I was born, and that was pretty damn old to be having a first baby in those days. She was on her second marriage and my dad, eight years her junior, was on his first. My father's side of the family was as conventional and conservative as my mother's side was wild and lawless. His father worked in a GM plant for forty-five years. My grandmother was a housewife who never learned to drive and was always dependent on others. They were Methodist churchgoers, teetotalers (in contrast to my alcoholic maternal grandparents), and racial bigots. They always brought me dresses and dolls at Christmas and on my birthday, which I cheerfully shredded as soon as they left. It was they who talked my mother into having kids. She had never wanted children. They definitely wanted a granddaughter. For reasons I can't even begin to guess, given my grandfather's sexism, they favored girl children.

But when my mother was pregnant with me she was so sure that she was having a boy that she and my dad picked out a boy's name—Renny—and didn't bother to pick out a girl's name. They wanted me to have the same initials as my dad, whose name is Richard, so they looked for a name that started with R. The story my mom told me when I was a kid was that they didn't like any of the R names for girls they could think of—Rachel, Roberta, Rebecca—and they sort of liked Rene, but it sounded too foreign so they turned it into Renny. It wasn't until I was in my late thirties that my dad finally told me the real story. Yes, it was a boy's name all along, and it was the name of somebody he'd known while he was in the Coast Guard at the end of World War II. Not only was I given a man's name, I was named after a particular man.

I don't know if I simply followed my own inclinations in preferring to be a boy, or if their expectation that I'd be a boy influenced me, but I was perfectly happy to be one. My mother thought she wouldn't have any more kids. My little brother, four years younger, was a surprise. My dad, I think, had no idea what to do with a daughter, so he just carried on as if I were his son, which was fine with me. Shortly after I got my PhD at thirty-five, my mother said to me, "You've always been your dad's oldest son." That was the best thing she ever said to me. That's how my family functioned while I was growing up: I was the older son, my brother was the younger son.

I wanted to be exactly like my dad in every way when I was a little kid. I wore my jeans low on my hips, like he did. I had a toolbelt that was a miniature copy of his. My brother and I each had beautiful toolboxes dad made us with our names inlaid in them, and wooden wagons he made for us, which we dragged around like they were hot rods, pushing each other downhill like daredevils. Although I lived a boy's life at home, I wasn't allowed to do so at school, so my life was split in two.

I got my first public lesson in gender when I was in kindergarten. There were two play areas in my classroom—a workshop and a kitchen. When we had our first play period I headed directly to the workshop because that's the kind of play I knew from home. I was dragged out of there by the ear by the teacher and tossed unceremoniously into the kitchen to the snickers of the students who had already, obviously, been thoroughly and "properly" gendered. Marked instantly as a misfit, I stood in the corner of that kitchen feeling isolated, exposed, and vulnerable. That feeling lasted through all my elementary and primary school years. I filled that emptiness with books, which made me academically successful, but took me further and further away from the working-class boyhood I'd been enjoying at home.

I also got my first lesson in heteronormativity in kindergarten. I made one friend, Eddie, another outsider like me. We had naptime in kindergarten, lying on spread-out towels on the classroom floor, girls on one side of the room, boys on the other. One day Eddie and I laid on the border and held hands across the gap. The teacher busted us, saying, "Look at the little boyfriend and girlfriend. No romances in this classroom!" and separated us. There wasn't a hint of infant sexuality in that handholding. It was purely for comfort. We were holding on to each other to keep from drowning in that sea of strangers. I didn't make another friend, male or female, until I was in sixth grade.

Although I went to public schools, the dress code required that girls wear skirts. My mother colluded with me in subverting this. She made all my school clothes, and she always sewed matching shorts to wear under my dresses and skirts so that I could hang upside-down on the monkey bars; I managed to feel like I wasn't really wearing a skirt at all. Nonetheless, as soon as I got home every day the skirts came off and my jeans and boots went on. That pattern continued throughout high school. Was I a boy in drag at school or a girl in drag at home? I was a spiritual hermaphrodite, bi-gendered from the beginning.

TEENAGE TROUBLE YEARS

When I was a teenager, working for my dad doing construction, I had great fun masquerading as a boy. I had very short hair and, until I was sixteen or so, had a fairly boyish body. Once, when I was hammering together the framing for a house on a new construction site, a delivery truck from a lumberyard pulled up and the driver jumped out and headed in my direction. I'd been facing away from him, and when I turned around, he did a literal double take as he realized I wasn't a boy. In those days it was unusual to see women working construction, so that kind of double take happened to me often. I loved it. I loved both parts—the initial perception of me as a boy, then the recognition that I wasn't, but that I was still working the job. It made me feel rebellious, defiant, and strong.

My dad never betrayed me. He never tried to make me into a girl. He never once told me not to do something physical. Rather, he'd teach me the best way to do it. My mother went along with that until I hit puberty, then her attitude toward me changed. She started warning me not to hurt myself. I've always wondered what that means, when adults tell girl children not to do something because they'll "hurt" themselves. Does it mean if you climb that tree, your uterus will fall out? That kind of cautioning makes too many girls grow up physically timid and insecure. I thank my dad (and my mother during my early years) for never making me feel physically insecure, for letting me take up room, project my body into space, and never be ashamed or humiliated by that body.

My mom tried to teach me to walk in high heels when I was sixteen or seventeen. I can't remember why I ever cooperated with that—to humor her, I guess. She soon gave up, telling me that, no matter what I did, I still looked like I was "clomping around" in cowboy boots. I took that as a major compliment. She also tried to teach me how to dance, but I couldn't dance without trying to lead, and she gave up again. Other girls I knew started badgering their mothers to let them shave their legs long before their mothers wanted to give them permission. For me, it was the opposite. One summer, when I was fourteen or maybe fifteen, my mother announced that if I was going to wear shorts, I had to shave my legs. I resisted. She insisted. Shaved legs felt weird and naked and strange. I always sliced my ankles with the razor, and my armpits broke out in red bumps. I stopped shaving the instant I hit college and discovered hippie style. My mother also plucked my eyebrows around that same time, when I was fourteen or fifteen. To my eternal dismay, they never grew back thick and heavy and across the bridge of my nose like they had been, so to this day I have delicate girlish eyebrows. These are the ways my mother betrayed my boyishness and tried to teach me girlishness.

Meanwhile, my own bookishness continued to exert itself as an influence that felt contradictory to my boyishness. I had the distinct feeling that books, poetry in particular, which I wanted to write, were effeminate. I felt distinctly uncomfortable doing anything effeminate, since I always modeled myself in everything other than bookishness after my dad. But the pull of books was too strong for me to resist. In the afternoons and on Saturdays and Sundays I'd climb up into the treehouse that my brother and I had built with my dad's help. I'd take a book up there and read for hours. I was consciously hiding my reading, as if it were a vice.

Up in that treehouse I read Robert Louis Stevenson's *The Black Arrow*, which I thought was the coolest book I'd ever read because it featured a character who was a girl masquerading as a boy and having lots of adventures. I had known all along that boys got to have more fun; that knowledge had always been part of what made me want to be a boy. By then, however, my body had changed, and I could no longer pass convincingly, even with a toolbelt around my hips and a hammer in my hand.

I got pretty tired of always being alone and having no friends. In the way many girls do, I discovered that one way to get attention was through sex. I had no interest in sex itself, no feelings of physical attraction for anyone, male or female, although I had plenty of intellectual curiosity about it, which arose through my reading. I read a lot of books with rather oblique references to sex, but was picking up some of the details through more explicit works like *The Godfather* and *The Last Picture Show*. I first learned about the existence of (male) homosexuality from Mary Renault's books about Alexander the Great, particularly *Fire from Heaven* and *The Persian Boy*, although I was still pretty unclear on how the physical details might work in practice.

I learned the heterosexual details when I acquired a motorcycle-riding, drug-dealing, leather-jacket-wearing dropout boyfriend, with whom I had sex for the first time when I was fifteen. It neither thrilled nor repelled me. I stayed in that state through quite a period of promiscuity, which wound up with me in bed with one of my high school teachers. And his wife. They were a hippie couple who'd recently moved to my small town, and were different (by a mile!) from anyone I'd met before. When she found out that her husband was having an affair, her response was to make it a threesome. My response was to discover that I was far more attracted to her than I was to him.

Somehow, I just didn't see my attraction to her as a problem, or as extraordinary in any way. (There's something to be said for ignorance and pigheadedness.) A bit later I fell head, feet, heart, and mind in love with a woman who was, at best, ambivalent about her feelings toward me. For the next eleven years we had an on-again, off-again relationship during which I went to college and graduate school, she got divorced, went to graduate school and completely changed her career, and we each had other lovers, and never once used the word "lesbian" until the day she told me we had no more future. She said she couldn't live a lesbian life while she was raising her children. While I was on-again, off-again with her, and having other rela-tionships with men, and, eventually, other relationships with women, I never heard, thought of, or needed, the word bisexual. I never thought about what I might be—I just was "it," whatever "it" was. Another term for it would have to be promiscuous. It was the late 1970s and early 1980s, that magic time in human history when there was easily available birth control, cures for syphilis and other STDs, and HIV/AIDS not yet on the horizon of cultural awareness. The way I looked at myself then, had I been forced to articulate it, might have been reflected by Margaret Cho's line from *I'm the One that I Want*: "I'm not gay or straight—I'm just slutty. Where's my parade?"

HIGHER EDUCATION CHANGES EVERYTHING

There was another development in my gender identity; it was becoming very fluid. I won a scholarship to Mills College, a private liberal arts women's college in Oakland, California. When I started there, a working-class girl on a campus in the big city, I went to class on the first day in a dress. I put no thought whatsoever into that choice. After all, I'd had to wear skirts all through public school, so I was used to it. Besides, I thought college was a formal occasion, and I was supposed to look nice, out of respect. Well. I found myself in a classroom full of middle-class women wearing ragged blue jeans and T-shirts. It didn't take me long to adjust to that, since the unisex blue-jeans-chambray-shirt look was at the center of my comfort zone.

Despite my easy adjustment to the dress code, I didn't adjust to the rest of the culture of the college. I had thought I was well prepared, having sailed through the academic work of high school, but I received a "C" on my first essay in my first English class. It turned out I didn't know how to write English grammatically. I didn't know a lot of things my fellow students knew. I couldn't understand why abstract thought, divorced from action, was desirable. In the world I came from, people didn't just think about things; they did them. College wasn't, it seemed to me at the time, about doing anything. It was just about thinking over abstractions. I was an English major because I loved books and wanted to write. But the books we were reading weren't the books I loved. We were reading what I later came to identify as the Dead White Men of the traditional canon, and reading them without discussing any of their social context. Understanding their social context might have helped me make sense of them. As it was, I didn't see why anyone was interested in nineteenth-century drawing-room conversations. I struggled academically, socially, and psychologically for a year and a half. Then I dropped out.

I did blue-collar jobs for the next few years, working a printing press and a typesetting machine, until I went back to college four years later. When I did, there weren't any skirts in my wardrobe. Once, when I went to a dinner party at a professor's house, the nicest clothes I had (most of which had come from thrift stores) were a pair of black narrow-wale cords, suede lace-up, flat-soled shoes, a white Oxford shirt, and a pullover sweater vest. Gender-ambiguous, but definitely not down-at-heel chic; rather, truly down-at-heel. I worked my way through college this time, as an independent student no longer part of my parents' household. I worked in typesetting shops, on the swing shift, and went to school during the day. Despite having to work thirty or forty hours a week, I had become a much, much better student. I had read numerous books in the four years I was a dropout, and made up many deficiencies I had entered college with. I had also learned to write, by doing a lot of it. I wrote a novel (which I eventually abandoned as immature), several short stories, and poems. When I reentered college, I was ready for the classroom.

When I got my BA I still didn't have the terms "working-class," "bisexual," "cross-dressing," or "butch" in my lexicon. I still simply felt myself to be an outsider, increasingly alienated by my academic interests from my family and world of origin, but not finding a place I wanted to be. In that slightly lost state, I went into a master's program. I also went back to work for my dad. During the year that I attended graduate school and worked on a construction site, I straddled worlds in a more obvious fashion than at any other time in my life.

Dad was working, that year, on a major commercial remodel job. I went to work with him in the morning, dressed in work boots, jeans or painter's pants, a T-shirt, and a rolled-up bandanna around my forehead. I did a lot of demolition and work with wallboard and joint compound. In the afternoons I took off for two and a half hours and went to class at the university. My change of clothes consisted of taking the bandana off and sticking it in my pocket. So there I was, a worker in men's clothes with a woman's body sitting in a classroom of higher education. My fellow students were very ambivalent toward me. I was getting the highest grades in class, and I studied with some students who appreciated my help, but it was quite a while before they invited me to join their group. Eventually one of them told me that most of the other students were afraid of me because I seemed so "tough."

In my second year, I took the first step into crossing over altogether into the white-collar world when I got a job as a substitute high school teacher, subbing three days a week and going to classes two days. I never wore what I call "work clothes"—blue-collar clothes—to class again. (And I've never learned to call a button-down shirt and slacks "work clothes," even though I've been working in them since leaving that last blue-collar job.) I have been teaching, in one form or another, ever since then, and never worked for a living in a blue-collar job again.

In my teens and twenties I was physically very strong, and the thinnest I have ever been in my life. I had taken up distance running and was working my way up to running a marathon. I ran about fifty miles a week. I lifted weights three days a week with a partner who was an amateur bodybuilding champion. I was fit, strong, and muscular, and cocky about my physical abilities. I still had broader hips and bigger tits than I would have liked. I joked that I wanted to get to the point where I could run upstairs without anything jiggling, but I never got below a B-cup bra size. Nonetheless, I was formidable, even though I'm short (five foot three). I have a photo of myself with as fifty-foot power cord coiled over my shoulder like an ammo belt, holding an impact drill as if it were a machine gun. The pose was a joke on the nickname a coworker on the construction job gave me: "She-Rambo." With short hair and bulging biceps, I felt positioned comfortably between genders.

During my first year in the MA program I met and became lovers with Gary, a bisexual man who first started teaching me terminology. He sent me a birthday card with a picture of a person who was dressed on the left side in men's clothing and the right side in women's clothing. The caption read, "Both of us wish you a happy birthday." It was the first image I was ever consciously aware of noticing in which someone represented both male and female. Gary also gave me a button that said "Working-Class Dyke." I still have it. When he gave it to me, it was the first time anyone had ever applied either of those terms to me. I knew what a dyke was, though I was struck by the term "working class," I didn't yet know what it meant.

PHD BLUES (AND PINKS)

I learned what it meant when I entered a PhD program. I learned all the terms for classes and genders and sexual orientations, all the meanings of the terms, and all the strengths and the restrictions that went with those terms. I was cocky going into the program. I wasn't so cocky coming out five years later.

The year before I started the PhD program, I taught at the same institution where I'd earned my MA. One of my professors recommended me for the position. Later I found out that he'd described me to the Dean as "cocky." I liked that a lot, because it implied rebelliousness and attitude. I could identify with the image of a bantam rooster. I decided that's how I'd always describe myself: as cocky. It wasn't so easy, as it turned out, because class and gender collided in a way that I never could have seen coming.

I entered the PhD program in literature at UC Santa Cruz in the fall of 1989. At first I felt utterly, completely lost. Eventually I learned to name that sense of being lost as being a first-generation college student, as being a working-class academic. Forming, defining, and claiming that identity took a lot of work and a lot of pain. I count it as the true subject matter and methodology I learned in graduate school, more than the disciplinary knowledge I was supposed to be learning.[1] However, one of the aspects of that dislocation I never looked at until I came to write this chapter was how the process knocked the hell out of my gender identity, as well as my class identity.

I had always been a cross-dresser—always wearing either gender-neutral or explicitly masculine clothes. I'd had my hair long, short, and in-between, but never considered my long hair to be "femme," since men of my generation adopted long hair as not only a fashion, but a political marker. I'd worn skirts when I had to, but had always worn them as a costume. I'd had very little consciousness concerning these practices. They were just the way I was. In graduate school I lost a great deal of my masculinity. It took me years to regain it. I knew how to be a working-class man. I had no idea how to be a middle-class man. Anyway, middle-class men looked pretty feminine to me.

When I started meeting a number of academic men of middle-class origin, I initially thought most of them were gay, especially those from the Northeast. I took their mannerisms, habits of speech, and attention to the details of dress as signs that they were effeminate because the masculinity that they performed was so different from the working-class masculinity I'd grown up emulating. Eventually I understood my error. They were displaying their masculinity, their power, through modalities that were completely alien to me, such as having elevated vocabularies, being able to quote literary sources (I'd always seen literature as an effeminate pursuit), knowing which wine went with which food, and which glass to put the wine in and which fork to eat the food with. I remember my utter astonishment when a fellow graduate student, a young man of sound body and middle-class origin, told a story about calling AAA to change a flat tire on his car. Changing tires had always been a point of pride for me. More than once over the years men had offered to help me while I was changing a tire, sometimes complete strangers, and I'd always insisted on my ability to do it myself, and do it well. I'd had to put both feet on a tire iron and jump up and down on it on occasion, but I'd done this to avoid ever having to ask for help. The idea of calling somebody to change your tire was so alien to me, and so unthinkable as male behavior, that I was stunned silent. I looked at the hands of the man who'd told the story. They were soft, smooth, pale, uncalloused, unscarred. Unlike my dad's. Unlike mine.

One of my problems in graduate school was that my fellow students, as well as my professors, usually classified me as too loud, as rude, as taking up too much space, as obnoxious. I was simply behaving as I had always behaved while I was wearing work boots and work pants, which didn't fit in the rarefied atmosphere of a research institution. I started softening myself, so people wouldn't physically pull back from me when I moved or spoke. Because I didn't "get" middle-class masculinity, it felt like what I was doing was feminizing myself.

I started wearing skirts. Voluntarily. I had read a magazine article that gave advice about job interviews. The article said that women in skirts were perceived as less aggressive than women wearing slacks. I took that to heart. My hair started going gray (I was in my early thirties). My hair was red, originally, and was the only aspect of my appearance I had ever been vain about. I decided to let my bi-level haircut grow out, to have it long for a few years before it went completely gray. Hair makes a remarkable difference in the perception of one's gender identity and sexual orientation. When I had my butch haircut, people generally assumed on first meeting me that I was a dyke. When I grew it out long, people generally assumed I was straight. The long hair and less-butch clothing I adopted had a profound effect on me, and on those perceiving me. I was transforming myself from a working-class man into a professional middle-class woman. While I was going about the class transformation consciously and deliberately, the gender transformation was largely invisible to me while it was happening.

In the late 1980s Santa Cruz, as well as on the university campus, an intense lesbian feminist movement was demanding a voice and a physical space for lesbians on campus and in the gay and lesbian community center downtown, which had been dominated by men. It was a time when a small but very vocal protest was being mounted by bisexual women for their inclusion in these spaces. I knew many of the women engaged in these culture wars, but I largely steered clear, without even realizing that I was doing so. I felt disenfranchised from claiming a bisexual identity too loudly because I was living in a monogamous relationship with a man, and among the lesbians I knew there was a great deal of animosity toward bisexual women involved with men because they could benefit from heterosexual privilege. Santa Cruz was very politicized about sexual orientation, but not about gender identity. And there were plenty of people around ready to tell me that I wasn't really gay if I were bisexual, and I couldn't take too many additional iterations of being told what I wasn't and should be—I was getting enough of those comments related to being a working-class person in a professional middle-class milieu. And my main concerns were elsewhere: in the intense struggle within myself over my class identity. I had practically lost touch with my family, who no longer had much influence over me. The man I was living with was helping, in subtle ways, to shape my new, professional-middle-class identity. I eventually came to feel like a Frankenstein's monster or Pygmalion's statue when I realized how much of my class identity had shifted before I realized what was happening. So while I was unconsciously being transformed into a sort of professional-middle-class femininity, I was (mostly) consciously not proclaiming my queer identity. "Queer" was not yet a term and a definition fully available to me at that point in the development of the idea and my own education. The need for definition and scholarly legitimation of every aspect of my identity was, ironically, eroding my longtime unconsciously held identity. I was lost in more ways than I even knew.

And I lost the body that had carried me so confidently through a construction zone. I had a knee injury that eventually required surgery, the timing of which coincided with my painful engagement with the professional-middle-class values of the PhD program, which took up a lot of the energy that I had previously channeled into long-distance running. I never got back to the same level of training that had made the body I had been so proud of. I gained weight, most of it in the hips, but some of it making that despised B-cup into an almost unbearable C-cup. In other words, I developed a very "feminine" body, which I hated and hid under loose, "feminine" clothes. I felt disenfranchised by that body, as well as by my class transformation, from proclaiming my former cockiness.

DOWN IN THE VALLEY, THE VALLEY SO LOW

I made it through graduate school, which was a breeze intellectually, if not emotionally. I didn't really know who I was any more. I had been an unhappy working-class boy, yearning for a world of books and ideas. Now I found myself a professional-middle-class woman, better educated but not any wiser, lost between worlds. When I started teaching full time, and therefore having a middle-class income, I discovered good wine, good food, and silk shirts, aspects of my new world that I liked. I typically wore black jeans and a silk shirt to teach in, and used so many "big words" in my everyday speech that my family were afraid to talk to me any more. The look was not gender-neutral, the silk shirts were obviously feminine, and the speech was not that of the working-class boy I had once been. I had clearly lost myself, in terms of my class identity, my gender identity, and my claim to my sexual identity.

I started looking for a job in the early 1990s, one of the worst times for the academic job market in my field, with few openings and many new PhDs looking for positions. It took me three years before I finally found a tenure-track professorship at California State University, Stanislaus, located in the small, provincial, socially and politically conservative Central Valley town of Turlock. It was the last place I wanted to be. I'd run away from a rural, working-class small town to go to college. Now I found myself back in the same kind of place I'd struggled to get out of. Ironically, though, I was in a milieu that helped me find some of the things I'd lost in graduate school. The campus and local community environments were profoundly homophobic. In response to this homophobia, I launched myself into a career as a campus gay rights activist. Quiet as I'd been in Santa Cruz, I now became equally outspoken. I became the advisor to the Rainbow Alliance, the campus GLBT club, organized panel discussions and poetry readings, brought speakers to campus, and eventually developed the first gay studies course ever offered at the university.

One illustration of how homophobic the campus atmosphere was when I first started at Stanislaus comes from the first Rainbow Alliance meeting I attended. The club members were planning to bring a comedian to campus and they budgeted double the necessary amount for posters because they knew from past experience that all the posters they put up would be torn down or defaced. We began building coalitions to change things. To my surprise, we received a lot of support from the campus president, an African American woman who had a reputation for being conservative. I met with her several times, and she always encouraged me in my work for gay rights on campus because it was important to her that Stanislaus not have the reputation for being one of the more hostile environments among the twenty-three campuses of the CSU system. One student in particular, April Dunham-Filson, who was also a staff member at the university, was instrumental in keeping the Rainbow Alliance alive and in helping to form an organization, Campus Allies United in Support of Equality (CAUSE). CAUSE sponsored panel discussions, speakers, and a Safe Zones campaign that eventually demonstrably changed the campus climate. When we first distributed our posters for faculty, staff, and administrators to put on their doors, declaring their offices "safe zones," a few people put them up. Many of them were torn down or defaced. We replaced them. The second year, more people put them up, and fewer were torn down. The third year, almost everyone put them up, and almost none were torn down.

In addition to these activities, I developed a general education course in GLBT studies. I anticipated having trouble getting the course approved, but the curriculum committee okayed it without comment. Then the general education committee approved it as meeting the campus's diversity require- ment. I was working with the chair of the general education committee in another capacity, and he told me informally that my course had been ap- proved, before official notification came. I said, "Without a fight? I was all ready to come before the committee and argue for it." He said, half-jokingly, "We know. That's why we approved it."

My department chair was reluctant to schedule the course, though, because she thought it might not draw enough students. However, when it was scheduled, in what turned out to be my final semester at the campus, the class enrolled twenty students, which made it an average-size class for the English department, and a large class for the Women's Studies program, with which it was cross-listed. The local newspaper ran a story on the class as a first on campus. It was a very sympathetic article by a reporter who was a lesbian. I was contacted by some people from the community, including Candy, a transgendered person who came to talk to my class. Candy wrote me a letter afterward indicating that the experience had been as useful for her—she lived a very isolated life in that rural, conservative area—as it was for the class. The experience of that class, overall, was the high point in a low time in my life, those seven years in the boondocks.

At Stanislaus I tried on middle-class drag for the first time. When I was named director of the new Women's Center on campus, I wore a jacket, shirt, and tie to the opening. My hair was still long, and I parted and combed it to look sort of like Marlene Dietrich. I thought of myself as Dietrich or Garbo in one of their drag performances. I did it deliberately to shock the shockable. It worked. It was the first step into the next stage of my evolution: from working-class boy/girl to middle-class woman to middle-class woman/man.

OUT OF THE VALLEY AND INTO A NEW SENSE OF SELFHOOD

After those seven hard years at Stanislaus, I moved to a new job at a startup campus of the California State University system, CSU Channel Islands in Ventura county in coastal Southern California. I thought, okay, a new campus with an explicit commitment to diversity, right there in its mission statement, in Southern California. This is going to be all right; this is going to be like being back in Santa Cruz. So, at the new faculty orientation, while we were introducing ourselves, I stood up and said, "I'm really glad to be here because Stanislaus was a very hard place to be a bisexual, socialist, atheist poet." I was wearing short sleeves, so my Celtic interlace armband tattoo showed, a tattoo that I consider to be terribly middle class and innocuous.

I was very wrong in my assessment of the place. Just about everybody in the room was shocked by my characterization of myself. Some were shocked by my sexual orientation, some by my socialism, and, I supposed, some by my atheism, although nobody ever said anything about atheism to me. I heard about all the other aspects of myself I had named, though. One of my colleagues told me that my idea that every full-time job in America should pay the same salary was "the most morally bankrupt idea" he'd ever heard. I also later heard that one mid-level administrator had said to another administrator, "Oh my god, we've made a terrible mistake. Have you seen that Renny has a tattoo?" Some people even seemed to regard my being a poet askance. Worst, though, I discovered that the people who had preceded me to the university (I was hired in its second year of operation) had already developed a remarkably homophobic culture. I repeatedly had to ask people to cease and desist from making homophobic jokes. I suspected that there was anti-gay discrimination going on in the hiring process when several openly gay candidates who did very well in their interviews were not hired. Someone taped a "why God hates gays" brochure to my office door. While I suspected it was not a colleague who had done it, but rather a student responding to something I had said in a class, clearly the university had not established an atmosphere in which students learned that such attacks were completely inappropriate.

I decided there was work to be done. I tried to get a President's Commission set up; it took almost a year. I suspected, but could never confirm, that there was more than just the chaos and incredible workload of a startup university involved in my not getting anywhere with it at first. Eventually I met with the vice president for student affairs and we jointly went to the president, who chartered the Commission on Human Relations, Diversity, and Equity. The commission was chaired by the university's one openly gay administrator (who is also Latino) and had representation from diverse elements of faculty, staff, administration, and students. The commission formed a subcommittee on GLBT issues, which eventually established a Safe Zones program and sponsored panels and speakers. Within a year, the campus climate had completely changed. Some people had left, and new people had been hired, including four new gay faculty, some of whom had been out during their interviews and some of whom hadn't. My colleagues no longer publicly made homophobic jokes, at least not in my presence. The Safe Zones program, after one year of operation, had a long list of people waiting to go through the training to join. I had developed and taught a new GLBT studies course. It had enrolled twenty-two students, making it a large class for our new, small campus, despite my department chair's fear that it would not draw students, a fear identical to that of my old Stanislaus department chair.

Before these changes had all taken place, I decided to get a little revenge. I was elected chair of the academic senate. I wasn't elected on my charm. I was the union's candidate, and had been chosen because the union members were looking for someone strong, who would confront the administration on behalf of shared governance. I won the election by a single vote. My very visible position as academic senate chair gave me a platform to do a little more educating, I thought. So at the initial all-faculty meeting of the fall semester, I wore a suit and tie. In my remarks, I said, "Please don't address me as Madam Chair. I'd prefer to be addressed as Mr. Chair." That got a laugh, although a bit of a nervous one. I heard later that someone said, "I know she's that way, but does she have to make a big deal out of it?" When I heard that, I thought I'd traveled back in time thirty years.

From then on, I put on middle-class drag for real. I started wearing a shirt and tie and men's slacks on any occasion that required me to get out of my usual black jeans. So, finally, I got my cockiness back. Once again "cocky" has become my favorite adjective to describe myself because it works for me on several levels. Not only does it imply rebelliousness and attitude, which I still have, but it also implies that I have a cock, which, in a metaphorical sense I certainly do. I'm fond of saying, in my current position as a faculty member who's often in an oppositional position vis-à-vis colleagues and administrators, that I have the biggest balls on campus. I've got the whole package. Who cares if it's only a metaphor?

I did an unexpectedly good job at being senate chair, despite the fears of those who didn't like my wearing a tie. I formed strong alliances with the student affairs vice president and with the new provost. I won over the colleague who'd previously told me my ideas were morally bankrupt. I even won over the president himself, who'd been clearly uneasy with my election and my public drag performances. Now, everybody just expects me to show up in a tie. I have a running joke with my colleagues and my department staff about how I look like Russell Crowe. I don't, not even slightly, but I cut my hair to look like his in *Master and Commander*, and joked about getting one of those eighteenth-century lacy shirts like he wore in the movie. So now some of the staff people call me "Russell." People who've gotten to know me, those who might once have been very put off by a woman in a tie called Russell, have become comfortable with it. My friend, the student affairs vice president, who's a very large (former collegiate football player), shaven-headed African American man, has adopted me as his "little brother." He gives me great hand-me-down clothes. He calls himself my "Straight Eye for the Queer Girl." When we see each other on campus we slap hands and he says "Hey, little bro!" People see that level of playing with gender (and race) coming from powerful and influential people on campus and they relax. That's what I want them to do.

I learned how to tie a tie sometime in the 1970s when ties for women were fashionable because of Diane Keaton in *Annie Hall*. A middle-class boyfriend taught me how. It was always difficult because I have a problem with left–right orientation, and doing it in the mirror was torturous. From time to time in my twenties I wore women's clothes with a tie, but had never worn one again until the Stanislaus Women's Center opening ceremony, when I was thirty-seven. When I started wearing them regularly at CSU Channel Islands, I got over the left–right orientation problem, but never reached the comfort level I might have had if I had grown up watching my father or my brother tying a tie. The only time I ever saw my father in a tie was at my brother's wedding. I'd seen my dad in bolo ties a few times, but never in a regular tie with a four-in-hand knot except on that one occasion. When my brother got a job as a fire department dispatcher in his thirties, he started wearing a tie to work, but it was a clip-on. And when you wear a uniform tie with a name badge on your pocket, wearing a tie isn't quite the same.

Although the gender-switching aspect of this cross-dressing feels perfectly comfortable to me, the class-switching aspect still seems alien and strange. I have some very lovely silk ties, a beautiful pair of wingtips, and Brooks Brothers shirts—clothes like no man in my family ever had. I will always feel like an alien in the professional middle class. I don't ever really want to feel comfortable in it, since I don't accept some of its core values: extreme individualism, striving, materialism. This class and gender cross-dressing has become the subject I've been writing about in my poetry recently.

I used to just be who I was when I was a working-class boy/girl. Now, because of my education, I spend a lot of time thinking about who I am and about how to account for it and explain it. Barrie Jean Borich (1999, 129) names a range of possible lesbian genders: "*butch* or *femme, femmy butch* or *butchy femme, femme top* or *butch bottom, femme-to-femme* or *butch-on-butch, transgender*."

Are any of those alternatives for me? Am I a "femmy butch"? It's close, but it doesn't sound quite right. I'll stick with "alternatively gendered" for now. When I do my laundry I've got men's shirts and women's shirts spinning around in the dryer together, and they're all mine. That's easy, and I feel good about that. However, performing class is a type of drag for me, as much as performing gender is drag. Putting on women's middle-class clothes is a drag performance for me. Putting on male middle-class clothes is double drag. I have a very nice wool men's cardigan that I had to get used to wearing because in the context I grew up in, no man wore cardigan sweaters. In my working-class eyes, a cardigan is distinctly effeminate, something only a "fairy" would wear. Although that makes it very appropriate for me, it just doesn't feel right with my masculine identity. Middle-class men wear cardigans, not the guys I grew up with, from whom I learned how to be a man. If I'm a drag king in terms of gender, am I a "drag doctor" in terms of class and education?

I had a girlfriend, a much younger woman who liked playing the girl while I played the guy. I asked her once, "Wouldn't you like me better if I had a flat chest that was just a little bit hairy, and a little bit of a beard, and just a medium-sized penis?" And she wrinkled up her nose and said, "No! I like you just the way you are. A little bit of both." I need to be a little bit of both. I can't imagine myself being all male or all female, just as I can't imagine myself settling comfortably into either the working class or the professional middle class; I need to straddle both.

I'm really not either–or, in sexual orientation, gender identity, or class orientation. I move back and forth. Shortly after I got my PhD, I briefly returned to my blue-collar roots when I spent part of a summer working with my dad again, laying a hardwood floor in a basketball gym. I spent another summer working as a horse wrangler in Yellowstone Park. After those blue-collar interludes, I returned to my professional-middle-class persona as a college professor. I move back and forth in gender identity, as well. I can wear a suit and tie to an event on campus during the week, then go out in a skirt on Friday night with my heterosexual male lover. I can feel fairly comfortable in the suit, and in the skirt. But I'm careful never to let anybody on campus see me in a skirt because they've gotten used to my "Russell" persona, and if they saw me in a skirt, that would be too shocking. One of my queer colleagues suggested that I should wear a skirt to the next faculty meeting, precisely because it would be more shocking than to wear men's clothes.

A friend I've known for years came to visit recently. He hadn't seen my new "Russell" haircut before. He'd only known me with long hair. When he saw me with the short haircut he said, "You look like a dyke!" I was wearing jeans, a short-sleeved men's shirt, and men's sandals, and had my hair slicked back. "No, I look like a guy!" I told him. "No," he insisted. "You look like a dyke." There are some women who look masculine, no matter what they wear, and would look silly and out of place in a dress. I'm not one of them. I've got "delicate" features. I have a "feminine" face. But I'm not sure that matters. I've been trying to look at masculine women and see what makes them masculine. I recently read an article in the *New York Times* (Bernstein 2004) about colleges establishing sections in dorms for transgender students. One female student interviewed in the article was described as being frequently mistaken for a boy. In the accompanying picture, she looked nothing at all like a boy to me. She had a buzz cut, but her face was cute in a girlish way. All right, I thought. If she can be mistaken for a boy, then my face shouldn't keep me from feeling authentically butch.

But I don't always manage to feel butch. While I was writing this chapter I gave a talk for a local lesbian community group. I wore a man's shirt and tie. After the talk, a couple came up to me. They were a generation older than I, a butch-femme couple. The butch woman started telling me her story. She was butch in the way that makes "butch" a noun—she was "a butch." She had that particular masculine quality that would make her look butch no matter what clothes she wore. Even in a dress, she'd look like a guy in drag. Yet she was clearly female. She had narrow hips no wider than her waist, but she had large breasts, and although her face had a mannish look, it was still a woman's face. There was no trace of a beard. She was what she was—a butch. A working-class butch.

She made me feel like an imposter, standing there in my middle-class gentleman's clothes over my feminine body with my delicate face and foppish hair. Imposter syndrome haunts me everywhere I go. I never would have felt inauthentic if I'd met this woman twenty years ago, while I was wearing my work clothes. Now, even when I have a carefully reasoned scholarly critique of the idea of authenticity, that's what I feel in my gut standing here with my class privilege and legal protection while she tells me stories of being arrested in bars in the 1950s for not wearing three pieces of women's clothing. Gender identity, including cross-dressing, has been added as of January 1, 2004, to the California nondiscrimination law, so nobody can arrest me or legally discriminate against me even though on this evening I'm wearing men's clothes all the way to the skin, except for my sports bra, which helps flatten out my chest. I have safety where she had danger.

Straddling identities is not always easy. I feel like a visitor in the professional middle class, and always will, but I can't go back to the working class. Lesbians can make me feel like I'm not gay enough with a single dirty look, even though I can talk till I'm blue in the face about the legitimacy of bisexuality as an identity and say, hey, we shouldn't reify the fluidity of sexuality into boxes with names like lesbian, straight, and bi- anyway, and then launch into a forty-five-minute explanation of queer theory. And whereas once, in my ignorant youth, my boyishness just felt normal and fine and I had no need to name it, now my attempts to claim it again in the clothes of another class make me feel like a double imposter.

A candidate for the position of provost came to my campus recently, and in one of her presentations she described herself as coming from a working-class family, being a first-generation college student. As I watched her through various interviews and presentations over the course of two days, I marveled at her. A colleague described her as "elegant," and that she was. Somehow she had mastered all the codes of style, of voice, of body movement, of gesture, of clothing, hair, makeup, jewelry—the whole thing—of the professional middle class. She got nothing wrong, at least in my eye. I have no confidence in my judgment, but others seemed to react to her as having it all right, so that bolsters my judgment. How did she learn to do that? She performed "PMC woman" in a way I never could.

Part of the challenge of performing middle classness is that if you get it wrong, someone will notice, and you're busted—revealed as an impostor. That's why I've always found it safer to challenge middle classness, rather than trying to pass. Gender drag is a different strategy. It's a displacement of class onto gender. If I perform PMC masculinity, and get it wrong, well, it's obviously, visibly, a transgression in the first place since there's no possibility I could really pass as male. If I get it wrong, well, people can say that it's not class I'm getting wrong, it's masculinity. It's not because I'm working class that I'm out of place; it's because I'm a (biological) woman acting like a man inappropriately. Having people perceive me that way feels more comfortable. Gender seems like a better playground, to me, than class, which seems much more serious.

CONCLUSION

> I saw myself as an adventurer, not a little girl. Gender expectations seemed to me to be formal middle-class rituals that did not fit into the realities of my life.
>
> —Joan Nestle, *GENDERqUEER* (2002, 4)

Costume

I finish the knot in my tie,
slide the clip into place,
check out the effect in the mirror.
I look like a little girl playing dressup
in her father's clothes. Except, my father
never wore clothes like these—fine-woven
shirt, silk jacket, slacks and wingtips.
My dad wore blue jeans or painter's pants,
a cap with "Ford" embroidered on the front.
For dressup, his shirts had snaps instead of buttons.
I dressed in miniature imitation of him when I was small,
learned to stand like him, walk like him, cock my head the way
    he did,
gestures that don't fit in this jacket and tie
any better than my female body does.
But somehow, I fit into his kind of clothes,
his kind of boots, and my hands were roughened and strong
like his those years I worked for him, before
I got a different kind of education, a "Dr." in front of my name
helping to hide not only my sex, but all the truth
of my origin. These clothes I'm wearing today
would be a costume for him as much as they are for me.

He taught me, with love and care, how to wear his boots.
There is no one to teach me how to wear these expensive shoes
that I have chosen.
—Renny Christopher

I see myself now as an adventurer, not as a woman. I do "gender studies" and started a gender studies program at my university, rather than a "women's studies" program, because just thinking about the idea of being a woman gives me the willies, so to speak. One reason I've never called myself a lesbian, even when it might have been more convenient than insisting on my bisexuality, is that lesbians, in my mind, are women. My girlfriend might (or might not) be a lesbian, but I could never be. Yet I'm not a man, nor do I think of myself as a man. I'm not really transgender or transsexual. I'm something else. Just genderqueer, like I'm class queer. If gender is a means of social control, well, I've spent my life resisting or eluding social control. Riki Wilchins (2002, 13) writes that "gender is the new frontier: the place to rebel, to create new individuality and uniqueness, to defy old, tired outdated social norms."

I live in layers of gender and sexual identity: I grew up wanting to be a working-class man, but became a middle-class woman trying to invent a middle-class male identity in an all-too-identifiably biologically female body. My deepest perceptions were formed during my working-class childhood, when I was learning how to be a rough-handed working-class man. Now I'm (more or less) a working-class woman occupying a middle-class economic and social position who sometimes performs middle-class masculinity. It's a Victor/Victoria thing: I'm a working-class woman who wanted to be a working-class man pretending to be a middle-class woman trying to pass for a middle-class man. It's dizzying sometimes. I think of myself as a gay (more likely, though, bisexual) man in a woman's body. I'd really rather be a hermaphrodite, but maybe that's another story—a science-fiction story (Scott 1996).

I'm perfectly happy in the in-between space I occupy in terms of gender and sexuality, in my multiplicity and lack of exact definition. My ambiguities make a few other people happy, too. Class is harder to come to terms with. I can't go back to the working-class world I came from, although sometimes I wish I could. I miss many things about it. I miss the straightforwardness of the way my parents and my brother live. They don't worry about existential dilemmas like I do. A few years ago I asked my brother what things in his life made him unhappy. He said the divorce he'd gone through and the fact that he'd never been able to become an airplane pilot. Purely practical things. I told him the things that make me unhappy are that I can't find any real meaning to life, that we live in a world filled with social injustice, and that my country wages wars on third world peoples. He looked at me as if I had become a Martian. I'm equally uncomfortable in the more rarified realms of academe, when people want to talk about nothing but abstractions and theories, never making any reference to the actual world. They look at me as if I were a Martian when I try to say something practical. That suspension between worlds is less comfortable for me than a suspension between genders, perhaps because I can form friendships with men or women or with men-women, but I can't ever really feel connected to working-class people or to middle-class people. Just as I'm more butch in my mind than in my body, I'm more middle class than I'd like to be, and I'm more working class than most of the people I associate with would like me to be.

NOTE

1. This process is the subject of a memoir, *A Carpenter's Daughter: A Working-Class Woman in Higher Education*, as yet unpublished, but a section of which appears in Dews and Law (1995).

REFERENCES

Bernstein, Fred A. (2004, March 7). "On Campus, Rethinking Biology 101." *The New York Times*, Section 9, page 1. http://www.nytimes.com/2004/03/07/fashion/07TRAN.html?ex=1393995600&en=d501013d7b45afe3&ei=5007&partner=USERLAND (Accessed June 20, 2007.)

Borich, Barrie Jean (1999). *My Lesbian Husband*. Minneapolis: Graywolf Press.

Christopher, Renny (1995). "A Carpenter's Daughter." In C. L. Barney Dews and Carolyn Leste Law, eds., *This Fine Place So Far from Home: Academics from the Working Class*. Philadelphia: Temple University Press, 137–150.

Nestle, Joan (2002). "Genders on My Mind," in Joan Nestle, Clare Howell, and Riki Wilchins, eds., *GENDERqUEER: Voices from Beyond the Sexual Binary*. Los Angeles: Alyson Books, 3–10.

Scott, Melissa (1996). *Shadow Man*. New York: Tor Books.

Wilchins, Riki. (2002). "A Continuous Nonverbal Communication," in Joan Nestle, Clare Howell, and Riki Wilchins, eds., *GENDERqUEER: Voices from Beyond the Sexual Binary*. Los Angeles: Alyson Books, 11–17.

FOUR

From The Altar Boy's Robes
to the Professor's Cap and Gown

The Journey of a Gay, Working Class Academic

TIMOTHY J. QUAIN

The Village of Cahokia, Illinois, sits across the Mississippi River from St. Louis, Missouri. Founded in 1699, Cahokia was the original settlement for what is now metropolitan St. Louis. Through the first half of the twentieth century, Cahokia remained primarily a farming community. The 1950 U.S. Census shows a population of about five hundred for Cahokia. The 1960 Census, however, indicates a population of about 15,500, a growth of over three thousand percent. Most of this growth came between 1956 and 1960 when a developer built several subdivisions of low-cost housing, primarily for veterans who were taking advantage of the GI Bill following World War II.

Many of the new residents came from public housing located at Jefferson Barracks, Missouri, a Civil War-era military base that had remained active through World War II but was decommissioned shortly after the armistice. Then, the barracks and officers' housing had been converted into low-rent apartments. Most residents were Catholic. The base theater was transformed into a Catholic church and the base hospital was converted into a parochial school. Other base facilities were used as a rectory for parish priests and as a convent for nuns teaching at the school. The church facilities were on the periphery of the base and would remain unaffected by a decision in the early 1950s to abolish the public housing for recreational facilities and middle-class housing.

The mid-1950s population boom in Cahokia included large numbers of poor and working-class Catholic families displaced by the planned demolition of the public housing at Jefferson Barracks. My family was one of these. My father, a veteran, bought our roughly one thousand-square-foot, three-bedroom home for one dollar down on a $15,000 thirty-year mortgage at one percent interest. Like almost all the new residents, my father was a blue-collar worker in St. Louis. He used to say that when he and mother decided to purchase the house, he had to compute the thirty-cents-a-day bridge fare into the monthly budget to determine whether they could afford the home. Since they had been paying rent without building equity in a home, they eventually decided if things did not work out and they lost the house, they would have lost only the one-dollar down payment. On August 1, 1956, my mother and father moved into the new home with their five children. I was the middle child, with two older brothers and two younger sisters. Within two years, there would be a sixth child, another boy.

Cahokia had been converted from a 250-year-old farming community into a village of almost exclusively poor and working-class Catholic families. For most of Cahokia during the late 1950s and through the late 1970s, the church was the central influence. With population growth, the original 1699 parish was split, and a second parish was established. Before even erecting a church, the new parish built and opened a parochial school and a convent for the teaching nuns. The two Catholic parishes dominated life in Cahokia. For the predominately poor and working-class residents, however, this was not all together bad. First, members of both parishes had access to very low-cost private education for grades one through eight, and most took advantage of this opportunity. (For families choosing public education, this was especially helpful in that tax dollars for education remained low but could go further because most children attended parish schools.) The parishes were also the center of social activity. The two parishes sponsored a little-league style athletics organization that provided baseball and soccer for boys and softball for girls, as well as basketball for both boys and girls. Parish organizations for adults also offered social activities, including dances that mimicked the high-society balls then occurring across the river in St. Louis.

There was, however, little expectation, either in my family or throughout the village, that any of the children would attend college. Across the highway from the church and parochial school, there was a small, Catholic, Jesuit college that had become affiliated with St. Louis University. It specialized in aeronautics. In the 1990s, the college moved to the university's main campus in St. Louis. During my childhood and throughout adulthood, I never knew one village resident who enrolled at the college. Perhaps because of this, the parish priests and nuns in the schools seemed quick to identify the boys who showed academic promise and plant in them at a very early age the idea they should become priests. At this time, the church still supported a system of major and minor seminaries. Boys would begin seminary in ninth grade and continue at the minor seminary through the second year of college, transferring to a major seminary where they completed the last two years of college and four years of graduate study in theology. It would be tempting to say the boys identified for the priesthood had shown early signs of being gay. However, both my oldest brother and I were among those encouraged to consider the priesthood and both of us went away to seminary after finishing eighth grade at the parish school. My oldest brother is not gay. Eventually, we both left the seminary. Significantly, we also both earned doctoral degrees.

For poor and working-class Catholic boys of the 1950s and 1960s, the priesthood was, much as it had been in medieval Europe, a readily available escape from their economic class. I did not perceive the priesthood as a way out then, but, in retrospect, I am quite sure the prospect of transcending my economic class was, at least subconsciously, one reason the priesthood was so appealing at such a young age. The community revered priests, who, in turn, drove nice cars and lived in relative luxury. By the 1960s, however, it occurred to many of these boys, especially the heterosexual ones, there might be other opportunities for escape. For poor, academically talented, gay Catholic boys, however, a career in the church was still often the only way out. The route from his economic class to a career in the church ran through a rigorous educational system that required extensive study in several languages, as well as mathematics, the sciences, history and humanities, and the more esoteric discipline of philosophy. The boy identified in grade school as potential priest material was often told, when his academic performance was not clearly above the norm, that he would never be admitted to seminary if he didn't study harder and do better. While academic achievement was acknowledged at home, recognition was retrospective and wasn't emphasized more than other forms of achievement. Proactive encouragement came from the parish priests and nuns; this encouragement was particularly important because they held positions of highest esteem in the village. Once a young boy said he wanted to become a priest, the encouragement was accompanied by praise and attention.

An ironic, and certainly unintended, effect of identifying young boys for the priesthood is that it allowed the gay boy to ignore the conflict between his sexual orientation and the general expectation for heterosexual activity. Consequently, my understanding of my own sexual maturation was tied closely to my academic development. I realized very early, even in grade school, that I was gay. I tended to seek a more academic understanding of my sexuality, reading everything in the public library I could find on homosexuality. For me, academic development and an understanding of my own sexuality are inextricably connected. Since I had, at puberty, expected to pursue the celibate life of a priest, I could delay my sexual exploration and develop a healthy perspective on my own sexuality. Simultaneously, because church officials had guided me toward the priesthood, I could pursue a college preparatory high school curriculum at a private boarding school, followed by schooling at a private liberal arts college that would have otherwise far exceeded the reach of my economic class. This opportunity launched my pursuit of advanced degrees and a career in higher education. As an academic, I have spent almost thirty years as a white faculty member at an historically black university in the South, where attitudes toward gay and lesbian faculty and students have lagged behind those at most other institutions of higher education.

My teaching discipline is English linguistics and grammar. Even my choice of academic discipline can be tied to the influence of the working-class Catholic parish where I grew up. Like many young boys in the parish, I was, early on, chosen to be an altar boy. Before we could serve the priest at mass, we had to memorize the extensive Latin prayers and responses required of the altar boy. As early as first grade, I remember kneeling in the church with one of the nuns during recess and staring at the altar cover on which was embroidered *Sanctus, Sanctus, Sanctus*. I was trying to make sense of these words, which resembled the word *See* in *See Dick run* and *See Jane run* in the oversized book at the front of the classroom that matched the smaller texts at our desks. Even before memorizing the altar boys' prayers and responses, I had gone to mass at least weekly with my parents and heard Latin recited by priests and congregants, including my parents. I was learning that there are different ways to say the same thing. We started every class by making the sign of the cross, followed by a prayer in English. The prayer ended with, "In the name of the father and of the son and of the holy spirit." Each schoolday began with mass, where we said the same prayer in Latin (*In nomine patris et filii et spiritus sancti*). Even though our working-class family and the other working-class families in our world were second or third generation in this country, our ancestors had quickly discarded their native languages and learned English, wanting so much to be Americans. If it weren't for the Latin prayers and the Greek *Kyrie* we heard daily in church, I don't think we would have realized there were other languages.

Knowing enough Latin to pray in mass and at other devotional settings was important in the working-class Catholic family in a way other intellectual pursuits were not. For the young boy inclined toward the priesthood, however, learning Latin prayers precisely and with impeccable ecclesiastic pronunciation was less a manifestation of religious piety and more a sign of academic talent; it marked the altar boy as having priesthood potential. As one of these altar boys, I realized this at an early age. I was not very good at sports, but I could memorize Latin prayers. I concentrated on my other studies. I was told I had to be good at everything if I wanted to attend seminary. In a working-class village like ours, this differentiated me from most others my age. But the priests and the nuns had identified five in my class as seminary material. We formed a clique. All five were the same age and in the same class. To my knowledge, none of the other four was gay. One died when we were in seventh grade. The other three went to the high school seminary with me. One lasted a semester and the other two stayed only until the end of the first year. Of the four of us, I am the only one who earned a doctorate. One earned a master's degree and works as a counselor at a college. One did not pursue formal higher education. The other earned his bachelor's degree after intermittent periods in a local commuter university. He was the most intelligent of the four of us.

None of the four families, at least not the parents, valued higher education. Some families were overtly antagonistic toward earning a college degree. My parents felt higher education was not a very realistic goal. First, college was expensive even if one went to the regional commuter university. Besides the costs of tuition and books, one would not be earning a living while in college. Finally, although my parents knew that many college graduates commanded high salaries, they could not really envision someone from their family in the types of jobs for which these graduates were qualified. However, they could envision someone from their family as a priest, so they seemed to accept the pastor's encouraging one, even two, of their sons to pursue this high calling. Nevertheless, they did emphasize the importance of finishing high school for all their children. My mother had finished high school, but my father had not, although eventually he earned a GED. Eighth grade graduation and high school graduation were major family events, with relatives and neighbors invited for the celebration. Like me, my oldest brother left home after eighth grade to enter the high school seminary. My second oldest brother attended the local commuter university on and off until he finished an undergraduate degree.

When I left home for high school seminary, three of my friends went with me, and I expected everyone else at the place would be like us. Not so. A few were, but most were not. About one-third of the students were from rural Illinois, a few of these coming from farming families that seemingly had more money than our families, while the others came from wealthier professional and retail families in those rural communities. More than half the students came from middle-class and professional class families in urban centers of Illinois, Minnesota, Missouri, and Wisconsin. I am not sure I would have adjusted to this more middle-class environment without my three hometown classmates whose socioeconomic status was the same as mine. Eventually, I established myself academically and socially and almost felt better being at school than being in my hometown. I remember my initial visit home at Thanksgiving of that first year: Everything seemed so small—physically and intellectually.

At high school, virtually all the teachers were Catholic priests or brothers with master's degrees. The librarian, though, was an older layman who resided with the priests and brothers, but was obviously separate. A conflict between him and the school rector led to his dismissal even though he had been at the school for about thirty years. Many of us retained a relationship with this favorite teacher, whom we called "Prof." Through the remainder of high school, throughout college, and after leaving the seminary following college graduation, I enjoyed visits with Prof, who challenged us to read, keep abreast of current events, and explore the arts and theater. At the time, I don't know if I could have articulated why I felt such an affinity for Prof. He was the most open-minded, although certainly the other teachers challenged us. In retrospect, it was through Prof that I learned one could be an intellectual and an educated human being without being a priest and without identifying so compulsively with Catholic ideology. The rector who had dismissed Prof from his seminary position once asked him why he didn't attend chapel. Prof replied he felt while sitting in the wooded campus he was closer to God than the priest on the altar was. The rector, of course, cried, "Heresy!" I don't know whether Prof was gay—he never married and he never made a sexual advance toward any student, at least to my understanding. In Prof I saw how one could live the life of an intellectual without being a priest.

One of the greatest ironies of my academic preparation was how much the Catholic setting and, in particular, the seminary environment, contributed to my psychosexual development. I know many gay men point to church teaching and the pronouncements of priests and nuns as having caused them great anxiety and stress as they discovered their own homosexuality. For me, quite the opposite was true. As odd as it may seem, the seminary helped me become very comfortable with my homosexuality—not because the seminary supported or advocated homosexuality, but because it encouraged me to take an intellectual approach to all aspects of life. In the working-class neighborhood and working-class village where I was raised, there was no discussion of sexuality and especially no mention of homosexuality. The same was true in the seminary. Apart from some pretty graphic treatment in biology class, the only veiled discussion of sexuality centered on the celibacy requirement for priests. Even those discussions concerned issues about remaining unmarried and living without a family. These are important topics for gay men as well.

Because I attended high school and college in a setting that emphasized celibacy, I didn't face the sexual tension that pubescent teenagers and young adult men encounter. Certainly, I did not face the sexual anxiety gay teenagers and young men faced in the late 1960s and early 1970s. I really did remain celibate. As early as about seventh or eighth grade, I had identified my sexual orientation. I didn't talk about it, but I knew where my emotions and yearnings were centered. When my classmates were beginning to talk about girls, I knew what they meant, but I felt that way about some older boys in the school. Watching television, I had warm feelings about characters such as *Bonanza*'s Adam. I thought the Mickey Mouse Club's Spin and Marty were an attractive couple. I remember when my dad took me to buy clothes and shoes, I felt a tingling all over when a salesman would touch me to see how well a jacket or pair of shoes fit. No salesman touched me inappropriately, but I enjoyed the feeling of a man's hand. No one in my family or in my community talked about homosexuality. I knew my feelings were real, but since I had decided to enroll in the seminary after eighth grade, I could ignore them. I don't remember ever thinking the feelings were wrong even though I knew my parents and the priests and nuns would certainly say they were.

I didn't talk about these feelings to anyone. Instead, I went to the small, local public library and began reading everything I could about homosexuality. I would sit in the library on Saturdays and read sociology and psychology books, works I feared the librarian would not let me borrow. Interestingly, the books were relatively current. There were some references to psycho-sexual maladjustment and to similar explanations of homosexuality. But most of these books discussed the harmful effects on gay men from prohibitions and prognostications condemning homosexuality. I thought I had discovered a secret. The high school seminary had once also included the first two years of college, so the library was quite advanced. I was surprised to find books with similar ideas in that library, although it also included moral treatises condemning homosexuality and exhorting Catholics to pray for God to cure the homosexual.

I had learned there was an intellectual basis for understanding my own circumstances, as well as all human phenomena. I became even more en-amored of academic life. I had not yet separated myself from the church or the seminary, although I now understood it was possible. I was, by this time, learning that some in the church did not condemn homosexuality. I also learned there were those in the seminary, both homosexual and heterosexual, whose commitments to celibacy meant rejecting marriage without necessarily denying themselves sexual gratification. While I knew I had to be celibate to stay in the seminary and eventually become a priest, I also understood the attitudes and personal circumstances of these others. While the Stonewall riots had already occurred and discussion of gay rights was gaining steam, gay men were still largely in the closet, at least in my world. I remember several of my classmates reported telling their bishops before ordination they were gay. Their bishops said it did not matter what kind of sexual activity they refrained from, heterosexual or homosexual, as long as they were abstinent.

I knew I was gay and I did not want to remain celibate. I left the semi-nary after college graduation in May. Although at the time it seemed like a difficult choice, I would later come to understand my decision was inevitable and had probably been made much earlier than I acknowledged to myself. In retrospect, I believe whatever conflict I may have experienced regarding the decision was less about my choice and more about communicating it to my family and to priests at home who had encouraged me to pursue a life in the church. The summer following my departure from the seminary I had my first sexual encounter.

By this time, I was relatively certain I wanted to teach. I had earned a BA in English with teacher certification. My first job, however, was teaching communications skills, values clarification, and sex education at a Catholic, inner-city, girls' high school. The school was in its last year of operation, preparing for merger with the boys' school the following year. I was offered a position in the religion department of the merged school, but I had also been offered a teaching assistantship at the local state university, where I had applied for admission to the master's program. I accepted the assistantship. I doubt my father understood my giving up a full-time job to return to college for a graduate degree. He and my mother responded as they would so often in my life and the lives of my siblings. They said, "It's your life and you have to live it in a way you think is right for you," the same response they would give a few years later when I told them I am gay and I had met someone who would become my life partner.

Working on the master's degree transformed me. For one, it was the first time I attended a non-Catholic school. Second, the university was large—more than 10,000 students compared to the 1,200 at my undergraduate college and seminary. (One of my freshman students would write that she transferred to this university because she wanted to attend a small school. She had come from another state university with an enrollment of more than 40,000.) Virtually all the undergraduate students and most graduate students at the university were from working-class and lower middle-class backgrounds, the majority from the region where I grew up. Most important, I was engaged with faculty who weren't priests, brothers, or nuns and with other students the majority of whom were not Catholic. Plus, all of this was happening in a setting not centered on Catholic culture and ideology. I easily saw that my prior education had been much broader and far more extensive than my peers.' My working-class background told me to get the best value for the tuition waiver that accompanied my assistantship. I pursued a linguistics concentration in the English Department. I took an overload of courses and earned a summer stipend, taking all the requirements for the literature concentration as well. I pursued a three-term program in editing. I even took some additional foreign language courses. I also immersed myself in the university's social and cultural life. Outside the classroom I was developing personal relationships, enjoying life as a single gay man in a diverse educational environment located within a major metropolitan area. I was becoming more politically conscious. The university sponsored an organization for undergraduate and graduate gays and lesbians and brought in speakers who addressed issues of importance to these students. I remember, in particular, attending a lecture by Leonard

Matlovich, the Vietnam veteran who was discharged from the military after disclosing his homosexuality. My undergraduate alma mater had been fairly liberal in its treatment of most social concerns, but it had avoided sexuality issues, including abortion and homosexuality.

When I completed the master's degree, I had difficulty finding a teaching job and had not yet committed to pursuing the doctorate. For a while, I worked for two faculty members in the Modern Foreign Languages department at the university, editing the manuscript for a first-year French textbook and translating foreign correspondence. Falling back on my Catholic roots, I eventually landed a job teaching sixth grade at an inner-city Catholic elementary school while pursuing projects with a local community theater. I enjoyed teaching grade school, and I was good at it. I could explore inventive teaching approaches in a school that encouraged innovation. By now, however, I had become sexually active. I had come out to my older brother but not to other family members. My brother was very supportive, but I was still not comfortable telling the rest of my family. I had seen friends' liberal middle- and professional-class families reject them for saying what I wanted to say. Although I felt close to my family, I knew my friends had felt close to their families, too. I wasn't ready to risk rejection. My brother said he thought I was underestimating the rest of the family, but I probably needed to wait to tell them until I had more confidence in them and myself. Of course, later he was proven right about their being open to what I wanted to say; my parents, siblings, and their spouses were enthusiastically supportive from the moment I told them about my sexuality.

I felt pretty certain the nuns with whom I was teaching would have been supportive, but I knew the organizational church would not. The school where I taught was in East St. Louis, Illinois, a severely decaying inner city across the Mississippi River from St. Louis. Because of its proximity to St. Louis and its decadent circumstances, East St. Louis was home to a great deal of adult entertainment, including the largest gay bars in the St. Louis area. It was the late 1970s and the bars operated without harassment from police or residents. And the bars were literally within blocks of where I was teaching. My sixth grade students talked often about seeing men dressed as women walking down the street. At school, we had discipline problems that were typical of inner-city schools. On one occasion, I took a knife away from a seventh grader. Another time, I confiscated a gun from an eighth grader. We were often breaking up fights. Overall, the students were good kids living in bad circumstances. I had, however, seen some parents blame the teacher when something went wrong. When I broke up one fight, a large eighth-grade student grabbed me by the neck and I had to wrestle him to the ground. The father claimed I mishandled the situation, but the principal supported me.

Because of these experiences, I became almost obsessed with fearing that someday someone would falsely accuse me of sexual misconduct with the young students, even though I had no such inclination and took care to avoid even the appearance of anything inappropriate. Part of my fear stemmed, I think, from observing that young children love and need to be touched, with a hand on the shoulder, a pat on the head, or a hug. The school had an innovative organizational structure with a team administration. Two nuns shared the principalship, one focusing on administration the other on academics. The academic principal was leaving for another assignment and I was offered that position after only one year at the school. By now, I knew I needed to break with the church and I understood taking the position would represent a commitment to certain values and beliefs I could no longer accept. Without having another offer, I declined the principalship and resigned my teaching position. I wanted to teach in a college or university. I had enjoyed my two-year graduate teaching assistantship and I thought the higher education environment was a safer place for a gay man. More important, though, I longed to be part of an academic community. I was anxious to discard my Catholic and working-class roots.

Times were getting better for those with a master's degree in English. I knew I would have to get the doctorate eventually, but I wasn't quite ready to return to school. I applied for teaching positions in several places. I was offered adjunct appointments at three institutions in the metropolitan area where I lived. I was also offered a job at an historically black university in Tennessee. The position would allow me to help establish a writing support center and develop instructional materials utilizing audio, video, and computer technology, although it did not include a faculty appointment. It seemed an ideal position, one that would allow me to accomplish something concrete that I could list on my curriculum vitae for admission to a doctoral program. The work would also help me in the future when I applied for full-time faculty openings. After my first year, I was offered a faculty appointment at this school. Almost thirty years later I remain on the faculty and serve in an administrative capacity, having earned the doctorate from another area university.

My early experiences at this university were mixed. I enjoyed the students. Like me, many were from poor and working-class families and many were first-generation college students. Their families, however, placed a premium on finishing college. A large percent of the students were from outside the university's locale. Many did not have the advantage of the rigorous high school education I had completed. Nonetheless, they were focused on their studies, albeit more pragmatically than I had been. It was exciting. I was really teaching in an environment in which instruction and learning were valued.

My colleagues welcomed me. I was respected as a peer with something to contribute. The department head was particularly supportive. We both had specialties in linguistics and rhetoric. I learned more about teaching from her and from a few of my other colleagues than I did in any previous or future pedagogical courses I took. Several colleagues, probably most of them, however, came from middle- and upper-class backgrounds. Many had parents who had been college professors or administrators. Some were children of physicians and lawyers. A few came from successful farming families. All were from homes where a college education was highly valued. Because of my educational background, many of them seemed to assume my parents were middle or upper middle class. The department head had become a friend and mentor. She had gotten me a tenure-track faculty appointment, and she encouraged me to enroll in a doctoral program, reminding me that the doctorate would be necessary for tenure.

Although it is a state school, unlike most northern and midwestern public universities, here there was virtually no recognition of gay and lesbian issues. In my early years, the late 1970s, there was a noticeable strain of homophobia, strongest among students but also noticeable among some faculty and administrators. There were reports, never officially recorded of course, that gay male students were harassed and even assaulted in the dormitories. Students were quick to make snide remarks about effeminate male students and faculty. In literature classes, students were equally quick to laugh at or scorn references to homosexuality in the readings. Faculty and administrators were more subtle in their homophobia. There were, of course, the frequent inquiries regarding my marital status or my plans for marriage. A few faculty would make derogatory remarks, not about me, but about gay people in general. These comments would escalate with the onset of the AIDS epidemic. One other English faculty in particular was a published poet who referred to gay men as "walking AIDS machines." When she read her poetry in class, a gay male student came to me appalled and hurt that a faculty member would express such opinions in a formal setting. When I discussed the matter with my colleague, she was unapologetic about her disdain for gay men, citing Old Testament and Pauline prohibitions against homosexuality. Many of my colleagues, however, personally supported me, although, in general, there just wasn't much discussion of gay rights or other issues of importance to gays. I began to consider seeking an assistantship in a doctoral program without requesting a leave of absence from the university. I wanted an environment more supportive of gay and lesbian students and faculty. When I discussed my future at the school with my department head and mentor, I told her about my concerns and she encouraged me to remain there.

About this same time, I met the man who would become my partner. Like me, he was from a lower-class family. He, however, had grown up in the Deep South in a rural Alabama farming and mill town not far from the Gulf Coast. His father was seventy years old when he was born and died when my partner was about eleven years old. My partner was one of only a few from his high school to attend college, having been encouraged by his mother. He graduated from a fundamentalist college and was married briefly while a student there. He never enjoyed school and did not pursue an advanced degree. He did, however, encourage me when I began to work on my doctorate. We were the same age and remained together for more than twenty-six years until his recent death from a prolonged illness. The similarities in our backgrounds did not have a significant influence on the development of our relationship, nor were they a hindrance.

I did not live my life at the university in the closet, but in the beginning I was open about my life and my partner only with those colleagues who had also become close friends. They included my partner in the same way they included the spouses of other colleagues. Throughout my tenure at the university, I have served in various academic and nonacademic administrative posts, including about seven years as the university's affirmative action officer. I became more public about my life and my partner, although I could not persuade the governing board to add sexual orientation to its nondiscrimination statement. Some at the governing board were outright antagonistic toward discussing gay rights. At a strategic planning meeting in the mid-1990s, governing board staff were discussing revisions to mission and vision statements, as well as the school's affirmative action standards. I asked a senior staff member when the board would add sexual orientation to the nondiscrimination statement. He tersely replied the board was not in the business of granting special rights to any group. He shared my Italian Catholic heritage, so I reminded him that Italians and Catholics had protection under the current statement prohibiting discrimination based on religion and national origin. He rightfully responded that neither group had special protection, but both were covered because the statement referenced categories, not groups. I agreed and explained I had not asked for special rights for gay and lesbian students and employees, but only that sexual orientation be added as a category. He argued that since we did not discriminate against heterosexuals, adding sexual orientation would, de facto, provide special protection for gays and lesbians. When I thanked him for making my point, he became irate and another participant suggested the discussion be continued later. Of course, the discussion has never been continued and the university and its system remain uncommitted to protecting the rights of its gay and lesbian students, faculty, and staff, although some schools in the system do include such references in their institutional statements.

An historically black, state-supported university (HBCU) in the South, my current institution has never upheld gay issues. Several colleagues have suggested reasons for this. Some, both here and at other HBCUs, say it stems from the church's strong role in the black community. They reason that Christian churches are notably homophobic and, given its historical responsibilities, the African American church plays a much larger role in the life of HBCUs than it does in other state-supported colleges. My school, for example, was embroiled in lengthy litigation, which it eventually lost, because Protestant and Christian prayers were recited at the opening of many meetings and at all convocations and commencements. Meanwhile, other colleagues insist that institutional homophobia at HBCUs stems from a history of closeted, married faculty and administrators using anti-gay rhetoric for self-protection; "They *must* be straight. Otherwise, why would they [closeted married faculty and administrators] be so anti-gay?" or so the reasoning goes. Finally, another group of my colleagues insist that the underlying attitude is: "Hey, we fought for our rights, so you fight for yours, but don't piggyback on our successes," as if there are not enough rights to go around. The fallacy in this argument is, of course, that rights are not part of a zero-sum game. I tend to believe HBCUs are so anti-gay because of the first reason: the African American church's role in the life of these universities.

Overall, it is easier for me as a white male on my campus to be out than it is for my gay black colleagues, many of whom remain closeted. Gay rights issues are often interpreted as important primarily to white males.

The atmosphere at the university is undoubtedly much more tolerant now than it was thirty years ago. But the operative word is "tolerant." Although no one is openly hostile toward gay rights issues, outright support for such causes is limited among faculty and administrators. One former senior-level administrator served concurrently on the city council as vice mayor and was instrumental in defeating a proposed ordinance to include sexual orientation in the city's nondiscrimination policy statement. Subsequent to this event, he received a university ambassador award for representing the school and its values to the public, especially in his role as vice mayor. Another city council member, a university alumna, was also very vocal in her opposition to the proposed ordinance and even more belligerent in her expressions of disdain for gays and lesbians. Subsequently, the university has spotlighted her as a prominent alumna and school supporter. In 2003, I was diagnosed with colon cancer. A university staff member with whom I had worked closely throughout my tenure on campus told me the cancer was God's punishment for my gay lifestyle. Surgery removed all my cancer; ironically, however, the homophobic staff member died from breast cancer less than one year later.

Following my partner's death, I was struck by the extensive outpouring of sympathy and support I received from throughout the university. My own boss, the vice president for academic affairs, had always been supportive and inclusive. His understanding throughout my partner's prolonged illness made it possible for me to do what I had to do to care for my partner. My boss sent an e-mail notice and statement of condolences to the entire university constituency, just as he would for any faculty member who had lost a spouse or family member. To my knowledge, this was the first time a university official acknowledged a faculty member's gay partner. As a result of this e-mail, I received numerous calls, notes, and other truly genuine expressions of sympathy from university friends, colleagues, and even students. Some of these came from persons whom I would never have expected to be supportive and understanding. Many colleagues attended my partner's memorial service. Still, several were noticeably silent and conspicuously absent. The university's president, with whom I had worked closely for a number of years, did not send condolences on behalf of the institution. The university does not yet include sexual orientation in its nondiscrimination clause. Nevertheless, it has come a long way from the almost rabidly homophobic environment I perceived when I first arrived on campus nearly three decades ago. Some religious zealots on campus still refer to homosexuality as moral transgressions, comparable to rape and murder. Others keep their bigotry to themselves. Still, there is hope. The student newspaper recently included several positive articles about same-sex marriages and civil unions, and a student organization has sprung up for gay, lesbian, bisexual and transgendered students and their friends. The recently appointed president of the university has not publicly addressed gay and lesbian rights. However, in a recent meeting, he agreed that sexual orientation should be included in understanding diversity. Similarly, he spoke of administrators' "significant others" rather than their "spouses." These developments suggest he might be empathetic to gay concerns.

I had at various times throughout my tenure at the university considered seeking a position elsewhere, somewhere perhaps where homophobia was less blatant. However, I settled into the southern city that is home to my institution and where gay businesses and organizations are becoming visible. I lived for a significant time in an historic neighborhood where gay singles and couples were leading its restoration. I have noticed gradual improvements in the homophobic attitudes of university administrators and faculty. The institution is moving more slowly than its majority-white counterparts, but it is progressing in its stance toward gay and lesbian students and faculty. I want to believe that my presence has made a difference and that my continuing efforts will help improve both policies and attitudes even more.

Today, I reside three hundred miles and thirty years from that house in the working-class neighborhood where my family moved when I was five years old. The house was sold after my father died. It wasn't the kind of house or neighborhood that eventually becomes home. Like so much of the late twentieth century, it was a product of planned obsolescence. It still stands, but it has become low-rent housing in a rapidly deteriorating subdivision. The further I get from that home, however, the more I seem to be drawn to it. My parents had been very active in their church and in their community. My father was a lifelong member of the Knights of Columbus, a Catholic men's organization similar to the Masons. He was a fourth-degree knight and served as an officer in local, regional, and state capacities. Not long before he died, my father received a lifetime service award at a banquet in his honor. When his family was recognized, my brothers and sisters were introduced along with their spouses. In one of the biggest surprises of my life, my partner and I were introduced together. I have no illusion that the Knights of Columbus or the small community where I was raised are supportive of gay rights. Recent political trends suggest quite the contrary. However, I know many of these working-class organizations and individuals are struggling with these issues in ways neither they nor I would have ever predicted. For the most part, they stick to the party line, to church teaching, to comfortable tradition. But when the issue has a face and a name they know, they are more likely to support the individual.

I have evolved from someone who had become almost ashamed of his background and perceived himself as having overcome it, to one who realizes his background is his life's foundation. I am quite happy to no longer be where I started. But my choices and my accomplishments grew from that background. Some of my choices involved using available opportunities, such as the college preparatory high school and liberal arts college educations I received because of the church's approach to academically talented poor and working-class boys. Some choices were reactions to or against that same church and opportunities I did not have because of my religion and the economic class I was born into. I am a better teacher because my education is complemented by an understanding of my students' social and economic struggles. I am a better administrator because I learned management from the most highly structured organization in the world, the Catholic Church. All the while, life has taught me that "rules are made to be broken." I am a better person because I like who I am, I better understand who I am, and I am always striving to know more about myself, especially how who I am is a function of who I was.

FIVE

One in Ten

Teaching Tolerance for (Class) Difference, Ambiguity,

and Queerness in the Culture Classroom

DENIS M. PROVENCHER

Between 1998 and 2005, I taught French and International Studies at the University of Wisconsin, La Crosse (UW-La Crosse), a regional comprehensive university in the upper Midwest.[1] My teaching assignment included courses in French language and culture and a course in intercultural communication, where students learned about "culture shock" and how to become better interculturalists during their study-abroad experience. Throughout my first several years as an untenured, junior faculty member at UW-La Crosse, I devoted most of my time to perfecting my teaching in these areas and doing research—the two most important "legs" of a three-legged academic stool, according to many university professors and administrators. Admittedly, I participated rather infrequently in both services-related activities and student-based organizations, except as faculty advisor for the French club.

In fall 2003, as I was finishing my tenure file, a member of the student organization "Straights and Gays for Equality" (SAGE) invited me to deliver a public presentation about my experiences as a "gay French teacher" at the second annual "Night of Compassion." This event brought together lesbian, gay, bisexual, transgender, and queer (LGBTQ) students and their allies from UW-La Crosse, the surrounding colleges, and the local community for an evening of music, poetry, personal narratives, and a silent auction to raise money for the local LGBTQ youth organization. Seeing this as an opportunity to engage in new ways with LGBTQ students on a campus where very few gay or lesbian role models existed for them, I willingly agreed to leave my teaching and research "comfort zone" to participate in this worthwhile event.

To publicize the occasion, a UW-La Crosse student reporter interviewed me for an article in the campus-based student newspaper *The Racquet*. She asked me various questions about my college education, coming-out experience, reasons for moving to the Midwest, and life as a college professor. On the day of the event, *The Racquet* published the brief article, "UW-L Teacher Speaks about Homosexual Experiences," which represented my very first media-related coming out. Initially, this headline struck me as funny because I had never thought of my own life as a series of "homosexual experiences," a provocative phrase, given its potential interpretation by both students and colleagues as "homosexual acts." Nor had I ever called myself a "gay French teacher" as described in the opening line of the article, given the taboo-like connotation evoked by the combination of signifiers ["gay" and "teacher"]. I could comprehend perhaps a term such as "gay researcher" as I understand how my sexual orientation informs my academic interests. In my own words, I probably would have said something slightly different: "I'm a professor who studies issues of gender and sexuality in contemporary French culture," since my research examines coming-out stories and other narratives of French gays and lesbians and compares them with stories told by Anglophone (U.S.-based and UK-based) LGBT populations (see Provencher, 2007). However, I did not know what to make of the reporter's journalistic shorthand "gay teacher." It had never really occurred to me, until reading her article, how my sexual orientation could have any significant bearing on my teaching philosophy or rapport with students in the classroom. How could sexual "difference" or "queerness" enhance the teaching of "foreign language and cultures" to American students? Is it possible to speak of a queer classroom pedagogy?

The *Racquet* article briefly mentioned other elements of my personal and professional life, including my French-Canadian heritage, romantic life, and general impressions of UW-La Crosse. For example, the reporter wrote: "The culture in which he grew up reflects French-Speaking Canada in that the family appreciates the small things in life, which can be attributed to his father's roots in Quebec." Although the journalist did not focus here on my family's socioeconomic background, it finally occurred to me in rereading the article both *how* I got to UW-La Crosse and *why* I enjoyed working on this campus during the first seven years of my professional life. For UW-La Crosse is largely composed of first-generation college students and many put themselves through school by working either part-time or full-time jobs. Hence, it was not only my "French-Canadian" heritage as described in the article that influenced who I was and how I approached teaching, but also the fact that I grew up in a rather modest Franco-American household (described below).

Indeed, the newspaper article and the eventual presentation at "Night of Compassion" provided me a fortuitous opportunity to retrace and reevaluate the personal and professional steps that led me to my position as a working-class queer in academe.[2] As will become more apparent, the *Racquet* article encouraged me to reflect not only on the role of "difference" or "queerness" but also on "socioeconomic background" and how it contributes to the creation of a productive classroom environment in which learning about linguistic and culture differences emerges in authentic ways. The remainder of this chapter—a revised version of the paper presented that evening—attempts to unite these two elements of my identity and situate them in the context of my professional life.[3]

WORKING-CLASS AND QUEER BEGINNINGS:
COMING OUT AS A FRENCH MAJOR

Like Jack Kerouac, my father was a first-generation Franco-American whose family fled the poverty of Francophone Canada (Québec) in the 1920s to pursue the "American Dream." My paternal grandparents eventually settled in Burlington, Vermont, where my grandfather worked as a laborer in a bobbin factory while my grandmother raised their nine children. Indeed, French–Canadian language and culture, including a strong Catholic faith, surrounded my father both at home and in the parochial school he attended that was run by French-Canadian nuns. The Baltimore Catechism he learned during his childhood "education" still represents one of the strongest guiding forces in his life. Yet, from a very early age, he also learned the importance of English as the language of opportunity to succeed as an "American."

Unlike Jack Kerouac, my father eventually dropped out of high school to work for an older brother who owned a furniture store. Dad did not go back to earn his GED until the 1980s when his employer strongly encouraged him to do so. In the meantime, he met my mother, another Burlington native of French-Canadian background, who had earned her high school diploma with an emphasis in secretarial management. They eventually married, settled in the Burlington area, and both found jobs working as support staff in higher education and had two children. My father initially accepted a position in the physical plant at the University of Vermont (UVM) and later became supervisor of their campus mail services. My mother worked for several years as a secretary in UVM's College of Education. However, she eventually resigned her position as she struggled regularly with mental illness. Although both my parents came from modest socioeconomic backgrounds, they certainly understood the importance of working hard—ironically both a French-Canadian (Catholic) and American value. Furthermore, they also came to understand the importance of a college education from seeing it firsthand in their work environment. Therefore, they always encouraged me to pursue my academic interests.

In public high school, I fit in quite well academically as I took all the college-preparation math and science classes as well as AP (Advanced Placement) English and AP French. I did well in my courses and established a good rapport with both my teachers and classroom peers. However, certain elements of an "invisible evidence" (Carroll 1987) of distinction surrounded me all the while, reminding me I did not completely fit in. Somehow, I was different from many of my college-bound peers, but I could not put my finger on why. I had friends in high school, but I did not win any popularity contests.

Although I was largely unaware of my "sexual identity" in such terms until my senior year of high school and freshman year of college, I often experienced a level of discrimination, mostly from male peers—either in social settings or during physical education—when my academic abilities could no longer mask other signs of difference. While my male peers were required to interact with me in the classroom as we worked in paired activities or group projects, they frequently ignored me in other settings. For example, because I did not participate in any organized team sports, my male classmates frequently picked me last for team activities in gym class. I preferred to participate in more individualized and apparently less "masculine" activities since I played piano and joined the jazz band. In retrospect, this silent discrimination or "invisible evidence" reminded me I did not fit in as a "straight" kid because I did not "perform" the typically masculine roles during my high school years.

Nonetheless, my sexual identity was not overly apparent to me in high school and I did not come out then. Hence, being a working-class kid presented an equally significant challenge for me as a teenager. The affluent children of many out-of-state families had moved to the Burlington area in the 1970s and 1980s to work for the university or the medical or computer industries (IBM had an extesnive workforce there). They lived in newly built homes and neighborhoods with panoramic views of both Lake Champlain and the Adirondack Mountains. Conversely, we lived in one of the "older" neighborhoods on the side of town largely inhabited by working-class and lower middle-class "Vermonters" of two or more generations. While the newer out-of-state "immigrants" could buy their children the latest fashions, sports cars, and high-tech ski equipment for their weekend trips to Stowe, my parents often struggled—mostly on one salary—to pay the weekly grocery bill, let alone pay for school clothes, recreational activities, or even birthday or Christmas gifts. I could not erase my visibly inferior social class status. Eventually, I discovered that my academic pursuits were my only means of liberation from the material reality of my childhood. The classroom allowed me to enter a world where equality based largely on pure intellectual capacities seemed attainable. In the end, this, combined with the strong work ethic of my French-Canadian upbringing, gave me the necessary discipline, persistence, and determination to survive high school and acquire the requisite intellectual capital (Bourdieu 1979) to find my way to college.

Despite my parents' modest backgrounds, they still provided me with an excellent college education opportunity. While my brother opted for vocational schooling and accepted a job directly out of high school, I took advantage of my father's employment benefits and received a full tuition waiver, allowing me to complete my undergraduate degree at the University of Vermont at virtually no cost. Ironically, my father's benefits would allow me to earn a college degree at his place of employment, which, in turn, would help me further erase any signs of class difference caused by his employment status within that institution—or so I thought. Being a UVM student allowed me to meet and socialize with a variety of people, including affluent out-of-state residents whose parents could afford "out-of-state" prices at a state university touted as a "public ivy." Since Vermont has long provided one of the lowest percentages of state funding to its universities and colleges—ranking in the lowest tier of the fifty states—UVM fiercely recruits a significant portion of students from families who can afford higher tuition rates (see Schmidt 2002). While visual minorities remain largely absent from UVM, a combination of privileged and less privileged students attend the university—enhancing on some level this institution's "diversity." Interestingly, many of my high school peers attended either private colleges or out-of-state institutions. High school friends who attended UVM were often from the same side of town as I. Although I eventually met many interesting out-of-state students at UVM, I developed my closest friendships with other Vermonters who were partially financing their own educations.

I had entered college as a biology (pre-med) major and planned on eventually attending medical school. My mother's own mental illness and dissatisfaction with the medical profession and our inability to cover her psychiatric bills largely incited my idealistic desire to change the medical world. UVM also touted an excellent medical school and especially encouraged in-state students to apply. Moreover, like a college education, a medical degree was another means of climbing the socioeconomic ladder, allowing me to move even further away from the life I had known as a working-class kid. Hence, during my first two years at college, I enrolled in several lab-science (biology and chemistry) and math courses.

Once I settled into undergraduate life, however, both my academic pursuits and personal life changed dramatically. While high school had prepared me well for pre-med course work, I discovered the more I enrolled in lab-science courses, the less time I had to take humanities and social science courses. I remained largely passionate about modern languages (French and Spanish), linguistics, anthropology, and comparative religions; trying to schedule science courses that included extensive lab components largely limited my ability to select classes in these other fields. Over time, I was growing dissatisfied with my lab-science courses. Moreover, I discovered how the "Romance languages" and other humanities courses allowed me to learn about other parts of the world and different ways of seeing and being. Ultimately, I had a change of heart, dropped the pre-med requirements, and "came out" as a French major.

It was no accident how or when this change of academic major happened. When I entered college, I had pictured myself earning a medical degree, practicing medicine, making a good living, getting married, and having children—in short, the upper-middle-class dream. However, during my sophomore year of college, I began recognizing my true intellectual interests and passions and in turn abandoned an old sense of self (i.e., being heterosexual and becoming a doctor) that both my family and I had known and discussed for several years. During this same period, I was taking humanities courses and questioning the (heteronormative) world around me. I began to understand myself better, including my intellectual and emotional interests as well as my sexual desires. Like the displeasure I experienced with my socially acceptable and respectable college major (i.e., pre-med), I became more dissatisfied with heterosexual dating relationships. During my first two years at UVM, I met a lot of new friends, including members of the campus GLB Alliance (there was no "T" in those days), and during the next year I came out as a gay man. In other words, I "dropped the requirements" established for me by a largely heteronormative and middle-class world. Thus, it was no accident these two college events occurred quasi-simultaneously: I left behind both an academic major and an ill-suited sexual orientation.

Abandoning the biology major and declaring a French major with an interest in cultural studies, I was free to explore and understand other parts of the globe, which, in turn, allowed me to better analyze my own situation in relation to the world. Interestingly, Wylie, the late professor of French civilization at Harvard University, explains why many Americans choose to study French language and culture. He states:

> Some of our best students are those who are eager to get away from their own personalities, so eager to find another personality, that they take to it genuinely, I think. There is, of course, the student who is so secure in his own ego that he can play a role, be a good French student, without feeling threatened. (Wylie in Santoni 1981, 23)

Indeed, as I became more aware of my own sexuality and secure in my own ego, I could comfortably play other roles and try on "another personality" in a new cultural setting. Paralleling my coming-out experience, in which I explored previously uncharted territory related to my sexual and emotional desires, I sought new cultural and linguistic paradigms that could effectively express previously unpronounced portions of my ever-changing intercultural persona. Likewise, the more I understood myself as a gay person, the more comfortable I became with myself and others and could adapt easily to both new social settings and cultural contexts. I was not one of those insecure French students whom Wylie refers to as: "scared to death to let go of themselves, the ones who sit back and are afraid to pronounce 'u' " (Wylie in Santoni 1981, 23). I sought new contexts where I could perform the new sounds of my "gay" and "French" self both at home and abroad. This desire eventually prompted me to spend my junior year abroad at the Université de Nice (France), where I experienced, firsthand, various linguistic and cultural differences.

In sum, French language and culture became my new vehicles in this journey of self-discovery. I could try or "perform" foreign (i.e., previously unknown) identities—in a Butlerian sense—to see which new ones would replace or enhance the older parts. Butler (1990, 136) argues that gender is a social construction performed and reenacted time and again in various sociocultural contexts. Indeed, learning both a new language and its related cultural persona replicates this "performative" process.

However, little did I know at the time how much my sexual orientation or class background were driving forces behind this desire to learn French, study abroad, and pursue a career in French studies. To cite Wylie again:

> My great grandfather was a farmer, and my grandfather started a little furniture store in Indiana, and my father became a preacher, and then I became a professor. I'll bet that if we talked about Americans who teach French . . . so often among my colleagues I find the same phenomenon of having learned French because it was part of our upward mobility. . . . And then there is that other group of Americans who are interested in French—I would call them, not the upwardly, but the outwardly mobile, that is, the people who are seeking a new identity or trying to get away from us. This would include the famous generation of the twenties, Ernest Hemingway and Gertrude Stein, and so on, but it would also include others of us. I participate in this too. As a preacher's son from Indiana, one of my main interests in French was that I was trying to get away from my background. (Wylie in Santoni 1981, 22–23)

Clearly, as a postal worker's son from Vermont, I sought the same upward and outward mobility. Like Wylie, I could acquire a new form of cultural and linguistic capital (Bourdieu 1979) through all things French and this would eventually allow me to escape my working-class roots and become a college professor. Ironically, however, this field of study represented the same language tradition my father had abandoned in his quest to succeed as an English-speaking Franco-American. Moreover, I would eventually gain "privileged employment" as an academic in the same institutional environment that gave my father a working-class subsistence.

Upon graduation from UVM, I accepted a graduate teaching assistantship in the Department of French at the Pennsylvania State University where I completed my graduate studies. I chose to attend another public university primarily for two reasons: Penn State's French program is one of a very few nationwide that offers a concentration in French civilization. This would allow me to continue my academic pursuits of language, cultural studies, and anthropology. Second, the department offered me a two-year assistantship to complete my master's degree in French literature and a four-year teaching assistantship to complete my PhD in French civilization. Hence, like UVM, Penn State allowed me to pursue academic work at a well-regarded public university at virtually no cost. As I will explain, little did I know how this choice of schools would irreversibly shape my intellectual marketability (i.e., intellectual capital) and eventual employment opportunities.

At Penn State, I enrolled in French literature and civilization courses wherein I discovered various schools of intellectual thought. These schools would eventually help me express my own worldview. Like coming out of the closet or coming out of "the desert of nothing" (Leap 1996, 125–139) into a newfound gay culture where a new language of desire exists, "coming out of the intellectual closet" in graduate school allowed me to acquire a new theoretical language. This, in turn, allowed me to express my intellectual desires in previously foreign or nonexistent ways. In particular, two influential streams of thought—the French *Annales* School and Birmingham's Centre for Contemporary Cultural Studies—helped shape my approach to (French) civilization and cultural studies.

The French *Annale* (initiated by scholars such as Bloch and Febvre in the 1920s) was an alternative to the chronological approach to political and diplomatic history—which proposed a more interdisciplinary method incorporating both social and cultural history (see Burke 1990). French social historians began building intellectual bridges between history and other fields such as geography, sociology, anthropology, psychology, economics, and linguistics. This movement eventually helped initiate newer fields such as the history of private life, the history of mentalities and daily life, women's history, and the history of sexuality. Similarly, the Birmingham School emerged in the UK in the 1960s (under Hoggart and others). These scholars wanted to move beyond traditional literary studies to create a more interdisciplinary approach that included examining noncanonical (i.e., popular culture) texts and everyday practices (see Turner 1996). Working-class academics and students who largely instigated this intellectual movement aimed to combat the elitism of the academy by encouraging study of both "high" and "low" cultures. In short, the *Annales* and the Birmingham School represented a certain democratization of academic disciplines whereby both a new generation of scholars and subjects found their way into the academy.

Hence, when I had to choose a dissertation topic, the French *Annales* and the Birmingham School largely influenced my decision to research both canonical and noncanonical texts in contemporary French gay and lesbian popular culture. Indeed, the interdisciplinary approach would provide a practical means for examining the everyday life of French gays and lesbians. While my dissertation director completely supported my choice of thesis topic, in our early discussions, she encouraged me to devote a section to images of French homosexuals during World War II. In choosing a more "historical" topic, she suggested I ground my research in time to legitimize my work and secure an eventual job in the conservative academy. Perhaps slightly out of naiveté, but certainly out of my working-class conviction of the intellectual merit of analyzing popular culture, I decided to hold tightly to my thesis topic. In the end, I worked diligently to finish my thesis on French gay popular culture in a timely manner. Along the way, I also earned an internal university grant as well as substantial moral and intellectual support from professors and peers. At the thesis defense, I also received high praise from many committee members for my engaging research. My hard work had paid off and now it was time to find a long-awaited job in the so-called conservative academy.

During my final year of graduate school, I had two job interviews with large state research universities. Although neither of these interviews at the annual meeting of the Modern Language Association (MLA) led to a campus visit, the professors I met during these interviews appeared genuinely interested in my research. Eventually, perhaps they decided my area of study was either too "sexy" (i.e., provocative) for their institutions or "pop culture" was not a "good fit" for their more traditional literature departments. I also wondered about the academy's "invisibly evident" prejudice against PhD candidates from large state universities and their silent preference for Ivy League graduates, especially in light of tough budgetary times and the academy's persistent elitism. Indeed, it is largely unproductive and virtually impossible to determine the vagaries or agendas of various hiring committees, so I decided to forego this analysis and focus on becoming gainfully employed elsewhere in academics.[4] Later in the same hiring season, I received an invitation to a campus interview at a regional state university in the upper Midwest (UW–La Crosse). A week later, after having returned from the campus visit, I received a phone call from the department chair who offered me their tenure-track position as a generalist in French to teach civilization and culture courses. I happily accepted the job approximately two weeks later.

I fared quite well during my first year on the job market, having landed this position in my subfield. According to data published by the MLA on trends in the job market, approximately 28.4 percent of new PhDs in French and Italian found tenure-track employment in 1996–1997.[5] What I did not or could not know then is that there is truly something to be said about being a "good fit" with a department or college. As I will discuss, my training in French popular culture and gay and lesbian studies, coupled with my working-class background, would serve me well at UW-La Crosse. It was no accident this working-class academic had found his way into a teaching job at a comprehensive university. Moreover, this new professor of French civilization would experience his own episodes of culture shock in the Mississippi River Valley.

TEACHING LANGUAGE, CULTURE, AND INTERCULTURAL
COMMUNICATION: AN EXERCISE IN QUEERNESS AND
CLASS DIFFERENCE

Before moving to the Midwest, I had at least heard of Wisconsin, but I did not know where exactly to situate the "Dairy State" on the U.S. map. Furthermore, as an "East Coaster," I had a hard time believing that a working-class kid from the Green Mountain State (Vermont) could ever adapt to the flat "heartland," where "not much seemed to ever really happen." Furthermore, despite how Wisconsin and Vermont tout their respective agricultural industries (mostly dairy products), the two states are quite distinct; the least of which is that Vermont's flavorful cheese is naturally "white" whereas Wisconsin's largely bland cheese is artificially colored orange.[6] Vermont had recently legalized same-sex civil unions and UVM currently offers domestic partner benefits to unionized couples, whereas neither Wisconsin nor the UW system provides domestic partner benefits for its employees. These types of comparative statements always provoked a loud gasp in the classroom each time I mentioned them to my UW-La Crosse students, who came primarily from Wisconsin and Minnesota. They were largely unable to comprehend my initial apprehensions about moving to their great state. Nonetheless, these instances of my own initial naiveté about the Midwest represented excellent examples in the culture classroom when I taught about ethnocentrism, culture shock, and cultural relativism. I would always explain to students, for example, how not all roads lead to their land of cheese (Wisconsin) or mine (Vermont), for that matter. I was also constantly reminded of how an educated person with a PhD in cultural studies who has seen other parts of the world could still cling tightly to certain stereotypes about foreigners or "unknown" groups. Curiously, as I soon realized while interacting with my new colleagues at UW-La Crosse, I was not alone in my cultural stereotyping.

For example, before I arrived at UW-La Crosse, my two new colleagues in French had prepared a mailing that included a brochure and welcome letter to recruit incoming first-year students by advertising the French program to them. The brochure included a description of the French faculty, including a biography of the most recent hire. I received these materials the summer before my arrival at UW-La Crosse. When I read the enclosed letter, I discovered the following description: "We would like to present our new assistant professor, Denis Provencher, of French Canadian ancestry, who recently completed his PhD in French Civilization and Culture from the Pennsylvania State University." Round one of culture shock set in.

Like the *Racquet* article, the phrasing of this letter struck me in similar ways. Initially, I was flattered by the recognition of my recent accomplishment and excited to join the academy. My colleagues' thoughtfully chosen words about me were an excellent means to market the French program to students, especially those interested in French culture. Nonetheless, I remained a bit startled by the description: "French Canadian ancestry." Highlighting my French-Canadian heritage alongside my French-looking name gave me an additional boost of legitimacy or authenticity (as a "native" or "near-native French speaker") to the earned letters "PhD" and "Penn State." However, till then in my teaching career, I never had "come out" to colleagues or students as such. This description was a curious paradox, or at least an intriguing juxtaposition of social classes as signified by—"Provencher"—derived from modest Franco-American roots (described above)—and "PhD"—suggesting an "educated, native or near-native speaker."

Like students who study abroad and eventually get targeted by foreign nationals as the cultural ambassador for an entire population, my new colleagues in the Department of Modern Languages had targeted me as an authentic ambassador of both French and French-Canadian cultures. While I feel capable of "performing" the former in the context of the French classroom, the latter still remains somewhat and ironically foreign to me. Like students who eventually assume certain exaggerated parts of an affected American persona in foreign contexts as they act as cultural ambassadors for their home country, I eventually began introducing myself in La Crosse as a person of French-Canadian roots to "foreigners" (midwestern colleagues and students) in this other land. My graduate education in French studies had ultimately and ironically led me back to my French-Canadian and working-class beginnings. This will become more evident.

The second round of culture shock happened during my first semester on campus. It came in the context of the first-year junior-faculty retention process. Tenured departmental faculty members would visit and evaluate classes taught by probationary faculty and then meet to discuss the candidate's progress in teaching, research, and service. While my colleagues appeared genuinely impressed with my teaching abilities and rapport with students, they justifiably questioned me about my transition from graduate school to department life. This included adapting my teaching style—developed largely from my contact with students at a Big Ten university in the East—to the learning styles of UW-La Crosse students. I received a glowing retention letter that elaborated all my talents and successes. Nonetheless, I found another most striking statement embedded in this letter: "You are making great progress in teaching, but we hope that you will continue to adjust your teaching style to our Midwestern students." This may have just been the chairperson's unconscious phrasing meant to encourage me to find new ways to adapt my knowledge to the classroom. Still, I could not avoid wondering how an educated person could put such words in a retention letter that other professors and administrators would eventually read. As my departmental colleagues were either foreign nationals or Americans who had traveled and lived throughout the world, it seemed apparent they (like I) should avoid such labeling and stereotyping, something some inexperienced students do.

I would often share these two anecdotes with UW-La Crosse students in my language and culture classroom. They found them humorous, shocking, and enlightening. These stories exemplify various components of my own identity and background as well as my experience with stereotypes, cultural identity, and culture shock. What I have discovered in retelling these stories is that I can best begin educating students about cultural differences by starting with a discussion of our own similarities and differences as Americans from different regions. From there, it becomes easier to better understand other cultures and ways of being. To achieve this, I integrate various components of my own identity in both explicit and implicit ways.

First, in my French culture courses, students learn about American stereotypes of the French and French stereotypes of American and how to debunk these myths. They also learn about various "differences" associated with French identity through discussions of marginalized groups in contemporary France. For example, we examine multiple identities based on ethnicity, race, class, gender, and sexual identity that "disrupt" a collective French consciousness or national identity of today. These include, among others, North African and Russian immigrants, first- and second-generation North African immigrants, Jews, women, gays, and lesbians. We also examine French history and colonialism and their effect on such regions or countries as Québec, Wisconsin, Tahiti, Martinique, Guadeloupe, Senegal, and the Maghreb (North Africa). We examine the potential of the underrepresented and the underprivileged French-speaking "others" to subvert the elitist and hegemonic nature of the *métropole* (France as the "mother country") and her mother tongue. Such French and Francophone studies courses solicit an explicit approach to cultural studies (mentioned earlier) that integrates an analysis of both "high" and "popular" culture to examine differences. My working-class background comes through in my choice to present socially marginalized groups alongside the study of highly esteemed literary texts and cultural figures.

Teaching difference through implicit methods presents an equally if not more effective way to reach students in my French language and culture classes. For example, each semester, I teach introductory and/or intermediate French language courses. Here, I use language to transport students to various parts of the (Francophone) world. For many first-generation college students from working-class backgrounds who work to pay for school, this becomes the most economic and feasible way to give them an intercultural or international experience. For example, every semester at UW-La Crosse, I met students who had never traveled outside the United States, or ridden in a plane, or seen the ocean. Hence, it is both possible and important to bring the world to students through a modern language.

In the language classroom, I perform "French" difference for my students by exposing them to both a strange (i.e., foreign) accent and alien grammar while inviting them to partake in that experience with me. As Germano reminds us: "A foreign language is a kind of endlessly working difference generator" (2004, B16).[7] Moreover, by assigning everyone a French name, students can better assume new French personae and acquire a language to express this newfound difference. Students can "find another personality" (Wylie) and display it in simulated cultural settings. This helps students understand culture as "both something you perform and something you learn," as Kramsch reminds us (1991, 228). Since the course is taught completely in French, students know they will not understand every word. They must embrace uncertainty and ambiguity (i.e., queerness) as it relates to linguistic and cultural norms. This does not mean students learn about queer French culture in French 101. Still, they begin to see the world differently by acquiring a new language and describing it in previously unutterable ways. Students learn what Rosello calls "the coming out of one's linguistic closet" (1994, 154). Rosello argues that this "coming out" requires reexamining and leaving behind a secure sense of self and belonging. Students of foreign languages learn to become "unanchored" or detached from their previous cultural narratives and thus to open themselves to linguistic and cultural ambiguity, which helps facilitate language acquisition (ibid.).

Interestingly, Rosello establishes a link between "learning" gay and lesbian cultures and learning a foreign language. She hypothesizes that if gay and lesbian cultures include their own so-called language, native speakers, and cultural narratives, then the process by which one acquires such linguistic skills resembles that of learning other "foreign" cultures and languages.[8] She further contends that queers have acquired a certain bilingualism and biculturalism that gives them a potential advantage in teaching and learning other languages. She reasons: "Queers who know how to speak a straight idiom may be compared to the bilingual children of immigrants who can be both alienated and empowered by their double origin" (1994, 160).[9] Hence, if a "gay teacher" has anything to teach students in the French classroom, it may be that everyone can at least be "bi" (i.e., inhabit two or more worlds, be bilingual or multilingual). As a "foreigner," "outsider," or "cultural marginal" in terms of both class and sexual orientation, I have drawn on my own "cultural marginality" (Bennett 1993) to provide a unique perspective related to difference in teaching French language and culture.

Finally, I adapt my role as a working-class queer academic into intercultural communication, a field that prepares students to be cross-culturalists. For example, at UW-La Crosse, I regularly taught a course in intercultural communication called "Orientation to Study Abroad" that provided an introduction to the various challenges—academic, social, cultural, linguistic, political, and economic—related to resident study and research in a foreign country. Students learned about the various stages and theories associated with culture shock, intercultural sensitivity and communication, and reentry shock (reverse culture shock when one returns home) presented in recent scholarship. They also learned to apply these theories to their own upcoming international experience in countries such as Australia, Scotland, Ireland, England, France, Germany, Spain, and Mexico.

In this course, I explicitly taught students about other cultures, ways of life, as well as other ways of thinking and being that do not necessarily match their "American" or "Wisconsin" lifestyles. I helped students learn to combat stereotypes, generalizations, and various images of the "ugly American." I would tell them the two stories about my initial culture shock when I moved to the Midwest. I incorporated much of what I learned on study abroad and my continued overseas travels to conduct research. Students completed a series of assignments that helped them explore various forms of "difference" based on language, socioeconomic background, class, gender, and sexual orientation. For example, students were required to attend one campus or community event that moved them beyond their "comfort zone." Many Protestant students attended a Catholic mass while Catholic students attended a more evangelic service. Then both groups reported how this activity prompted them to adjust and rethink their own "anchored identity." During the latter part of my tenure at UW-La Crosse, students started to visit gay bars, or would attend an event organized by the sign language club, ride the city bus around town while mingling with local bus patrons, offer their time tutoring Hmong students (the local "immigrant" population), or travel to an urban environment (Milwaukee) to volunteer in a community cleanup project. These various activities illustrated ways to draw out cultural and linguistic differences in real-life situations.

In this course, I also integrated my working-class background and gay identity. However, I did this quite differently from the French language and culture courses. Interestingly, it is not necessary to "come out" in the French language or culture class as "different from my students" since I already act out or "perform difference" by speaking a foreign or "queer" tongue—challenging students to embrace such difference. I am already an authority of "difference" of French culture when we are in the French classroom because I am a "guardian of native knowledge" (Rosello 1994, 157). In other words, as the professor, I represent the "near-native" French speaker who has lived in and is familiar with the target culture. In the intercultural classroom at UW-La Crosse, I was not an authority on all parts of the world where students would travel. I had to "come out" as different in some way to initiate the learning process associated with intercultural sensitivity and cultural relativism. I "came out" as a Vermonter who had moved as a "foreigner" to the Midwest, as a gay male who has not always felt "at home" in a heteronormative world, and as a French speaker who does not always see things as the typical "American." I would also come out as an American professor of French-Canadian ancestry whose modest roots resurfaced while working in a regional state university in the Midwest. The latter helped me maintain common ground with them through this class distinction. This approach provided the necessary pedagogical leverage for teaching them about sameness and difference, including but not limited to being a "Vermonter," "Wisconsinite," "American," "gay," "working-class," and "bilingual speaker." In short, the students learned other ways of being.

When I started teaching as a graduate student, I did not understand the reason for divulging one's sexuality (or other background information) in the classroom. Gradually, I recognized its merits, which are not necessarily related to the content of the disclosure per se. Haggerty (1995) shows us the importance of "'promoting homosexuality' in the classroom":

> What a gay or lesbian studies classroom can accomplish is an open confrontation with the various essentialisms that threaten to silence difference in any classroom: we must liberate students from the various oppressions that have shaped their social 'identities.' (15) . . . 'Different organizations of the real,' then, are precisely what we as lesbian and gay faculty members owe our students. For if we leave them [students] as we found them, if by our silence or our shame we teach our students that the dominant culture was right about us all along, then we are merely replicating the traditional function of education. By acknowledging our own complicity, by challenging our whiteness, gayness, empoweredness, we help to point the way toward change. (17)

In the intercultural classroom, and particularly in study-abroad programs, students learn about "different organizations of the real" in preparing to live, study, and work abroad. Whether they know it or not (or like it or not), students experience their first dose of culture shock by dealing with a familiar "foreigner"—someone who is like them (working class) but not exactly like them (gay, Vermonter, professor). Although they may initially see this as my disclosing various if not inappropriate parts of me, it implicitly teaches what culture shock is. As Paige et al. (2002) explain, culture shock is: "caused less by one single incident and more by the gradual accumulation of anxiety, frustration, and confusion from living in an unfamiliar environment" (85). Hence, by seeing an accumulation of the subtle disclosures or "invisible evidence" of difference portrayed through my various performances of sameness and distinction, students experience culture shock in a familiar setting.

Interestingly, students who study abroad are their own minority group, since the national average of undergraduates who study abroad is twelve percent, or about one in ten (see Gomstyn 2003). Like LGBTQ students who supposedly represent one in ten students on college campuses, students in study-abroad programs constitute approximately one in ten in their graduating class. According to Madeleine F. Greene, vice president of ACE (American Council on Education) and director of its Center for Institutional and International Initiatives, only one in four U.S. institutions surveyed currently includes internationalization as a top strategic priority, and only one in three addresses internationalization in its mission statement (Gomstyn 2003). Consequently, it is extremely important to take this brave minority and prepare them for one of the most exciting and memorable experiences of their lives.

In sum, students in the intercultural classroom and study-abroad programs must learn to tolerate difference of new cultures and ways of being. They gain an appreciation for ambiguity and adaptability to new situations, peoples, and forms of communication. My courses at UW-La Crosse taught students a tolerance for ambiguity (or *queerness*) in intercultural contexts and this appreciation of difference helped reduce their level of culture shock as they embarked on new journeys. These brave study-abroad (i.e., "minority") students had to abandon old ways of seeing and being in the world when they entered a new land. They simultaneously discovered a new sense of the "other" and the self whereby artificial divides such as national boundaries began to disappear. Indeed, my disclosure to them as a working-class queer at UW-La Crosse ended up being an effective way to both prepare them to participate in study abroad and become educated global citizens.

CONCLUSION

It is not coincidental or accidental that I taught language, culture, and intercultural communications to first-generation college students at a regional university for the first part of my professional life. Working at UW-La Crosse taught me a lot about stereotypes, culture shock, cultural relativism, and tolerance for difference. It also allowed me to retrace both my gay identity and working-class Francophone roots while living in a "foreign" land. I learned to apply a queer pedagogy for all my courses that address linguistic and cultural differences while fostering an understanding of other ways of being. Moreover, by working with first-generation college students, I learned to "reexamine my allegiance" to the working class. As bell hooks (2000) writes about her experience of earning a graduate degree:

> I finished my education with my allegiance to the working class intact. Even so, I had planted my feet on the path leading in the direction of class privilege. There would always be contradictions to face. There would always be confrontations around the issue of class. I would always have to reexamine where I stand.

Although I attempted, like Wylie, to "get away from my background" by pursuing education, teaching at a regional university led me back to my working-class beginnings. Like hooks, I have experienced contradictions along the way. Nonetheless, through all the contradictions, I have come to understand my place in academe and how to educate students effectively in the culture classroom. Working with college students will always present me with intellectual challenges and remind me to reexamine my place in academe in light of such challenges. This continues to be true as I have discovered in my recent move to a new academic position at the University of Maryland, Baltimore County (UMBC), a research intensive and "honors" institution in the University of Maryland system. Indeed, this new position will require me to "reexamine where I stand" by confronting a new series of contradictions, as I move more in the direction of privilege as a professor with more research opportunities and fewer teaching responsibilities. Still, it will allow me to continue to come into close physical, intellectual, and social proximity with students from various backgrounds, including many transfer students from the local community colleges. Hakin Hasan argues that many academics who teach at the best colleges and who conduct research on the urban poor have little or no contact with their own research subjects. For this reason, he stresses the importance of academics and community to "give lectures and share ideas with low income-students who are on the front lines of social problems (see Hasan 2004)." Over time, my commitment to ideas and actions like "Night of Compassion" that engage my queer and working-class identities in meaningful ways can only grow.

NOTES

1. I want to thank Jennifer Quizler and the other SAGE representatives at UW-La Crosse for inviting me to prepare an earlier version of this chapter to share with them at the second annual "Night of Compassion" on November 6, 2003. I

also extend special thanks to Andrea Wagner who interviewed me for *The Racquet* and who was my student in International Studies 250 (Orientation to Study Abroad) at UW-La Crosse during fall 2003. I dedicate this chapter to all the UW-La Crosse students with whom I have worked.

2. My use of "personal and professional steps" is largely inspired by Stivale (2003, 9–39).

3. While working at a "teaching institution" within the UW-system, my tenure and promotion committee encouraged me during my pre-tenure years to publish in the area of teaching by uniting my research area (French cultural studies and gay and lesbian studies) with pedagogical issues. While I do not believe this is the type of work they intended, it is what has emerged from many of my interactions with students during various teaching moments in and beyond the classroom at UW-La Crosse.

4. For more on the MLA interview process and hiring committees, see Stivale 2002.

5. For more information, see "Career Information for Graduate Students and Junior Faculty Members."

6. Indeed, this statement was informed by my own cultural bias.

7. Germano continues: "Foreign grammars—with their separable prefixes and deponent verbs and markers for formality and falling tones and a hundred other things invented by the language gods—are mysterious worlds within our own."

8. For more on gay and lesbian languages and linguistics, see, for example, Leap 1996 and Leap and Boellstorff 2004.

9. Similarly, Bennett (1993) refers to this "double origin" as "cultural marginality."

REFERENCES

Bennett, Janet M. (1993) "Cultural Marginality: Identity Issues in Intercultural Train-ing," in R. Michael Paige, ed., *Education for the Intercultural Experience.* Yarmouth, ME: Intercultural Press, 109–135.

Bourdieu, Pierre (1979). *La distinction: critique sociale du jugement.* Paris: Editions de Minuit.

Burke, Peter (1990). *The French Historical Revolution: The Annales School, 1929–89.* Cambridge: Polity.

Butler, Judith (1990). *Gender Trouble: Feminism and the Subversion of Identity.* New York: Routledge.

"Career Information for Graduate Students and Junior Faculty Members." MLA Com-mittee on Academic Freedom and Professional Rights and Responsibilities. http://www.mla.org/pdf/careerinfo.pdf (Accessed August 5, 2006.)

Carroll, Raymonde (1987). *Evidences Invisibles.* Paris: Seuil.

Germano, William (2004, June 11). "Parlez-Vous Anything?" *The Chronicle of Higher Education.* http://chronicle.com/weekly/v50/i40/40b01601.htm (Accessed August 5, 2006.)

Gomstyn, Alice (2003, November 7). "Few Students Get an 'Internationalized' Educa-tion, Report Says." *The Chronicle of Higher Education.* http://chronicle.com/prm/weekly/v50/i11/11a01202.htm (Accessed August 5, 2006.)

Haggerty, George E. (1995). "'Promoting Homosexuality' in the Classroom," in George E. Hagerty and Bonnie Zimmerman, eds., *Professions of Desire: Lesbian and Gay Studies in Literature*. New York: Modern Language Association of American, 11–18.

Hasan, Hakim (2004, March 12). "Working-Class Voices in Scholarly Discourse." *The Chronicle of Higher Education*. http://chronicle.com/weekly/v50/i27/27b00501. htm (Accessed August 5, 2006.)

hooks, bell (2000, November 17). "Learning in the Shadow of Race and Class." *The Chronicle of Higher Education*. http://chronicle.com/weekly/v47/i12/12b01401. htm (Accessed August 5, 2006.)

Kramsch, Claire (1991). "Culture in Language Learning: A View from the United States," in Kees De Bot, Ralph B. Ginsberg, and Claire Kramsch, eds., *Foreign Language Research in Cross-Cultural Perspective*. Amsterdam: Benjamins, 217–240.

Leap, William (1996). *Word's Out: Gay Men's English*. Minneapolis: University of Minnesota Press.

Leap, William L., and Tom Boellstorff, eds. (2004). *Speaking in Queer Tongues: Globalization and Gay Language*. Urbana: University of Illinois Press.

Paige, R. Michael, Andrew D. Cohen, Barbara Kappler, Julie C. Chi, and James P. Lassegard (2002). *Maximizing Study Abroad: A Student's Guide to Strategies for Language and Culture Learning and Use*. Minneapolis: Center for Advanced Research on Language Acquisition.

Provencher, Denis M. (2007). *Queer French: Globalization, Language and Sexual Citizenship in France*. Aldershot: Ashgate.

Rosello, Mireille (1994, March–June). "'Get Out of Here!': Modern Queer Languages in the 1990s." *The Canadian Review of Comparative Literature/Revue Canadienne de Littérature Comparée*: 149–168.

Santoni, Georges (1981). "Lawrence Wylie: The French Civilization Course." *Société et culture de la France contemporaine*. Albany: State University of New York Press, 1–63.

Schmidt, Peter (2002, January 18). "State Spending on Higher Education Grows by Smallest Rate in 5 Years." *Chronicle of Higher Education*. http://chronicle.com/prm/weekly/v48/i19/19a02001.htm (Accessed August 5, 2006.)

Stivale, Charles J. (2003). *Disenchanting Les Bons Temps: Identity and Authenticity in Cajun Music and Dance*. Durham, NC: Duke University Press.

Stivale, Charles J. (2002). "The Loneliness of the Long-distance Interviewer." *The ADFL Bulletin* 34.1: 41–46.

Turner, Graeme (1996). *British Cultural Studies: An Introduction*, 2nd ed. New York: Routledge.

Wagner, Andrea (2003, November 6). "UW-L Teacher Speaks About Homosexual Experiences," *The Racquet*: 10.

SIX

Flying the Coop

Liberation through Learning

NANCY CIUCEVICH STORY

I grew up in the 1950s, reading comic strips with my dad on the living room floor on Sundays, while mother cooked dinners of roast beef, turnip greens, and sweet potatoes. My father claimed he could only read the comics, his prayer book, and technical manuals on welding and plumbing. In 1931, he left school in eighth grade when my grandfather, the son of a Croatian immigrant, caught his third son (of nine children) skipping class. On that day, my dad became his father's plumbing apprentice, a trade he followed until 1940, when he, at age twenty-three, married my mother, then twenty-two, and was hired at the local shipyard as a welder-in-training. At age sixty-five, he retired from the same shipyard, a proud member of the Boilermaker's Union.

I say "proud," but he is also humble to the point of being self-denigrating. He describes himself as an ignorant worker, not smart enough to get a desk job like some of my schoolmates' fathers. When I chose him for the subject of a "Hero" essay in sixth grade, he reminded me that biographies are written about the rich and important, not peons like him.

As Calvin tells Hobbes in a Bill Watterson (1995, 183) comic strip, "Birds don't write their memoirs" because they "don't lead epic lives." But my dad was a master of several trades, rising to the highest non-company position in the fabrication shop of a major shipyard. He would sometimes chuckle at white collars who could not fix their own leaky faucets or tile their bathroom walls. "What good is all the learning when you can't flush your own toilet?" he would ask.

Every Friday, when he hurried to the bank after work to cash his paycheck, he would act deferential and out-of-place, trying not to dirty the teller's hands by touching them with his greasy ones. I watched him closely and learned to walk in two worlds, a skill I would need later as I negotiated the society of higher education and discovered my lesbian identity.

My mother quit eighth grade in 1918. She lied about her age so she could work at a McCrory's department store. This was not unusual among her peers. She tells of feeling both regret and relief when she decided to leave school to help her mother support her two younger sisters. Mom regretted that she would not finish high school, yet was relieved at not having to wear her older aunt's "grown-up" hand-me-downs to school anymore. She would have been the first in her family to receive a high school diploma.

Shame was already a way of life for my mother. Her father was an alcoholic who abandoned his family, forcing his oldest child to join his wife in the labor pool much too soon. It is not surprising that my mother's main desires for me were to be accepted in school and church, to hand her and my father a high school diploma, and then marry a "good Catholic boy" to support me and her future grandchildren. One out of three was not good enough.

When just "being yourself" is antithetical to the values and expectations of your culture, a double bind exists within the individual (Wegsheider-Cruse 1987, 48). Not meeting the criteria of family or social institutions like church, school, and government can lead to feelings of shame, low self-worth, and alienation from the community. Shame that goes unaddressed and builds over a long time eventually finds expression. Sometimes it becomes anger turned outward in aggression toward others. Turned inward, it can trigger acts of self-sabotage (McKay, Davis, and Fanning 1997). To avoid feeling shame, one might avoid, or even ruin, opportunities for success. In the worst cases, self-shame can lead to self-destruction.

When a poor or working-class person dreams of going to college to enter a profession, numerous personal, cultural, and socioeconomic conflicts emerge. When gay, lesbian, bi, or trans people decide to be "out" as their authentic selves with family, peers, and colleagues, they face possible discrimination and rejection because of their sexual orientation.

Being from a working-class background is a socioeconomic fact. Being lesbian is a biosocial one. Neither has been a choice. Both have contributed to *my sense of being an outsider* from my family and culture of origin and from my adopted culture of higher education.

"MISTAKEN ZYGOTE SYNDROME": OUTSIDER TO FAMILY AND CULTURE OF ORIGIN

In *Women Who Run with the Wolves* (1992), Estes, a Jungian analyst and Chicana *cantadora* (storyteller), uses the Mistaken Zygote to explain the origin of the outcast, the stranger in her own family: "You were indeed destined for parents who would have understood you, but the Zygote Fairy hit turbulence and, oops, you fell out of the basket over the wrong house ... right into a family that was not meant for you" (195). Estes's goal in telling this story is to encourage her readers to approach being an outsider "from a lighter side, for levity can shake some of the pain out of a woman" (192).

As a child, I recall my mother asking me again and again, "Where did you come from?" "Why are you like that?" "Why aren't you more like your cousin, Dolores?" "Why do you have to be so different?" "Why can't you just fit in?" I had no answer for her except to say I felt the difference too, and I felt the shame it produced.

Intellectually, the difference between my family of origin and me was in the arena of critical thinking. If I had simply been an A student, consistently on the honor roll, I would not have been much different from some of my cousins. In that case, my parents would have still labeled me as "smarter" than they were, but maybe not so different in other ways. Mostly, however, I was not an honor roll student, but a problem.

In third grade, Sister Mary Sara requested a conference with my parents. I was on the verge of heresy in religion class for using the methods of skepticism to challenge St. Thomas Aquinas's proofs of the existence of God. In creative writing, I cast God the Father as the supporting character to the Virgin Mary in a one-act-play titled, "Whose Child Is This?"

My parents and teachers worried I was becoming anti-Catholic via the influence of a Protestant friend. The truth was I would have argued against any doctrine presented as authoritative, as most young independent thinkers would. In the context of my late 1950s traditional southern culture and Catholic education, questioning authority was not permitted, especially for a "young lady." The nuns instructed my parents to "watch" me closely for other evidence of straying from the fold. In response, my folks prayed for me.

Being different continued to cause me shame and it isolated me from my family. I was consumed by literature, its allure, its ability to transport me to other, sometimes taboo, places where people talked about ideas my family never discussed and did not value. I would rather read than eat; my family could not understand. I did not understand either. I wanted to fit in, wanted to be like my friends who loved to talk about boys and clothes. I found these topics boring and that unnerved me. My sense of being different escalated as I entered high school in 1964.

Then I met Ellen.

Ellen was not a "pretty" or popular girl. She was not an A student either, but she loved to read and write and imagine being in other places, like New York City living with the bohemian poets, or London, riding motorcycles with the "Mods" or the "Rockers." I had never met another young woman with this kind of imagination and disregard for acceptability. We became best friends.

With Ellen, I felt understood and accepted. It seemed miraculous to me. We spent all our time together, in and out of school. She also came from a working-class family. Her mother worked outside the home (my mother disapproved), so we had the run of her house in the afternoons.

Ellen and I invented scenarios in which we were the heroines. As writers in New York, we shared a Greenwich Village apartment and wrote novels about women detectives. Our heroines, "Sam and Jo," dressed like the men in their department and combined their keen intellects with female intuition to close "cold" cases that had been unsolved for years. In London, we dressed in tight black leather pants and jackets bearing the logos of all-girl gangs and rode through the wet streets at night stopping to brawl with other girl gangs.

Ellen dared to think outside the box of our patriarchal culture. She was daring and vital, a free thinker in a society of followers. She was unpopular with girls, boys, and teachers. I fell in love with her.

When we kissed, we always pretended one of us was a man. We played out the fantasies we invented, but never as two women. We skirted the idea of being "queer" by identifying ourselves as bohemians and rebels. In our dramas, one of us would become involved passionately with a man for a short time, but we would always end up leaving him to return to our female partner in an investigation or gang violence. For almost a year, we thrived in our taboo relationship.

One afternoon in early fall, our relationship ended by parental decree, enforced by fear, shame, and the Catholic Church. My mother was hysterical. A female family member a decade older than I had told my mother I should stay away from Ellen because she wasn't "right." I was not to see her outside of school or associate with her in school. If I didn't agree with mother's decision, I could talk with our parish priest.

I felt devastated at the thought of losing the only friend who understood me. With Ellen, I felt whole and acceptable. Now I was hearing from family and church that my feeling of being okay was wrong. I pleaded, "Why? Why? She's my best friend, the only one who really likes me. Please don't make me stop seeing her! I don't understand." My mother looked relieved but would not explain further. If I did not understand what she meant about Ellen, it was I because I was a "good" girl, and, by God, she would see I stayed that way.

I told Ellen the next day I could no longer be her friend. She cried and called me a traitor. I was heartbroken and scared. Indeed, I felt like a traitor, but I was also afraid and ashamed of my feelings for her. I put my feelings for Ellen away with my toys and stuffed animals I had outgrown. I buried my feelings so deep it would be years before they resurfaced. Because I still had not named the feelings, they were not difficult to deny and forget. That fall, I quit being Ellen's friend and began dating boys (with a vengeance). I also began cutting myself to acknowledge inner pain, an impulse that resurfaced throughout my youth and young adulthood.

Santos (1995), editor of *From Wedded Wife to Lesbian Life,* describes her self-loathing at discovering her desire for girls. "By the time I was sixteen, I was so terrified of being queer, and so isolated with my fear, that I tried to kill myself by eating a dozen aspirin" (32), she explains.

Whatever the reason for alienation from one's family and culture, it will inevitably bring a sense of shame and loss.

LEAVING THE NEST

In 1968, I was a senior in an all-girls Catholic convent school in a traditional old southern town. The cultural and family expectations were that I would graduate, marry within the religion, produce a family of however many children God chose to send us, and be the family's spiritual and physical backbone. There is nothing wrong with this path if it is one you freely choose to walk. The problem was my apparent lack of choice.

The nuns and priests at the Catholic schools warned us against the dangers of attending secular (non-Catholic) schools and colleges. They feared we would be swayed from our faith by skeptical thinking and materialistic values. Another danger was the possibility of falling in love with a non-Catholic. The greatest fear was that we would lose faith in God. This institutional bias against secular higher education fueled my parents' distrust of higher education in general.

My parents' view of themselves as intellectually inadequate was passed to me in cautions against trying to fit into the world of the educated. The family message was that college was meant for the more entitled, upper classes, not for me with my working-class background. "Don't try to fly out of your element or you may be shot down," they cautioned.

My parents understood, though not by personal experience, that attending college could lead one far away from home and family, a distance measured in miles and values. Even so, in the 1960s, they could have accepted my brother's wanting a college education. After all, it was appropriate for a young man to pursue a career. But in the late 1960s and early 1970s especially among working-class southerners, a woman's role was still mostly restricted to marriage and home.

If a woman did go to college, it was usually a "finishing school" or a teachers' college. Moreover, college was an expensive endeavor for a working-class family. The message to me was clear; by embarking on higher education, I would be putting unnecessary economic strain on my father. He had already sacrificed for years to keep me in Catholic school. Furthermore, I would be putting my family's values second to my own. In response to such thinking, and my pattern of not living up to my parents' expectations, I developed an image of myself as intrinsically flawed.

Most girls from my high school came from wealthy families who could afford to send their children away to universities. Our junior and senior years in high school were focused on getting accepted by the best schools. Not to be left out, I applied to a couple of colleges in state but out of town. All the while, my folks were saying they could not afford to send me to college. Their lack of resources was a fact. They would have to borrow money to pay my tuition. My father was fifty-one years old and still working twelve-hour days at the shipyard to support us. He needed a financial break, not a loan.

In the middle of my senior year, one of my teachers requested a conference with my parents. I had no idea why she wanted to see them, and they were clearly nervous I had done something wrong. Sister Mary Ann tried to convince my parents I should go away to college, and they should do whatever is required, even borrowing money if necessary, to make that happen. She said she had taught girls like me before, and if I didn't follow the path of higher education, I would likely marry too early and perhaps badly, for lack of other opportunities.

My parents came home angry. How could Sister Mary Ann ask them to sacrifice more for me after they had spent every extra penny and even gone into debt to send me to Catholic high school? I continued talking about the colleges my classmates would attend. Almost everyone was going away to school in the fall, but a few girls were not going to college at all. Ellen was one. By the time of my high school graduation in May 1968, my parents reluctantly agreed to pay for me to attend the local college for a year. I was also awarded a work-study job on campus.

As I went to "send off" parties for my peers that summer, I saw how proud their parents were of their daughters' acceptances into college. Some of these young women would be attending their parents' and even grandparents' alma maters. In contrast, my parents were acting under pressure, going against their beliefs about what I should be doing. The atmosphere at home was grim. I knew I was being selfish again, further stretching their limited resources. It was hard to be happy knowing I would begin classes the following fall and cost my parents so much money.

I did not find satisfaction in college my first year. Nothing much had changed for me. I was going to school and still living at home. It was 1969 and my focus turned to moving out on my own. My dad had struggled to pay for two semesters of college and still I was not happy. Desperate to change my living situation in the least offensive way to my parents, I left college and married my high school boyfriend at age nineteen. He was non-Catholic, but my family prayed he would soon convert. For both of us, marriage seemed to be the only acceptable way to leave home with our parents' (reluctant) blessing. At least we were following the path most often taken by working-class people.

The patriarchal view of marriage permeated every level of my life: the woman was seen as the center of the family, the keeper of hearth and religion. I wanted college, but I wanted children too, and, according to my family and culture's rules, that required marriage. As Rich (1986, 59) explains,

> Women have married because it was necessary, in order to survive economically, in order to have children who would not suffer economic deprivation or social ostracism, in order to remain respectable, in order to do what was expected of women, because coming out of 'abnormal' childhoods they wanted to feel 'normal' and because heterosexual romance has been represented as the great female adventure, duty and fulfillment.

Within two years, my husband and I were living apart, I with our baby son in a small apartment. In the shadow of a divorce that left me in poor standing with our tight-knit Catholic community, I decided I had little to lose. On the advice of a knowledgeable older friend, I enrolled in social services programs to help me survive economically while I returned to school. I used all available resources to help me finish my degree, with hopes of attending graduate school and entering a profession. I had studied enough American history and government to know I was using the social services system legitimately to help me effect socioeconomic change both in my life and my child's. Unfortunately, my actions caused my family shame. My family viewed reliance on social services as a failure of willpower and an abandonment of values.

After the divorce, returning to college was my next giant step away from my family and culture of origin.

A DUCK OUT OF WATER: OUTSIDER IN COLLEGE

In 1973, when I was twenty-three, I enrolled my toddler son in a social services-funded community day-care center for twenty hours a week so I could return to college. My mother was shocked and outraged I could be so selfish. She exclaimed, "I will never understand you as long as I live!" (She was right.) My mother did not live long enough to understand me. She died before I knew I was a lesbian.

Being a mom in college in the early 1970s in the South was fairly unusual. I was also pursuing a nonteaching degree in literature. Family members and friends would ask, "What in the world are you thinking?" Among parenting, attending classes, doing homework, and working part-time, I often asked myself the same question. The answer was always the same: My happiness lay in raising my child and finishing my degree. The challenge was to balance the two. Pursuing a college degree became more than a way into a profession. Our living in a college community gave my son opportunities he would not have had as the child of a single, working-class mom.

Despite my limited economic resources, my son was growing up among educated people from all over the world, playing and studying with their friends, learning about their cultures. Sean attended public schools taught by university-educated teachers in the forefront of their fields. We went regularly to free, university-sponsored, cultural events, exposing him to music and art we could not otherwise have afforded. Living in the university community gave us access to a life I had dreamed about for years. Meanwhile, my mother continued challenging my choices, "How can you be a good mother when you're still going to school?" she asked.

As a college sophomore, I met and married a fellow student. His field was world revolutions and political science. I was studying literature and philosophy. His socioeconomic background was even more dire than mine, but we shared a drive: to break into the world of academia and change our destinies. As undergraduates, we survived on a shoestring budget from financial aid and whatever part-time work we could get. After we earned our BAs, I took a job as a bank teller and he worked as a shoe-store manager to earn enough money to move to the state where we wanted to attend graduate school. Later, as a teaching assistant in graduate school, I would take three classes and teach two to three during the semester. In summer, I was employed part-time as a bank teller. By piecing jobs together and staggering our work schedules, my husband and I could study, work, and be active parents to our son. Sometimes, usually toward the end of the semester, chaos overtook us. With final projects and papers due for both of us, Sean would inevitably develop an ear infection and fever. The added cost of doctor visits and medications would drain our bank account, resulting in a bounced check to one or more of the utility companies. They would call, threatening to disconnect us. At these times, my feelings would vacillate between anger at my lack of family support and envy for fellow students from middle- and upper-class families who could write home to Mom and Dad for extra money.

Mostly though, I would lose sleep worrying, feeling ashamed at my lack of resources, and not be able to focus on my schoolwork. The only way to get back on track was to remind myself of my next goal, a master's degree in English that might one day lead to a teaching position.

In graduate school, I encountered other obstacles: academic snobbery and elitism. In the 1970s, in the South, the "academy" was a sacrosanct institution for an economically and socially favored few. It was no place for an academically underprepared, working-class person. It was only beginning to be a place for women and students of color. One result was a lack of mentoring and other resources to help working-class "foreigners" like me find our way through the land of academe.

It was assumed if you were not already "in the know" when you came to graduate school, you obviously did not belong there. Discussion of financial struggles or child-care issues was treated as inappropriate and irrelevant. Overall, I felt my peers, graduate school faculty, and the school's administration preferred I not disclose my working-class background or ignorance of academic culture. Although this attitude was discouraging to encounter, it was not surprising. I was new to higher education, but, hey, I was accustomed to feeling out of place and being treated like an outsider.

I knew when I started on the path to higher education I was stepping out of my social class. In the mid-1970s, entering a prestigious graduate program at the University of North Carolina at Chapel Hill from the base of a working-class background, not to mention as mother to small children, was daring, if not foolish. It is comparable to launching an expensive venture in a foreign land, purely on credit, with no savings or collateral, and no backup plan. Oh yes, and in my case, there had been little or no preparation in the language and customs of graduate education. But desperation is a strong impetus for success.

What I had, in the way of preparation, was a desire to break out of the restraints of my working-class background and enter the world of the academy, supposedly the place of free thinking and ideas. My father had been on a picket line more than once in his life. He was among the original strikers who brought the union into the shipyard where he worked. I remember seeing him on a black and white television, standing with a group of other grim men wearing work clothes. My mother said, "It is dangerous for them to stand there, but more dangerous to keep welding with no eye-goggles and no gloves, running machinery in unsafe conditions." It was dangerous to my identity for me to proceed toward the MA, but it would have been death to return to my former life.

DUCK OR SWAN? OUTSIDER IN THE INSTITUTION

I have spent much of my life migrating from one culture to another, feeling and being treated like a visitor at home and in the university. It is unsettling living in two worlds, especially when their values conflict so much. I remember my feeling of validation at reading "Sonrisas," by the Chicana poet Mora (1986), wherein she explores the experience of living between cultures. The speaker in the poem lives "in a doorway/between two rooms." One room is peopled by "careful women in crisp, beige/suits, drinking "black coffee" and examining "budgets" and "curriculum." In the "other room, senoras/in faded dresses stir sweet/milk coffee" and laugh while they prepare tamales (777). The speaker stands in the doorway, never entirely at ease in one room or the other.

Of course, outsiders are nothing new. Only the names change. Outsiders come in all forms and are found in the literature of most cultures. By definition, the concept of society implies the presence of outsiders to it. Sometimes being the outsider can be empowering. This has been my experience.

After finishing my master's degree and taking more coursework, I began looking for a job in higher education that would not require me to finish a PhD. I had gone deeply in debt attending an excellent graduate school, but was ignorant of my employment opportunities. My academic program trained PhDs to teach in regional universities, so I presented my professors with something of a problem. Unsure of how to direct me, they suggested I visit the university career advising office. A career counselor there guided me to jobs in community college teaching.

I had not attended a community college so I began researching them as I sought employment. I liked what I learned, and my years of experience in community college work around the country have verified my original impression. Most community colleges are open-entry, meaning standardized test scores like SAT and ACT are not used to exclude marginal people from higher education (Weissglass 2002, 332). Instead, entering students take assessment tests that match their skills in reading, English, mathematics, and sometimes study skills to appropriate levels of classes offered in these areas. The philosophy is to meet people where they are and lead them forward, teaching them how to function in the new world of higher education.

I have been "accused" by some self-appointed gatekeepers of "academic standards" of viewing community college as a form of affirmative action. I do. Community colleges provide affordable academic and technical certificates and degrees to women, students of color, displaced workers, economically disadvantaged adults, and working-class students. Moreover, community colleges usually have a variety of academic and cultural support services meant to assure the academic and professional success of their various "nontraditional" students. In this case, "nontraditional" is another term for "outsider."

RISE OF THE PHOENIX

In 1998, I transformed from wife to widow in one day without much warning. My husband of twenty-five years, and father to (by then) our three children, hanged himself in our home. He had been severely abused and neglected as a child and teenager by members of his family who were supposed to protect and nurture him. Raised in abandoned houses, living on government food, with parents who were intellectually bright and emotionally damaged beyond repair, he had, nevertheless, earned a doctorate in history by age forty. At forty-two, having gained tenure at a local university, he committed suicide. His abusive childhood and the struggle to break into academia and live a middle-class life had taken a great toll. Along the way, he had tried unsuccessfully to relieve his stress and heal his wounds by substance abuse and serial affairs. While writing his dissertation, he had what psychiatrists called a "psychotic break." At times, he thought I was his enemy, although I was his strongest and most faithful supporter. Finally, he became abusive to our children and me despite his great love for us, which I never doubted. He could not stand the person he had become or the pain of living as that person.

There was another, perhaps deeper, struggle for him as well. When I met him, my future husband was bisexual, though he always denied it. He had just ended a relationship with a young man before he and I began to date. Although this was common knowledge, he claimed the relationship was nothing more than a brief, abnormal affair. I could not understand his need to deny this part of his identity, but he heatedly refused to address the topic. He could not understand my interest in this relationship or my desire to explore this aspect of his life. I could not tell him because I could not admit to myself that my interest in his bisexuality was deeply rooted in my own sexuality. Ironically, after his suicide, and with great support from my children and friends, I uncovered a deeply buried secret—my own, hidden, sexual identity.

A few months after my husband's death, a relatively new friend visited our home for the first time. Although we had known each other for less than a year, a strong friendship was growing between us. As we sat in my house making small talk one afternoon, she began looking at my book and music collection and asked about my interest in lesbian literature and music. I told her I'd always had a strong interest in women's literature, history, and music. She noted that my collections of favorite poetry and music were mostly of lesbian artists. I had never made this distinction before. I was surprised, but, yes, it was true. Later that day, after her visit, parts of me began emerging that had been in the shadows. I felt as if I were seeing myself for the first time since I was a child. It was as if I had been looking at myself through a kaleidoscope for years. The vision was multicolored, beautiful, but fragmented in some underlying way. That afternoon, as I turned the kaleidoscope just a bit to the left, all the pieces converged to form a beautiful flower, and I thought, "Oh, that's me, then! I'm gay." Suddenly, so much made sense. I felt whole for the first time I could remember. Pieces of my past suddenly made sense to me: feelings I'd had for women, high school relationships I hadn't understood, my attraction to gay and bisexual friends, music, and culture, all were clear. I had not known the feeling of wholeness until then. The year my husband, and best friend of twenty-five years, committed suicide was the year of my rebirth.

In retrospect, the signs were there in my history had I known what to look for. But my family culture and society had programmed me not to look. Homosexuality was taboo; there were too many reasons I would not have wanted to look even if I had known how to see. Homosexuality was rarely mentioned in my home or school as I was growing up, except as put-downs among students. Back then "those people" were called "queers." I did not hear the word lesbian used in conversation until college. It sent shivers up my spine for reasons I later came to understand.

Even if I had recognized myself as a lesbian earlier in life, there were other pressures to live a straight life. In the 1970s and 1980s, the barriers to childbearing or adopting as homosexuals were enormous, nearly impossible, without wealth and power. I had wanted children since I could remember. I would not abandon that dream.

Friends have asked me, as I have asked myself, were you always a lesbian? I was married twice, a total of twenty-nine years (four and twenty-five), and during that time I was not conscious of being gay. This may seem mysterious, but it is common among lesbians in the United States, especially those born before 1970 (Frantz 1995, 11). The legislative reforms and consciousness-raising groups that came about because of the women's rights movements of the 1970s changed all this.

Some might say I turned to lesbian life in response to some hideous experiences in marriages to men. But lesbianism is not defined as a relationship of women to men. It is a preference of women for women (Damon 1970, 336). Or I could be considered chronologically bisexual, as I was continually in heterosexual relationships from age seventeen until I was forty-eight years old, when my relationships became exclusively lesbian. I prefer saying I was a lesbian all those years, but did not "know" it.

According to Damon, writing in the collection *Sisterhood Is Powerful*, lesbians range from unconscious, to conscious and closeted, to uncloseted. Damon (1970, 337) explains, "First of all, lesbians cannot be counted by any of the existing methods of statistical estimation, so long as these studies continue to be based on conscious sexual experience." Not all lesbians are "out," even to themselves. Damon points to two groups: "the women who make up our vast sea of lifelong spinsters" and the married women who finally understand they are lesbians. Some of these women will identify as lesbian but subvert their personal identities to the values and perceived needs of their community of origin. Others will "come out" as lesbians and engage in same-sex relationships, revealing their sexual identities to those they trust to accept them. A minority will live bravely, and some might say foolishly, openly gay in a largely homophobic society. Many of them are, "whether expressed or not, Lesbians" (ibid.).

RECONSTRUCTING THE NEST

I do not feel comfortable in either my family of origin or my professional life. In college, as a student, teaching assistant, faculty member, and student advocate, I have felt estranged from higher education. Working in the community college setting with students who are also "outsiders" to higher education allows me to live in both worlds. It offers a way to bridge them.

I am a working-class person who has raised my standard of living via higher education yet who retains working-class economic values. I am an "out" lesbian in a culture and society that denounces homosexuality as sick or evil, or both. My home is my safe house, a haven where I am comfortable. Outside home, I am aware of being a discomfort to society. As a lesbian, I am often treated as an undesirable presence. Just last weekend, in front of our home, a neighbor stopped and introduced his girlfriend to my partner and me. The woman was clearly uncomfortable at having to make brief eye contact with us. When I shook her hand, she looked disgusted and shivered a little.

In expressing myself, I know I am challenging my family and community's basic values and assumptions about whom I should be and what I should want to do. One of the most effective tools used to induce conformity within a community, small as a family or large as a state, is shame.

Invoking shame in others always represents an effort at control. In parenting, it is a psychologically damaging tool used in the absence of more rational, humane methods. In governing a state or a religion, it is an equally powerful means of keeping the disenfranchised of whatever stripe in their place.

In the world of school and work, gays, lesbians, bisexuals, and trans people by the score feel compelled to hide their identities from their peers and supervisors in fear of discovery and discrimination based on their sexual orientations. Living under cover involves a daily source of shame and resentment, but coming out as gay or trans can cost people their families, friends, jobs, and even their lives. Much of the time, these stories go unnoticed by the public because they are not considered significant by the police or newsworthy by the press. Mathew Shepard, a gay college student who was beaten, pistol-whipped, tied to a fence post, and left to die near Laramie, Wyoming, in 1998, is an exception ("Matthew" 2005). Another notable exception is Fred C. Martinez a sixteen-year-old trans, or "Two-Spirit," Navajo student in Cortez, Colorado, beaten to death in 2001 ("Fred" n. d.). The brutal murders of these two young men are bloody witness to how "being yourself" can be fatal. No wonder some of us live in self-denial all our lives (the most profound disconnection from soul).

As marginalized groups in the United States gain greater access to higher education, little do they know how much they are stepping into an alien world and, in turn, how they must struggle to succeed largely by hit or miss. In the United States, higher education is still considered a privilege, not a right. It is available to some in the poor and working classes by virtue of government grants and loans. Even then, there are not enough college and university programs available to help outsiders, such as newcomers (first-generation college students), understand and navigate the higher education system, to acculturate and learn the methods of success the more privileged know from having grown up in educated families.

Many bright and talented people, living on the outskirts of society, decide their worth and futures in response to feeling shame. They believe the message: "You get what you deserve in this life." My father thinks this way. He has always said that if he had worked harder and been smarter, he could have been more successful. Whatever he gained, it was by the grace of God and what he called "fool's luck." Whatever he did not achieve was his own fault, or so he thought. "It's a damn shame!" he would say.

The poison in this belief in the notion of the class system is that the whole operation is based on justice, where material success equates to human value, and, thus, our social class is part of our destiny. Such thinking can lead to lives in unfulfilling, low-paying jobs, with no hope of change. Ironically, for the marginalized among us who succeed in breaking into higher education, the prize is tainted. We have succeeded in a system that has traditionally barred our families from full participation in the benefits of this society.

According to Overall, in "Nowhere at Home: Toward a Phenomenology of Working-Class Consciousness," working-class academics "must buy into academia in order to get out of the working class, but in doing so, we also buy into the denigration of our origins and the preservation of class inequities" (1995, 219). The shame associated with success is not unique among those who "make it" in a society that has historically oppressed their families and culture. In some ways, we may always feel like traitors to our class origins.

As those of us from marginalized backgrounds continue to infuse our nontraditional talents and energy into the U.S. higher education system, we can find ways to influence societal change. In academe, we can choose to promote the status quo or change the system from within. We can act as mentors to junior faculty and our students from the poor and working classes. We can continue to infuse the standard curriculum with multicultural educational programs, create and help institutionalize more support programs for first-generation college students, GLBT students, and other traditionally marginalized groups in higher education. We can advocate for hiring minorities in college counseling, teaching, and administrative positions in schools, and act as mentors for others in need.

In my twenty years teaching and working in community colleges in four states, I have helped several other working-class students "break into" and succeed in higher education. Not all students I have helped enter college complete a degree. Some take a few classes and go back to work, hoping to return to college when their home situations allow. Some complete certificates that help them get better jobs. Some students graduate with associates degrees and transfer to four-year colleges and universities. I consider each and all these cases a measure of success. Just walking in the door of a college can be a huge breakthrough.

Each day, first-generation college students, whose parents have no more knowledge of higher education than mine did, tell me of their struggles. They follow similar patterns. There is the thirty-year-old single mother who circled the campus in her car during open registration at the start of three different semesters before working up the courage to park and walk through the door of the community college. She cried tears of shame and relief in my office when I helped her fill out an application to the college. She wants to be a role model for her children, to show them the value of getting a higher education, to show them they have the right and strength to succeed in formal learning.

Unfortunately, recent changes in TANF (Temporary Assistance for Needy Families) regulations require that single mothers with small children work to receive their benefits, including day care for the kids. Some of my students had to leave school this past fall because their TANF benefits would no longer pay for day care if the parent is "only going to college." This is a good example of barriers the poor face when trying to better themselves and their children.

Then, there is the twenty-year-old ex-gang member trying to change his family's destiny after his brother was killed in a drive-by shooting in their neighborhood. This student remembers a high school counselor saying he was "smart," and he wants to see if he can live up to that label and bring more hope to his life. When Adrian took his assessment test to place him in appropriate college classes, he scored into English and math classes, needing no remediation. Last semester, he made the president's list and is now a Phi Theta Kappa member, the national community college honor society. This fall, he brought two cousins to sign up for college classes too. "Hey ma'am," Gerardo said, "if Adrian can pass, we can too. He is no smarter than we are!"

In a way, Adrian is atypical because most of our students require remediation in math, reading, and English. This adds a couple extra years to their finishing a degree, but, with academic support labs, tutors, and mentoring programs, many of them ultimately succeed.

Most of my students work thirty to forty hours per week, support families, and take three to four classes each semester. They are fighting within the system to raise their standard of living. They are struggling within themselves, and often against their families of origin, to change their lives.

Working as a teacher and student advocate at a community college has validated my own struggle to break into the institution of higher education and into a profession where I can help change the system. I particularly like teaching at inner-city colleges where diversity reigns. In my courses, diversity is a given. Whether I am teaching English composition, Introduction to Philosophy, or reading, I use texts that reflect the rich mixture of my classes. These texts include assignments that promote a variety of learning styles. In my work as a student advocate, I mentor a group of first-generation students in how to navigate the system and succeed in this culture of higher education, one so foreign to them. We focus on their strengths instead of deriding them for their "lack of college preparedness." I also help them work through the inner struggles involved in accommodating a social structure that has excluded them and their families for generations.

As their advocate, one of my most important jobs is assisting students with the financial aid process. For most of our students, money is a very real barrier to higher education. The financial aid process is confusing enough to those of us who know the system, but to a first-time college student, it can be a daunting challenge. In our first-generation programs, we have found that assisting students with financial aid issues is vital for retaining them in college. All our student-mentors are trained in the financial aid process, from the initial filing of the Free Application for Federal Student Aid, to completing the financial aid file at the college.

A challenge in the 1970s was opening the doors of higher education to the disenfranchised. In the beginning of the twenty-first century, the task is very different. Today, it involves, among other things, revising the curriculum so it better meets the needs of those previously excluded from college, including more minorities in teaching, advising, and administrative higher education positions, and building support networks to help first-generation students finish their degrees. First-generation programs often begin on grant money, but they require financial support from the colleges if they are to continue after the grant ends. The work is ongoing. Some four-year colleges and universities are beginning to implement these programs as well. In so doing, we are removing some traditional barriers to higher education that have excluded so many working-class families from fully participating in our society.

We who fly out of formation to places we are not expected to go and then assert who we are when we are there, now have the credentials and standing necessary to effect significant change in the demographics of higher education. Certainly, we must expect, given the conservative nature of most bureaucracies, that many in the academy will reject our arguments about democratizing colleges and universities. Still, we must persist. By definition, we have the power to chart the course of others who, like us, were raised by parents who lacked the education, opportunity, and resources necessary for accessing the benefits our society so readily supplies to those with considerable financial and social capital. We must commit ourselves to helping others spread their educational wings, as we have. By smoothing their path we can change how they think and live. In turn, we will reward ourselves with one of life's most cherished goals: the knowledge that as we near the end of our days on earth, we can say our lives were indeed *very* fulfilling.

In Our Own Time
(for Fred C. Martinez, Jr.)

We are weary with waiting
on what we all deserve,
tired of hurting
for being who we are,
who the universe gloriously
created us to be.

Father Sky cries
dark tears for us.
Mother Earth groans
deeper than birth pangs,
watching her children
walking in shadows,
feeling our brothers
bear the pain,
holding our sisters
in arms that cannot
protect them from hate.

We are weary with waiting
for the right
to live and die
in our own way,
in our own time.
—Nancy Ciucevich Story

REFERENCES

Damon, Gene (1970). "The Least of These: The Minority Whose Screams Haven't Yet Been Heard," in Robin Morgan, ed., *Sisterhood Is Powerful: An Anthology of Writings from the Women's Liberation Movement.* New York: Random House, 333–342.

Estes, Clarissa Pinkola (1992). *Women Who Run With the Wolves: Myths and Stories of the Wild Woman Archetype*. New York: Ballantine Books.

Frantz, Marge (1995). "Introduction," in Deborah Abbott and Ellen Farmer, eds., *From Wedded Wife to Lesbian Life: Stories of Transformation*. Freedom, CA: The Crossing Press, 5–16.

"Fred C Martinez, Jr." (n.d.) *FUAH* (Families United Against Hate). http://www.fuah. org/fuah_cortez.html (Accessed June 23, 2007.)

"Matthew's Place." 2005. Matthew Shepard Foundation. http://www.matthewsplace. com (Accessed June 23, 2007.)

McKay, Matthew, Martha Davis, and Patrick Fanning (1997). *Thoughts and Feelings: Taking Control of Your Moods and Your Life*, 2nd ed. Oakland, CA: New Harbinger Publications.

Mora, Pat (1986). "Sonrisas," in Carl Bain, Jerome Beatty, and J. Paul Hunter, eds. In *The Norton Introduction to Literature*. 5th ed. New York: W. W. Norton, 777.

Overall, Christine (1995). "Nowhere at Home: Toward a Phenomenology of Working-Class Consciousness," in C. L. Barney Dews and Caroline Leste Law, eds., *This Fine Place So Far From Home*. Philadelphia: Temple University Press, 209–220.

Rich, Adrienne (1986). "Compulsory Heterosexuality and Lesbian Existence" in *Blood, Bread, and Poetry, Selected Prose, 1979–1985*. New York: W. W. Norton, 59.

Santos, Robin Teresa (1995). "Nao pica daloroso, nao saber sabrosa—As Marias," in Deborah Abbott and Ellen Farmer, eds., *From Wedded Wife to Lesbian Life*. Freedom, CA: Crossing Press, 31–39.

Watterson, Bill (1995). *The Calvin and Hobbes Tenth Anniversary Book*. Kansas City: Andrews and McNeel.

Wegscheider-Cruse, Sharon (1987). *Learning to Love Yourself: Finding Your Self Worth*. Pompano Beach, FL: Health Communications.

Weissglass, Julian (2002). "For Equality's Sake, the SAT Should Be Abolished," in Marilyn Anderson, ed., *Keys to Successful Writing*, 2nd ed. New York: Longman, 331–332.

SEVEN

NO MORE RENTED ROOMS

BONNIE R. STRICKLAND

Once when I mentioned my rural southern roots for the umpteenth time, my mother with some exasperation said, "You know, your grandfather was a very rich man and our family was pretty well-off." What she didn't add was that although my grandfather lived on several hundred acres of Florida land on the Apalachicola River and ran a general merchandise store in the community, he could not read or write and made his money on illegal whiskey. She also failed to mention that he and his son, my uncle Cliff, spent many years in jail for murdering a man who was hanging around one of their bootleg stills. No wonder I'm still confused about the social class status of my maternal grandparents. My father's side of the family was much easier to classify. My grandfather and his three sons all worked in the steel mills of Birmingham or on the railroad and were from the quintessential working class.

In summer 1934, having just finished tenth grade, my mother left the Florida swamps for Birmingham to visit her sister who was dating my father. My mom and dad took one look at each other and fell in love. My seventeen-year-old, tenth grade dropout mother and my twenty-three-year old unemployed father married three weeks later.

In her mid-eighties, shortly before she died, my mother was reminiscing about my father, the first of her four husbands. She said he had promised her a home of her own, but she remembered with some anger and great sadness, "We always lived in rented rooms." For the first years of their marriage, they lived with my father's family or in apartments in Birmingham and, when my father finally found work on the railroad, they lived in Louisville, Kentucky. I was born in 1936 and my brother in 1940. His crib was a dresser drawer and I assume mine had been as well.

EARLY YEARS

Although my mother quit high school and didn't receive her GED until she was in her sixties, my father and his two brothers were all high school graduates, not a mean accomplishment at that time. There were books in their home and union newspapers. I remember how my dad's oldest brother, my Uncle John, would occasionally read to me from an encyclopedia, one he would take from the leather set carefully shelved in a bookcase in the living room. I assume whatever trappings of a higher class that were available were a consequence of my paternal grandmother's influence; she was, after all, a Lee from Virginia. My mother, too, would read to me and taught me the alphabet and numbers well before I started first grade.

While class is, of course, a major dimension in shaping one's upbringing, I want also to note the enormous impact of being raised in the South. We were still fighting The War when I was a child, not the war in Europe and Japan, where we sent a disproportionate share of southern boys, but the alleged War of Northern Aggression. My great-grandfathers on both sides and most of my great-uncles fought for the Confederacy; we admired their pictures and kept their firearms. When I was growing up and taking Alabama history, slavery was barely mentioned. But we continually embraced a set of martyr-like beliefs that the dreaded Yankees had ravaged our cities and towns, occupied our country, and elected their own to represent us. No child of my time could have escaped the loathing southerners felt for the North, or the twisted, convoluted notions we held about segregation. As an adult, when public transportation was finally integrated in Birmingham, I watched with great sadness as my grandfather refused to go downtown because he would have to share the trolley with African Americans.

Perhaps there were private preschools and kindergartens in Birmingham in the 1940s, but none were available to us. I did, however, happily start first grade and immediately fell in love with my teacher (but then, doesn't everybody?). I loved school and have been enthusiastically returning every fall including the last three years since I have been retired. I started school at a time of considerable turmoil and transition in my family. The ardor of my parent's love at first sight quickly cooled in the economic desperation of the Depression and in light of their personal difficulties. My mother, especially, took a second look and would regularly leave my father and return with my brother and me to the Florida swamps. Since my mother was the twelfth of thirteen children, this meant we joined countless cousins in life by the river. Then my mom and dad would reconcile and we would return to Birmingham to live in rented rooms. In the summer after my first grade, my mother left my father for good, but did not return to Florida except for extended vacations. At age twenty-seven, she was determined to have her own home even on the limited wages and tips she earned as a cocktail waitress in a downtown hotel. She and her sister bought a house in Birmingham.

The move across town was dramatic for all of us. Although we continued to visit Florida regularly, we finally settled into one place in Birmingham without constantly moving around. The conflict and turmoil between my parents lessened and they both held steady jobs. Any number of people moved through our home to take care of brother and me, including my grandmother, two aunts, and finally a series of housekeepers. I was in school and was reading and writing well enough to skip second grade and go to third. I adored each of my schoolteachers and determined I would be a schoolteacher when I grew up—that is, if I weren't a librarian. My mother's home was across the street from a public park with a library and tennis courts. I received my first library card when I was about seven or eight and I learned to play tennis about that age. The Baptist church was on the next block. I started attending every available activity and since women couldn't be ministers in the Baptist church, I thought of becoming a missionary.

Because my mother was away every day until midnight and I only saw my dad about once a week, I suspect I was raised mostly by institutions, including schools, the church, the library, and public parks. However, some institutions were unavailable to me. I never entered a museum, saw a ballet, or heard an opera. Looking back, it's also interesting that the only occupations I ever considered were ones that were immediate models for me: schoolteacher, librarian, or missionary. I secretly wanted to be a major sports figure, but assumed that was only open to men.

I was determined to escape the working world of railroads, steel mills (they didn't use women anyway, except in clerical positions), and factory jobs. Surely, I would never have to wait tables or be a sales clerk, but neither did I aspire to more lofty professions such as physician or attorney. No, it would have to be schoolteacher, that is, if I didn't return to Florida to live in the swamps, a distinct possibility in my mind.

The river forest near my grandparent's home was dark and mysterious. I spent hours alone in a boat sliding through the shadows. I learned to swim in the murky water or at the nearby beaches. With cousins, I hunted and fished and went frog gigging. My first job ever was grubbing worms for fish bait. Before dawn, my Uncle Jennings would start his pickup truck and whatever cousins were around or awake would jump in the back. He would take us to some burned off palmetto fields and drive a two-by-four into the ground. Then he would rub another two-by-four across the top of the first one. The ground would vibrate and worms would surface. We would pick them up and put them into tin cans that Uncle Jennings delivered to neighboring stores.

Our Birmingham home was in a working-class neighborhood a couple of miles from the steel and textile mills. When I thought about it, which was seldom, I considered us a bit better off than the mill workers. Our home seemed somewhat bigger and better kept; our neighbors didn't work in the mills. One was a baker for a large bread company, another drove a public bus. Two women lived together on one side of our home and seemed to get along perfectly well without any men around. Another neighbor was epileptic, but was always available to drive me across town for tennis matches. And, of course, there was my single mom who was always inviting people to come and live with us, especially cousins from Florida and waitresses she worked with. Once she casually told my Uncle John (my father's older brother), a paranoid schizophrenic who was on leave from the VA hospital, to come see us sometime. He took her seriously, packed up his few belongings, walked across town, and moved in with us. This is the same Uncle John who read books to me when I was a toddler. I loved having him there. Conveniently ignoring that I was a girl with absolutely no chance of ever playing professional baseball, he taught me the intricacies of the game. He sat on our front porch at an old card table and wrote letters to the president. I had never met a politician, but I was impressed with my Uncle John, who, I assumed, had a personal relationship with the government. Unfortunately, he threatened to kill my cousin Charles who was also living with us and Mom made Uncle John go home.

Growing up I had two great passions: playing sports and reading. My passions were critically shaped by ease of access to the playing fields of the public park and library. I read voraciously and took my first paying job in the library at about twelve. Not only did I re-shelve books, I bound new books in cellophane to keep them clean, and repaired old ones. My pay was miniscule, but I dutifully gave the check to my mom who much preferred I spend my time in the library instead of playing sports with boys. She was definitely not pleased when she learned I had been named center on the ninety-pound YMCA boys' football team; she forbade me to play with boys at all. Little did she know I would later walk across the park and find a women's softball league that welcomed me.

Although I still secretly scrounged some pickup games with boys, I put most of my energy into tennis and won a few tournaments. It was through tennis, where some of the tournaments were played at an exclusive private club, that I met the first wealthy people I ever came to know. I recall eating lunch at the home of a doubles partner just a few blocks from the country club. The lawn was lush, the walls beautifully decorated, and there were oriental carpets on the floor. This was the first time I realized our home, with its linoleum floors, gas space heaters, and people sleeping on sofas, was really poor and shabby.

Of course, the Birmingham house was a palace compared to my grandparent's home in the Florida swamps. While once it may have been imposing for that part of the world, during my growing-up years the roofs and walls were collapsing. The hand pump for water was in the backyard and there was no electricity or indoor plumbing. My aunts and uncles who lived there always planned to make improvements, but money was sparse and life was lived outside anyway. The trips to Florida were always a joy and I loved the outdoor activities.

Still, growing up in a working-class neighborhood in Birmingham shaped most of my adult life. The public schools were good and I did well there. I won spelling bees and awards for essays and poetry reading. I had a chemistry set at home and spent hours mixing various concoctions. My favorite was a magnesium flare I would detonate in the backyard, leading me to fast becoming a public menace. All my activities were boyish and I had little or no time to play with girls. I was forced to wear dresses, but I longed for boy's clothes. As I moved into adolescence, I continued hanging out with boys, but never in a romantic way.

In high school, I began dating because I was supposed to, but I became much more interested in spending long hours with close girl friends. They were much more interesting and attractive to me than boys. I began sensing a strong difference between the girls I knew and me. With only one or two exceptions, my feelings for them were never reciprocated.

In high school, sports and schoolwork continued as my great passions. I was nationally ranked in tennis and I played on the boys' varsity tennis team. My teachers were attentive and encouraged my scholarly pursuits. I took Latin and math and hated typing and home economics. I tried out for cheerleading and failed to make the squad but, if allowed, could probably have made any of the other boys' varsity teams.

COLLEGE LIFE

No doubt, the major event of my high school days was my decision to attend college. Once I realized I could combine sports and school, I was sold on the life of a physical education teacher. I, of course, had a crush on my own physical education teacher who was straight and happily married. I was also enamored of the student teachers who came from a local Baptist college. I began to figure out how I could attend their school.

My mother, with whom I had a rather stormy relationship, took me aside and said to forget about college. There was no money and it was assumed I would take a job and get married. Never having been one to listen to my mother, I simply ignored her. My physical education teacher arranged for me to apply for a scholarship at her alma mater, a small liberal arts women's college. I received a half-time scholarship and a half-time job waiting tables in the dining room. The two gave me enough money to cover my housing, tuition, meals, and health care, which cost $536 an academic year. I quickly found other part-time jobs. I was a lifeguard, I had a paper route, and I delivered picture show announcements to get into the movies free. I also threw myself into the various athletic activities available through the college and was elected to some leadership positions.

College became my beloved home. I was independent and had found a place to pursue my own interests. Looking back, I realize how much my mother tried to shape my femininity (I had little). The endless criticisms about dress and appearance, the bitter fights over curfews were, I realize now, primarily directed toward having me be more feminine. She wanted me to be the stereotypical southern belle. I wanted to be a butch. When I finally admitted I needed a formal gown for some college events, my mother bought me not one but two evening dresses. I wore one with my sunburned neck from my physical education shirt giving mute testimony to my preference for the ballfields over the ballroom.

College was also the turning point for my sexual orientation. I had crushes on girls in high school, but I was confused. No one I knew admitted to being gay or lesbian. Those terms were not used and all I heard was how homosexual equals pervert—no great comfort for a kid who increasingly knew how she was different from her peers.

Sexual status was a more powerful obsession with me than social class. I was much more interested in which women might be lesbians than I was in their socioeconomic backgrounds. I realize now that when I went home with friends their families were much better off financially than mine were and there were always two parents in the home. One father was a college professor, another was a wealthy landowner; all the mothers were homemakers. While I was generally oblivious to my social class, I was exquisitely sensitive to being lesbian. Although I never talked with anyone about my attraction to women, I was obsessively curious about who else on campus might be inclined toward homosexuality. My entrance into the gay life was an emotional attraction to a feminine friend and the dramatic dance of determining whether she was attracted to me. At first, we were cautious about showing our real sentiments toward each other. Once we finally acknowledged we were both interested in having a relationship, we could talk openly about our real feelings toward one another. In those early days of my coming out, it was difficult to speak freely to other women about being attracted to them. My confidence was bolstered by learning that there were other out lesbians on campus. The butches were easy to identify, but, being one, I was not particularly interested in them. I preferred more feminine women and they were more difficult to find. Nonetheless, I became involved with a number of wonderful women across my four years in college.

As far I was concerned, college was the best home I had ever had. My meals were prepared for me; my laundry was done; my room, while not spacious, was my private space, even while shared with roommates who were like the sister I never had. I gave up attending the Southern Baptist Church and began participating in a Unitarian Fellowship. I went to my first opera, although I never quiet made it to a ballet or a museum. Best of all were the classes taught primarily by strong, independent women and the joys of being a physical education major. Besides our gymnasium, tennis courts, swimming pool, and ballfields, we had a good-sized lake and small golf course and I used them all. My grade point average was such that I graduated first or second in my class, although this was purely by virtue of my enthusiasm for sports and having taken over ninety hours of physical education.

Of the few courses I took outside my physical education major, I particularly enjoyed biology and psychology. I suspect this had less to do with the content of the subject than the attention I received from faculty who taught these courses. The biology faculty took me along on many an Alabama morning to collect water samples from our college lake—my first taste of hands-on research. The two psychology faculty not only encouraged me in research but Dr. Herbert Eber played tennis with me as well. I beat him in 1957 and I beat him again twenty-two years later when we played at a Georgia State Psychological Association meeting.

Eber was very supportive of any number of students and sent many off to graduate school, whether they had planned to attend or not. He and I often talked of my career plans. In my junior year, I had begun inquiring about physical education jobs in Alabama and even in Georgia where one could coach women's sports as well as teach. Salaries were about $2,700 a year. Eber suggested I think more carefully about my future and suggested I might want to pursue some other subjects of interest. I told Dr. Eber I had always been interested in English. He said that was good because I'd always have to write clearly in whatever profession I pursued. I mentioned philosophy. He suggested I think some more. Finally, he confronted me about my interest in psychology. He knew I had been practicing hypnosis in the dorms, becoming altogether frightened when suggestion seemed to work. He also knew I had just finished reading *The Return of Bridey Murphy*, a book about age regression. He said if I were to be accepted into a graduate program with support I would be making close to a physical education salary for half the number of formal work hours required. We decided to experiment. I would apply to several different graduate programs. If admitted, I would try a year with the understanding I could always return to Alabama and teach. Like my high school mentor, Dr. Eber helped me complete applications and I simply applied to schools he wished he had attended.

GRADUATE SCHOOL

Still rather oblivious to social class, I knew that attending graduate school would take me farther from my beloved southern roots. For me, the major goal was going to be how to remain an unreconstructed rebel if I indeed had to live among the Yankees.

One sunny spring day, on my way to a golf tournament, I went by the campus post office to collect my mail. The long white business envelope in my box had a return address of J. B. Rotter from Ohio State University. I stood in the sun and turned the letter over and over. Except for Harvard, I had been admitted to every program to which I had applied and I received financial support at every one except Ohio State. Dr. Eber and I sat down and laboriously wrote a letter to Julian Rotter, director of the clinical program at Ohio State. We explained that Ohio State was my first choice, but I could not attend without financial assistance. We said my father still gave my mother $30 each month for my support and perhaps that would continue and come to me. I knew the letter I held in my hand was Dr. Rotter's reply and would determine whether I would attend arguably the best clinical program in the country. I opened the letter and found Dr. Rotter had offered me a research assistantship to work with him for $2,400 for twenty hours a week. I knew next fall I would be packing and leaving for Ohio. I also suspected Dr. Rotter thought a kid named Bonnie Ruth from Alabama College had to be African American. He was always gracious about my acceptance, but I know he was surprised to have admitted a poor white hillbilly kid.

During my graduate school days, as far as I was concerned, socioeconomic class continued to be a non-issue. Weren't all graduate students poor? The most dramatic change for me was living among Yankees and meeting Republicans for the first time. I responded by finding an African American, southern roommate; we spoke the same language and ate the same food. I was very aware that most of my colleagues had attended very prestigious schools and had likely never taken an hour of physical education if they could avoid it. I was quiet in classes, having recognized early that my graduate student colleagues were much better prepared than I was.

I can recall only one time my southern rural background worked to my advantage. I was in a psychological testing laboratory and we were practicing a nonverbal, supposedly culture-fair intelligence test. One item asked what was the defining concept running through a picture of a watch, a clock, and a tree stump. I was amazed my colleagues didn't immediately know the answer was time. They had thought of time, but couldn't integrate the tree stump. I had known from early childhood that rings on a tree denoted years of growth. Perhaps my colleagues had never seen a tree stump in the wild. Perhaps they didn't have country cousins who told them about tree rings. Whatever, I savored my brief moment of glory. I suspect also my having learned to work hard when I was growing up, whether it was collecting worms or binding books, helped me succeed in graduate school.

THE ACADEMY—A PRIVATE SCHOOL

When I was graduated from Ohio State University in 1962, my class background and lesbian identity, especially since I wasn't out, were much less important in regard to my finding an academic position than the simple fact of my gender. Few women were being hired for college and university positions. I still have a copy of a letter from a prestigious midwestern university saying, "while [your] record [is] very good [they] had decided to hire a <u>man</u> (their underline) instead." My major advisor had been consulting on developing a clinical psychology program at a prestigious private university in Atlanta and recommended me for a position there. I soon received a job offer and accepted it. I was delighted to return south, finally home again, where the weather was pleasant and I spoke the same language as the natives. Like my mother, I immediately bought my own home at age twenty-five.

Living in Atlanta, I crossed several communities and classes. Weekdays I dressed up and went into the genteel halls of the university. Late afternoon I would return to my suburban home, and evenings and weekends I would dress down and join lesbian friends in softball and basketball games. One boundary, however, was impermeable. My gay and lesbian friends never met my straight colleagues and vice versa. I was either trying to pass as straight or living openly in the gay world. And my straight friends were matchmaking at every turn, never knowing I would rather *have* a wife than *be* one.

Being a graduate student is a class unto itself, while being a faculty member at a university brings one into a social class of some prestige and stature. As I walked the academic halls, I was as far from family, the steel mills of Birmingham, and the Florida swamps as one can imagine. My life was no longer one of waiting tables in the college dining room or binding books in a dusty office, nor would I face the prospect of making a living through physical labor. I had also escaped the early marriage and children that were the fate of so many of my high school peers. I was single, made a good living, and worked at a job I loved.

Life within the academy was pleasant but sometimes embarrassing as well. I learned to quit saying *De*troit and *po*lice, but I remember my humiliation at mispronouncing *A*rab in front of my class one day. I began to think I would never speak the English of my students. I was also one of the first of the very few women faculty in my college. As had been true in graduate school, all my mentors were male. Looking back, I am not surprised they had a difficult time relating to a young, working-class lesbian from an entirely different culture.

Then one afternoon, I was at home reading a psychology journal. I vividly remember the telephone call from the Dean of Students asking if

I would consider becoming the Dean of Women. This was my second year at the university and the administration had few women to turn to when the current Dean of Women abruptly resigned. I took the position and was quickly caught up in a round of social activities where I was expected to host gatherings and model manners for college coeds. Perhaps the most jarring responsibilities were supervising the strong sorority system that was deeply entrenched in the campus culture. Not only did I deal with the sorority sisters but with their parents and national representatives of each group. I appreciated the opportunities for the young women to gather in small groups and expand leadership roles for themselves, but I abhorred those moments with a crying parent whose daughter had been "cut" from her preferred sorority. First the group "rushed" you and encouraged you to think of them as "sisters."' Then one's sisterhood was abruptly denied and the poor girl was rejected via some unknown criteria that brought her very being into question. As an outsider myself, I could appreciate the pain of being excluded. I could do little to change the sorority system, although we tried a number of approaches to open doors to everyone who wanted to belong. I never mentioned my sexual orientation, but was somewhat attuned to class differences. I had never attended a "tea" before and now I had to pour it. I admired the elegantly dressed parents and sorority representatives and had no clue where they shopped or how they had attained a taste for fashion. I wore pearls, but preferred blue jeans.

Bowing under the intransigence of the sorority system, I turned my attention to women's government, trying to enhance a sense of freedom and responsibility for the students. At that time, women still had curfew while the men could stay out as long as they liked. Women at the college also had to wear dresses to class even when they rode bikes to school in winter weather. We changed all that.

After three years as Dean of Women, I was happy to return to my department to continue my research and teaching activities. Although I was not conscious of it at the time, class issues permeated every aspect of both my research and teaching. My research increasingly centered on understanding psychological issues in diverse communities. One of my earliest studies, which later became a Citation Classic, was an investigation of the attitudes held by black activists about internal versus external control of reinforcement. Internal individuals were significantly more likely to engage in important social action than were their more external counterparts. I also looked at delay of gratification and trust issues among African American schoolchildren and eventually began researching gay and lesbian topics. With colleagues, I was among the first to show that gay men and lesbians were seemingly as well adjusted psychologically as heterosexuals.

I was fortunate to be in Atlanta during the heady days of the civil rights movement. I would invite well-known figures to speak to my classes, trying to balance both conservative and liberal approaches. At one point, I scheduled a bus to take my social psychology students through the working-class neighborhoods of Atlanta in an effort to broaden their understanding of the city where they lived. No doubt, I felt isolated as a liberal lesbian from the working-class teaching at a wealthy and extremely conservative school. Yet, in ways, my southern and working-class background helped me in that I could speak the language of the demonstrators and share their frustrations and disappointments. I knew what it was like to be an outsider and discriminated against. But, while I saw African Americans empower themselves and appreciated their enormous efforts, I never dreamed gay and lesbian people would someday use the same tactics of boycott and demonstration to attain their freedoms—a struggle that will likely continue far into the future. Although I didn't know it then, I realize now I was desperately trying to bring some integration to myself across gender, race, and class, and I saw this effort manifesting itself in my social activism during the 1960s.

THE ACADEMY—A PUBLIC UNIVERSITY

After over a decade in Atlanta, I was offered a position at a large public university in New England. The long journey north was poignant for me. I was leaving a familiar life and a wealth of friends. I had enjoyed working with my straight colleagues who until the day I left were still trying to marry me off. Little did they know that all the handsome men I would bring to our social gatherings were gay and not interested in me. I was happily settled into a partnership that would last for eighteen years. I was also leaving a large group of lesbian friends. We had been through a lot together—a softball league, the opening of several gay and lesbian bars, innumerable private parties, and at least one raid by the police. I had owned a home for almost the whole time I was in Atlanta, and I loved my job.

Even before I left Atlanta, I came north to search for a home to buy. I didn't find exactly what I wanted so I bought a condominium instead. I would live in it for three months until I settled on a lovely home in the woods. No rented rooms for me.

The differences between my old and new schools could not have been greater. While I had been involved in the civil rights movement, students at my old university were demonstrating against school integration. When students throughout the country began holding peace rallies during the days of Vietnam, students from my old university sponsored aggression rallies. They rented the Atlanta stadium to affirm Vietnam. One visiting scholar said he had never seen such a university where faculty and administration were so much more liberal and socially active than their students, students whose tongue-in-cheek college motto was "Apathy." So, I left the privileged students and the well-endowed private university for a rowdy, working-class "people's" public university. On the day of my interview, I walked through a crowded student union with tables and posters espousing every liberal position imaginable. The scent of marijuana drifted through the halls. Although I was once again living with Yankees, the students were predominantly like me—the first in their family to attend college.

Just a few years ago, I was walking across campus with a colleague and we passed what was yet another building takeover with a couple of hundred students demonstrating out front. My colleague looked at the protesters, smiled broadly, and said, "That's what I love about this school." I also reveled in the openness and diversity of both the university and the community where it was located. Beginning with the days of Vietnam, peace vigils were held on the town common. Peace vigils are still commonplace there. While my southern students had affirmed Vietnam, the students of my new university had shut down the campus to protest the war.

I had been closeted in the South, but I quickly found my new university and its community were open and affirming of my being a lesbian. My partner and I quickly joined a softball team composed predominantly of lesbians. We played in a feminist softball league. Most teams were not competitive and didn't want to keep score. We, on the other hand, kept score and wanted to win every game. Some of us secretly called ourselves PIGS—Politically Incorrect Girls Softball. Our motto was "Kill."

At school, my partner and I were warmly welcomed to social events and gatherings, just another faculty couple. Being an excellent athlete, my partner was especially welcomed to compete on our departmental intramural sports teams. At first, I was not entirely open about my sexual orientation, but most faculty suspected I was a lesbian and seemed relieved when I came out to them. My class background seemed to have much less impact in my new situation and sometimes my being lesbian was more of a blessing than a burden. Once I was meeting with our undergraduate curriculum committee. We were trying to determine whether the university was offering all the courses we thought it should. A colleague asked if I might develop a course on health psychology, an offering not on our books. For whatever reasons, I blurted out I wasn't interested in a course on health psychology, but I would develop one on lesbian psychology. Well, you would have thought I had endowed a building. The curriculum committee was ecstatic and when the course was proposed the Dean jumped at the chance for such an offering and made the class one of the diversity requirements in general education. The faculty senate voted unanimously to approve the offering and I found myself preparing a new course. We called it The Psychology of Differences: The Lesbian Experience, but it quickly became known affectionately as Dyke Psych.

During this time, I also became very active in my professional association. I cannot say to what degree my being a lesbian helped or hurt. I suspect most members did not know of my sexual orientation and voted for me because of my academic and research background. However, in smaller groups, such as the board of directors—to which I was appointed—the members knew or quickly learned I was a lesbian. Still, they were especially welcoming of me and my partner who was invited to join other spouses in the activities planned for them. Here again my class background was particularly salient. I was eventually elected president of the association and found myself in a whirlwind of activities with high-status individuals and groups. I was invited to thousand-dollars-per-person political fundraisers. I met U.S. senators and representatives. I visited congressional offices and testified before congressional committees. I hosted elaborate parties at our various conventions and moved in a world of rare wealth and sophistication. By this time I was well aware of class differences and often wondered how a kid from the south side of the steel mills in Birmingham could walk the halls of the senate.

Just before my mother died, she was talking about my father. She recalled his good looks and the better parts of his nature, but she never forgave him for keeping her in rented rooms. I count myself most fortunate to have escaped rented rooms, although I may have overdone it a bit. I now have homes in Massachusetts, North Carolina, and the Gulf of Mexico. I live very comfortably and travel extensively; most of my friends are "professionals." I still visit my cousins and kinfolk in the Florida swamps. I love walking the outlines of my grandparents' house and returning to the old boat landing. I enjoy being with my relatives and imagining what my life would have been like if I were still in the swamps, though talk of fishing and deer hunting is not as interesting to me now as it once was.

After eighteen years my partner and I—we had been in a very traditional relationship—separated. We had simply moved in different directions. I remained single for about the next ten years until I met my new partner and settled into an exciting and loving relationship. Beyond my wildest dreams, we can get married in Massachusetts, unlike my old home states that passed laws against same-sex marriage.

Although my family gradually came to know that I was lesbian, we seldom if ever discussed it. Until her dying day, my mother kept trying to marry me off. She seemed proud of my accomplishments but, I think, could never admit I was lesbian. In some ways, she lived our improved social class life vicariously through me (I even bought her a house once), but my being lesbian was simply beyond her comprehension. My mother, bowing to the social norms of the 1940s and 1950s, wanted male children. Likewise, she only felt secure with a man on her arm, and she never knew what to do with me.

For over forty years, I have lived in my own home and worked in the academy. My life has been full and happy and a long way from my southern roots. Poor southern kids have only limited ways to escape poverty—primarily through education or sports. I was lucky to have a bit of both. The public library brought me books. The public tennis courts brought me a national ranking and scholarships. The public schools eventually awarded me a PhD. I count myself among the most fortunate to have spent the better part of my life doing all I ever wanted to do—reading, writing, playing, and talking to people, and even getting *paid* for my efforts. It has been a very rewarding life, one that children of poverty and working-class origins are seldom encouraged to pursue. I have sought, in my own special ways, to remedy this problem, and perhaps that has been one of the most gratifying parts of all.

EIGHT

Escape from the Bronx

The Making of an Unlikely Leader

RICHARD GREGGORY JOHNSON III

FIGHTING FOR MY LIFE

I was born on June 1, 1964, in Harlem Hospital. I came of age in the Bronx, New York, during the 1970s and early 1980s. As a child and young adult, I always knew I was different. I was unlike my only brother, my parents, and most everyone living in my working-class, multiethnic, multiracial neighborhood.

My sexual orientation was the first difference people noticed about me. My perceived effeminate behaviors led to continuous torment and ridicule from family members and classmates. It did not help that I enjoyed playing with Barbie dolls until age six or seven. I had no sisters, which made getting access to dolls especially challenging. Every occasion I had to visit my father's oldest sister, Aunt Katherine, I went there because it meant I could play with her daughters' dolls. Aunt Katherine and her husband had five girls and many dolls in the household. Things got worse for me when my doll playing became public—not to mention that Aunt Katherine had three masculine sons who hated me for playing with their sisters' dolls. I could not help myself. I loved escaping into the world of Barbies and more or less pretending to be a little girl myself. It is hard to admit this even now. However, as a little boy, I was compelled to want to become what I saw in Barbie, with her long flowing hair and beautiful clothing.

My parents were not pleased with my doll playing and they ordered me to stop. Once I was playing with my cousin's Barbie and my father ordered me to put the doll down and stand in the middle of my aunt's living room and say, "I am not a little girl." This was one of the worst moments of my life. My father wanted to show he controlled his little boy and his little boy was not a "fag." I thought I was going to die when this happened. The living room was packed with relatives. I felt like a puppet on my father's strings: *dance, fag, dance*. To make matters worse, I received no sympathy, hugs, or "poor baby" from onlookers. My father, on the other hand, received pats on the back and high praise for making his sissy son relinquish his girlish ways. I did not know then that I was up against a force that would be with me for the rest of my life: homophobia from the African American community.

My father is a man of considerable athletic ability. He stands six feet, four inches. He was quite the ladies' man before he married my mother and also while he was married to my mother. Of course, he wanted his older son to mirror him. Instead, I was on a slippery slope traveling far from my father's dream.

Eventually, I stopped playing with my cousins' dolls. It was not because I wanted to or could have at that stage of development. I stopped playing with dolls because my father was beating the sissy out of me, or so he thought. During the 1970s, beating children was still a proper way to raise them, at least in my family. There were no public policies against hitting your kids. Nor could I call 911 or the Child Protection Agency. Therefore, I had to stop playing with dolls because I was tired of having my ass beat all the time.

My mother was not sympathetic to my cause either. She agreed with my father and did not want her older son playing with dolls. She did not beat me for playing with them, but she continuously bought me an array of football jerseys and macho-type outfits in an attempt to "reorient" me.

When I was about nine, a new phase of my life started. I would wear my mother's wigs when she was not home. I think I was practicing to be a drag queen later on, although, oddly enough, drag does not appeal to me as an adult. My parents did not know I had entered this stage. It was fun wearing my mother's wigs. I really enjoyed looking in the mirror with my mother's wig fitting just right on my head. My younger brother was at home during these times. However, he either called me "fag" or "sissy-pooh." (I wonder if my brother remembers calling me these names.) My parents and I both hated hearing these insults. My brother always threatened to tell my parents about my new stage in life. Candy, toys, and comic books were the only way to get him to keep quiet about my wig adventures.

My wig phase lasted about two years, and then I got busted. Eastern Star Club is a Masonic community service organization for women. One evening, my mother returned home early from one of their meetings and caught me wearing a wig. I tried to get rid of it before she entered our apartment, but I was too slow. Mother saw me with the wig and started to scream and rant and then beat me. For two weeks, my mother did not speak to me except to call me "fag," a term she had refrained from using in my doll-playing years. My disgusted father refused to look at me. He would leave the room when I entered.

Finally, my parents wanted to take me to a counselor. Before doing this, my father spoke with Aunt Katherine about my effeminate nature. After all, she still pulled rank as his older sister—much to my mother's disapproval. Aunt Katherine said God would heal me of my desire to become female. My parents agreed that going to a counselor was expensive and that God was a cheaper solution; my parents liked the idea because it was both financially and spiritually acceptable. My mother stopped wearing wigs after that incident, and quit calling me fag as well. My father also quit calling me "fag," more or less. Unfortunately, my father never talked to me much after the wig affair, other than taking pokes at my sexual orientation every chance he got, albeit more subtly.

I grew up in public housing, commonly called the "projects." My neighborhood was very diverse. I never really noticed or appreciated this until I was an adult. Although my community contained many races and ethnic groups, African Americans were the force I had to reckon with. My life through junior high was mostly having one fight after another. I was constantly picked on for being effeminate and short—not a good combination at Albert Einstein Junior High School 131 in the Bronx.

I was academically gifted. This only made things worse. I did not realize growing up working class and gay was going to be so difficult. However, at 131, the African American students seemed to delight in making my life miserable. The Hispanic and white students rarely hassled me. Meanwhile, the African American boys and girls made me feel unimportant, and unattractive. During junior high, I would ask girls out on dates—even though I was more interested in dating boys. My father mentioned to me more than once that he was disappointed I had not started dating girls yet. This is why I had tried to date the 131 girls. However, none would date me because I wasn't in the cool group and I seemed to associate with every other race but black kids. *But why would I hang out with a bunch of people who taunted me endlessly?*

During seventh grade, I got into a fight that was so bad my parents transferred me to another school. That whole year had been one of endless fighting, and no dates. I had one good African American friend. His name was Calvin and he was also very talented academically. He and I often vied for top grades in our classes. Despite being black and effeminate, nobody picked on Calvin because he came from a family of six children and all of them were good fighters. Calvin and I remained friends until I transferred to another junior high school. We never connected again and I sometimes wonder what happened to him.

Transferring to another junior high school transformed my life. The new school gave me a sense of independence and freedom because it was far enough away that I had to take a bus. (Junior High School 131 had been just a ten-minute walk from my house.) My new junior high school had smart students of diverse backgrounds and, perhaps most important, they were not interested in fighting. The African American students enrolled at the school were very nice to me and I thought I had overcome all my 131 "issues."

The year away from 131 was fight free and wonderful. Much to my dismay, the next year, I had to return to the same junior high school that had caused me so much suffering. By this time, my only brother started attending the same school. Unlike me, my brother was big and masculine. My mother said my *younger* brother would be there to protect me—the humiliation and indignation I felt from that statement still resonates. Fortunately, my brother did not have to join in the fights or protect me.

My last year at 131 was not too bad. I still had fights and no dates with girls, but I did become good friends with Raymond. He was so cute. Raymond was biracial (African American and white) and had stunning good looks. I could not stop thinking about him. He was my best friend that whole school year. We hung out during and after school. We even cut school one day and got away with it.

Toward the end of that year, I really wanted to kiss Raymond because I knew we would be going to different high schools next term. One day we were in the boy's bathroom and I told Raymond I wanted to kiss him. He said, "Go ahead." However, fear got the best of me and I did not do it. Raymond promised he would not tell anyone if I kissed him. I decided not to chance it. Paranoia was already a looming part of me. If the African American students knew I tried to kiss Raymond, who was well liked and accepted, out of shame I would have to quit school, which was bad because I would have to stay home with my parents for more time than I ever wanted.

Raymond and I graduated from the Albert Einstein School in June 1978. I never did get to kiss him. Nor did I ever know which high school he attended. All these years later, I still think about Raymond and wonder what it would have been like to kiss him in the bathroom that day in school. I am sure it would have been a lovely experience. Like Calvin, Raymond was another one "who got away."

DAYS OF PENTECOST

My high school years were filled with church and sex. By age fifteen, I had already determined I was gay, not bisexual. Fortunately, my parents probably also knew this and no longer pressed me to date women. I was active in church and somehow my parents did not believe I would go to hell for "being different." Oh, the wonders of rationalization. Nonetheless, they encouraged me to have my "soul saved," just in case.

I met my first true love in church. His name was John and he matriculated at the High School of Performing Arts in New York City. We dated for several months during my junior year at Adlai E. Stevenson High School, a working-class institute in the Bronx. John was smart and had the charm and grace of someone from a well-to-do family. Instead, John, like me, lived in public housing in the Bronx.

One night John dropped me off at my parent's apartment after a great date. My father saw me getting out of his car and got very angry. Dad screamed at me all the way up to our apartment. My mother came out of their bedroom to see what was wrong. My father was yelling at the top of his lungs saying he had seen me "getting out of some punk's car!" "Punk" is the African American term for "gay." I did not protest. I acted helpless against my father's onslaught. I had had some knock-down, drag-out fights with my parents, but, on this night, I did not want to battle them. It was after midnight and I was much too exhausted. Without saying anything, I went to my room, donned my pajamas, and got into bed.

John broke up with me the next week because he claimed God told him to turn from his wicked ways. What a lame excuse. I wondered why God would give him such a message and not me as well. Had God given up on me? Had God abandoned me, but not John, to hell? I cried and wondered about this for the next month. Sadly, there was nobody around to comfort me.

During high school, I started finding more gay friends. Despite the messy breakup with my first boyfriend, I continued dating other men. In my first year of high school, I tried to be bisexual. I started writing about this topic for my English classes. I assumed God would not mind if I dated men *and* women. In a way, I reasoned, dating women would cancel the sin points I accumulated when I went out with men. My essay did not amuse my teacher. She said I could write on any topic except bisexuality. She was adamant in her demands. I would really disrupt her theology when I attended class wearing a light blue "Jesus Saves" T-shirt my older cousin had given me. Eventually, I complied with my teacher's request. I was a good boy, but I was seeing the manipulative effects of formal education in practice. It was clear whose side my teachers had chosen in the sexual identities wars.

I sang in the church youth choir throughout high school. I played the role of a good religious boy by going to Bible study every Wednesday night. On Sunday, I spoke in "tongues." I remember when our pastor chastised some men in the congregation for being effeminate or for wanting to have sex with other men. His voice reeked with loathing. I knew escaping such church dogma and my parents' rules would be my only salvation. For the next few years, I plotted my escape.

My self-acceptance was not as difficult as I had expected thanks mostly to Darren, a good friend who had just opened up to me. It happened during my last year of high school. On Darren's urging, I joined a support group for gay teens. All of us met on Christopher Street in Greenwich Village in

New York City. Ironically, given my recent history with the Apostolic Church, my support group made me feel I had died and *gone to heaven*. For the first time I felt celebrated as a complete person. There was a male facilitator and a female facilitator. I remember so well the time the male facilitator told the group, which met on weekends, that he had been married, but secretly kept dating men. One day he left home to hang out with friends at a gay bar. He told his wife he was going to a baseball game with some buddies. Upon entering the tavern, he looked in the corner and saw his wife hugging another woman. Talk about a coming-out story—it reminded me of "The Pena Colada Song."

After the support meetings, the group hung out along the "pier" in the Village. My new associates gave me friendship and knowledge. For the first time in my life I was excited about being black and gay. I was *liberated*!

The Village was an amazing place. It was very different from my working-class Bronx neighborhood. The train ride from the Bronx south to the Village took almost an hour using the Number 6 and the Number 1 trains. The trip was well worth it. I was transformed upon entering the Village. As soon as the train entered Christopher Street station, I knew I would feel at home for at least the next few hours.

When it was time to return home, I got depressed. Unlike my Bronx neighborhood, in the Village I saw men holding hands with men and women holding hands with women. I also noted that people in the Village spoke well. I remember a tall, white guy who was so gorgeous I would have married him on the spot. I overheard him talking to someone in a store and he sounded so smart and sophisticated. My friend Darren thought he just sounded stereotypically gay—I did not care. Unfortunately, my newfound freedom and self-awareness were causing me great grief because I was still living in an oppressive working-class neighborhood with my parents. The Bronx made me feel even more isolated and alone.

I remained an active church member to fake heterosexuality. I did not need God to save my soul. However, I needed a good cover for why I was away from home all the time. Being "out" for me meant only my friends knew my sexual orientation. It would be years before I came out to my parents and family.

CONSIDERING COLLEGE

I was accepted to New York University during my last year of high school. I planned to move completely into the world I had grown to love: the Village. Unfortunately, my excitement about NYU was short-lived. My parents were unimpressed. My father made one of his haunting statements about my trying to live in an environment with "those people." He declared he would not pay for his son to attend school with "a bunch of fags." Instead, my parents wanted me to go to Temple University in Philadelphia. Temple was about a half mile from my paternal grandparents' home. I would have died before submitting to this lunacy. When it came to sexual orientation, my grandparents were at least as tyrannical as my parents were. Given that Temple and NYU were now out of the question, it was on to plan C, attending a Historically Black College/University (HBCU).

During the early 1980s, television sitcoms such as *The Cosby Show* and *A Different World* were contradicting stereotypical perceptions of how African Americans viewed formal education. The Cosby family was headed by a happily married couple. He was a doctor and she was an attorney. They had a daughter at an Ivy League university and four other children. All five kids were well adjusted. These two shows represented a monumental and exciting shift away from other sitcoms, such as *Good Times*, which featured a father who was often unemployed and two sons who shared a pull-out sofa bed. In short, *The Cosby Show* and *A Different World* presented African Americans living upscale lives and doing remarkable things, including their kids attending college.

A Different World depicted college life at a HBCU in Virginia. Most HBCUs were located in the southern United States and the schools usually had religious affiliations, two things that turned me off. However, going to a United Negro College Fund (UNCF)-supported school pleased my parents and thus provided some peace in our household.

A DIFFERENT PLACE OF BEING

My parents and I agreed I would attend Johnson C. Smith University (JCSU). JSCU was founded in 1867 and is located in Charlotte, North Carolina. My parents felt good that I was attending JCSU because I would be away from "those people" in New York City. Likewise, I would be close enough to other family members then living in South Carolina should I need help. I never did. My father spent weeks before my departure telling me how to behave and that my effeminate mannerisms and high-pitched voice would not be tolerated in the South. He reasoned that one justification for my going to JCSU was that it would "straighten me out."

If I had good sense, I would have left JCSU during orientation week. When it came to my sexual orientation, this school was not the bastion of hope and goodwill I had expected based on what I saw in *A Different World*. One of the most surprising things was something I never anticipated would affect my view of higher learning. It was the role of social class within the black community, just like in every other community. Somehow, I thought we, the African American community, were all in this together. It was like this in the television shows I mentioned, but I never paid that much attention to social class stratification.

I had never seen so many middle-and upper-middle-class African Americans in my life until I went to JCSU. Until then, my sexual orientation and my race were what distinguished me from the majority. However, from my first days on the JCSU campus, I had a growing awareness of my social class origins, something I had simply always taken for granted.

My first awakenings to my class background came when I watched as other students moved their belongings into the dorms. There were long lines of moving vans outside the buildings. Every vehicle was full of expensive furniture, stereo equipment, and other modern luxuries. I had arrived the day before with only a modest-sized trunk that housed all my clothing and a thirteen-inch television. This was it. This was all I had to bring with me. Still, I was only beginning to notice the class differences that should have otherwise been obvious to me at JCSU. In those early days, I was just glad to be away from home and far from the misery of growing up in the Bronx.

The school paired me with a junior for my first-year orientation sessions. My "Buddy" was supposed to introduce me to campus life at JCSU. Ours was a horrible coupling. Rather than help me adjust to campus, she continued the "Richard Johnson Jr. Self-Esteem Destruction Process" the African American students at Junior High School 131 had started. Within the first hour of meeting her, I learned she was the fourth generation in her family to attend JCSU. In the late 1860s, her great-grandfather had been one of the university's first graduates. She wore a sorority jacket and explained that her mother, grandmother, and her three sisters had pledged the same sorority. I later learned this sorority was one of "The Elite Eight" (Ross 2000).[1] Next, my Buddy questioned me about my lineage. "I am the first one in my family to attend college," I said proudly. She appeared to pity my humble origins. It was as if she believed she had somehow chosen her family members and I had chosen mine, and I had selected the wrong people. It has been twenty years since my Buddy asked me about my family background, but I still vividly remember how this woman made me feel like a second-class citizen at a place I thought would be free of such prejudices. (Today, I keep asking myself why JCSU officials did not pair me with a Buddy who was also first-generation college. That would not have made my life carefree, but it would have probably helped me better appreciate the importance of social class in everyday events, both on campus and beyond.)

Unfortunately, that was only one of many discouraging episodes I had during my stay at JCSU, and certainly, as you might expect, not all of them based on my social class origins. The next affront came during my sophomore year. I "pledged" a fraternity—big mistake, at least in the beginning. As noted, nobody in my immediate family attended college. A couple of cousins who had gone to college did not join a fraternity or sorority. Thus, I didn't know what to expect from my fraternity "brothers." I wanted to be a traditional college student, which to me meant joining a fraternity. In part, I thought this might help me escape my class-background problems. I selected the Alpha Phi Alpha fraternity. It is the oldest of the predominantly African American "Greek" organizations (Graham 2000, 92). Because there are no "professional people" in my immediate family, I thought joining one of the most sought-after international fraternities would assure me success after college. Even though most of the "brothers" came from families where the men were both college educated and fraternity members, I felt Alpha Phi Alpha was the fraternity for me.

I had all the requirements needed for membership, including a stellar GPA, community service, and kick-ass recommendations from alumni brothers of the organization. I had met the latter at various campus functions. I knew many current Alpha brothers liked me. I was even selected to become a sweetheart for Alpha's sister sorority, Alpha Kappa Alpha. Many women in the sorority knew I was gay but still welcomed me into their noble circle. To this day, I consider the time I spent with these women among the most enjoyable episodes of my college days.

However, one event greatly changed my world. I was a residential advisor (RA) when I was attempting to join Alpha Phi Alpha. I also started to date a first-year male student named Terry. He was dark-skinned with expressive eyes and a strong intelligence. I thought he was truly the one for me.

One evening Terry was spending the night with me. As an RA, I had my own room. There was no rule about males staying over at each other's rooms. About midnight, someone knocked on my door. I thought it was a resident. I opened the door slightly to see who it was. Horror covered my face and body when I discovered it was two Alpha brothers. They were also RAs. They had come to my room to discuss a rumor circulating on campus about my sexuality. I denied the allegations and said there was a woman in my bed that very moment. I never expected one of my visitors would have the temerity to push my door open, only to find my boyfriend in my bed. The brothers looked disgusted, even though I suspected one was gay based on my past conversations with him. The two men shook their heads and walked away quietly. I would have left the university if I could have.

Neither Terry nor I could sleep that night. The news of "the Scandal," as my friends and I call it now, spread immediately. JCSU had less than two thousand students. Therefore, rumors traveled fast around campus, especially gay news, whether it was about men or women. I went to the cafeteria the next day and immediately noticed there was a conspicuous iciness toward me. Due to my bad timing, I came to eat just when the place was packed with students. There were no empty tables. I asked another student if I could sit with him. He said I could and in the same breath explained he wasn't gay. This was the beginning of a long, uphill battle for me.

I knew the spreading stories about my homosexuality were reducing to zero my chances of becoming an Alpha. Nevertheless, I applied during rush period. I received an interview invitation. I took this as a good sign. Wrong! At midnight, I went to Biddle Hall and ascended the steps to the third floor. I was wearing a black suit and tie. I was ushered into a room filled with Alpha brothers. Of course, the two brothers who saw Terry in my bed were there. They were sitting with their arms folded.

The questioning period began without niceties. Thus, I was not shocked when the brothers lowered the boom on me. One asked me to describe the worse thing I had ever done. (In hindsight, I should have said, "Pledged your fraternity.") I knew this was a setup question, but I responded without missing a beat. "I have never done anything I am ashamed of," I replied. The brothers asked me about other issues that night, but the question about shame was the only one that sticks in my head.

An alumni brother escorted me out of the room immediately after the interview. Ironically, I noticed how beautiful he was, including his wonderful smile. As we stepped into the hallway, he quietly mentioned he thought I had interviewed well. For the first time in weeks, all seemed right in my world.

A couple of days latter, I received a letter saying Alpha Phi Alpha had rejected my application to join their fraternity. I was devastated. It took me two more times to get into Alpha Phi Alpha—but I was determined to join. It is comical now to think that a homophobic organization could work so hard to reject someone because of his sexuality. Because Alpha Phi Alpha is private, it has the right to discriminate against gays, both officially and unofficially, without sanctions. Eventually, after being admitted into Alpha Phi Alpha, I served as alumni chapter president, regional director, membership director, and secretary. I wonder how active the "infamous" two brothers who came to my door that night were as Alpha Phi Alpha members, and how successful they have been after college.

Men with an undergraduate degree may still join Alpha as alumni members. My greatest accomplishment in terms of my own fraternity resume has been getting as many gay brothers and brothers without family connections into Alpha Phi Alpha as possible.

I end this section by suggesting that attending JCSU was one of the most disappointing experiences of my life. Although I maintain close relationships with a couple of my college classmates, I still remember how, as a working-class, gay student, I found little support at an institution that had promised to nurture me. Instead of cultivating all facets of my personality, most JCSU administrators, faculty, and students seemed to be saying, "Shut up and graduate." One of my JCSU classmates at the time even said I was attending a HBCU to learn how to be black. I found his statement highly offensive. Although I grew up in a very diverse Bronx community, I didn't need any lessons in blackness. I was "black" long before ever stepping foot on the JCSU campus.

Almost none of the JSCU faculty encouraged me to pursue an advanced degree. It was probably because I wasn't in the "elite group of students." Likewise, I had never developed connections with any "real scholars." Nonetheless, I learned about master's and doctoral studies. Something inside was motivating me to achieve these advanced degrees. My grades at JCSU were stellar during my first year but nose-dived during my second year, after Alpha Phi Alpha blackballed me. (What an ironic term to use in rejecting an applicant.) During my junior and senior years, I began getting high grades again.

Being an urban studies major was especially challenging at JCSU because most of my classes were with the same professors and same students; there was not a lot of intellectual variety. As a faculty member today, I look back and shake my head at what was being passed off as an urban studies major. The program had only two full-time professors and neither was tenure track. Both were good teachers, but only one had a doctorate. Neither did much student advising. Not surprisingly, I drifted aimlessly through the program; I had no real direction. Thus, it is funny that my vita indicates I graduated with honors in my major, something that helped me get into graduate school. I finished at JCSU in 1987. I left campus with many psychological battle scars, wounds that are life lasting and deep. As the years away from JCSU pass, I keep thinking I should "forgive and forget," yet I am still very resentful about what happened to me there. When I tell other African Americans about my many unfortunate experiences at JCSU, they look at me in disbelief. HBCUs are supposed to be the pinnacle of higher learning for all African Americans. I have even heard some African American students say the educational quality of HBCUs exceeds what Ivy League schools offer. (Of course, had many of these same African American students been invited into the hallowed halls of the Ivy Leagues, I am sure their own classism would carry them to Cambridge, New Haven, and all points expensive and Ivy, but that is another story.) I took my degree from this HBCU, leaving with high student loan bills and low self-esteem. I still believe I paid far too much for my undergraduate schooling. In my case, time has not brightened the halo people usually place on their alma maters. Oh, how I wish I had come from the sort of family that already understood the nuances of campus life and the importance of shopping for the right college.

I wish I could be upbeat and generous about my treatment at a university that sells itself as nurturing and supportive. I can't. There are too many bad memories, recollections I cannot relinquish no matter how hard I try. Every day I consider penning a letter to the current JCSU president chronicling my experiences there. Perhaps when this book is published, I will have the emotional wherewithal to send her my chapter. Even writing these sentences pains me. I am trying to work through my anger, though it is challenging, to say the least.

LOST IN SPACE

After JCSU, I was determined to leave the South and attend graduate school. I had no idea what I would do with a graduate degree. All I knew was that I wanted to gain more formal education in a different setting and definitely not in urban studies. I had had enough of that by not having enough of that, if you will. I focused on reviewing information about master's of public administration (MPA) programs at schools in large U.S. cities. Much as it was with my decision to major in urban studies, I don't know how or when I became interested in public administration/affairs. DePaul University and Northwestern University accepted me into their public affairs programs.

I chose DePaul because of my father. He and I had evolved into having a passable relationship while I was in college, although we were still not best friends. At least now we were civil toward one another. DePaul had admitted my father on a basketball scholarship during the mid-1960s. He opted to join the Marines instead. I decided to attend DePaul for him. One of the first things I did when I was at DePaul was buy my father a university sweatshirt. That was in 1988. My father still wears that sweatshirt. After all, blood is thicker than homophobia, I guess.

DePaul was very different from JCSU. For one, I had to study a lot harder and longer to maintain a B average at DePaul. I also noticed how my class background haunted me again. I was a black, gay, working-class kid with a college degree, but my graduate professors were not the least bit interested in my struggles and what it took for me to get to graduate school. They only cared about what I could produce without much assistance from them.

There were several reasons I had problems my first semester at DePaul. One was the culture. I remember standing among several tall (over six feet) white men who were wearing business suits and waiting for the elevators at the downtown campus. All these guys looked as if they had just gotten off the same Ivy League train. Likewise, they were all taking the same courses I was, and some were in my classes. Suddenly I felt panicky and inferior to all these well-groomed and well-spoken white men.

DePaul intimidated me for other reasons as well. While I was right out of college, most of my classmates had worked for at least three years before attending graduate school. They had far more practical understanding to draw on than I did. I know my lack of "real-world" knowledge caused me to get lower grades than I would have achieved had I been as practiced as my classmates. For example, my lack of experience affected my performance on my writing assignments and tests. I received a C on my final paper in a human resources management class. The course was supposed to teach graduate students how personnel systems work. Obviously, I did not learn much about such things. Certainly, my lack of professional experience in personnel matters did not help.

In my capstone paper, I detailed the issues associated with supervising staff. I had never supervised anyone in my life! This was a daunting assignment. My father was a correctional officer at a New York City prison and my mother served meals in an elementary school. Neither had ever supervised anyone, so I could not call on them for advice. My capstone paper was not an award winner, but it was the best I could do given my limited administrative experience.

I learned something from this episode. As a faculty of public policy, I teach HRM each spring term. I don't use my DePaul capstone paper in this course because I know it is incomplete. Nor do I penalize students who lack work experience or who have never had supervisory responsibilities. Instead, I gauge what individual students bring to class and, in turn, I help them produce acceptable products for my course.

Another problem I faced at DePaul was the big change from my undergraduate academic culture. At the end of my first semester at DePaul, I was not feeling good about myself. I had been receiving mediocre grades in the three classes I was taking. I did not realize I needed to change my study routine and how I was approaching my classes. As an undergraduate, I always completed my work on time and got at least B grades. However, I found that the same strategies that worked at JCSU were not cutting it at DePaul. Being a graduate student is a very challenging task, especially when your parents cannot help you with advice about completing assignments, nor can they counsel you about dealing with the stress associated with being in seminars where there is so much open discussion and your lack of practical experience inevitably shows. There are no places for a graduate student to go and say, "Hey, I'm first-generation college and I need advice on surviving the academic challenges and emotional demands of advanced study." If I went around asking where I could get help, most of those my age would have probably looked at me with puzzled faces and said, "Just call your parents. That's what I always do. I simply call my folks and get their advice." "But that's why I'm coming to you in the first place, my parents don't . . . Oh, forget it."

I remember thinking I was crazy to pursue a master's degree at a major university. I was preparing to leave graduate school at the end of my first semester. After speaking to some of my professors, I found enough answers to survive, if not prosper, during the remainder of my program. While some of my professors were encouraging, others were condemnatory. Rather than offering to work with me, one faculty member said my writing skills were weak, at best, and the committee probably was mistaken in admitting me to the program.

These last remarks were devastating, but they motivated me to get the help I needed. I met with a book editor who held a doctorate in English and he tutored me for several hours to help me improve my writing skills. I received straight Bs that semester and stayed in the program. I am a creature of ritual and I had promised myself I would not eat another Demon Dog until I successfully finished every one of my courses that term. Demon Dogs are hot dogs named after the DePaul Blue Demons sports teams. A nearby café sells them. I tasted many Demon Dogs during the rest of my MPA days.

Two year later, I entered a doctorate of public administration program at Golden Gate University in San Francisco. Again, no one assisted me with the application process. I got the idea of going to GGU based on a comment one of my DePaul professors made, although I never thought to consult with him about the application process. I was attracted to GGU partly because I always wanted to live in San Francisco. As a high school junior, I told my cousin, who was seventeen years my senior, that I already knew I wanted to live in San Francisco. Her response was, "Why would you want to live with all those faggots?" For the next several years, I never mentioned living in San Francisco again. I still don't know if that cousin understands I completed my doctorate at a school where I was gloriously surrounded by faggots and dykes. Graduating from GGU in 1995 with a doctorate in public policy and administration remains a high point in my life.

BEING A PROFESSOR AT THE UNIVERSITY OF VERMONT

Evidently, I have always been chasing the American Dream of upward mobility. Only now I'm smart enough to understand that few poor and working-class kids ever achieve this goal, thanks to countless psychological, social, and financial barriers they must overcome.

It has been over twenty years since I left my parents' working-class neighborhood. I live a nice life in gay-friendly Burlington, Vermont. My social class background is not as much an issue today except when I encounter faculty who have attended prestigious boarding schools like Exeter or Choate. Few of them understand that simply by choosing the right parents, they were allowed to receive the private and prep school educations that readied them for prestigious undergraduate schools like Harvard, Georgetown, and Yale. I appreciate my education, but I know top-tier institutions rarely if ever sought to recruit students from my working-class high school. I also resent I had to incur so much student debt to get my education. Yet I know I should feel fortunate living in a country where some students growing up in poverty and with little family money can ascend at least to the middle class. I only wish more kids like me had the chance to attend college. The system is overlooking a lot of talent by not seeking out more of us. We have so much to offer.

I am proud to be a professor at the University of Vermont, a place where my department and other faculty across campus support my social class research efforts. No matter how many times it happens, I still marvel when I hear colleagues causally describe growing up in homes where one or both parents had at least an undergraduate degree and, in turn, spent considerable time and effort grooming their kids for the professorate.

I only realized that becoming a professor was possible during my doctoral studies. My first inkling of this career option came when my mentor and now friend Dr. Larry Brewster suggested I interview for academic positions. Larry remains a key figure in my life. For years, I worked hard to keep my social class background secret. Instead, Larry taught me to embrace my origins, not hide them. He supports my being gay and constantly encourages me to pursue the family life I desire.

As one of only a few tenure-track faculty of color at the University of Vermont, I work hard to ensure that all my students receive support and affirmation. As a single gay man, I find my life in Vermont to be very isolating at times, despite having many close friends within the state. I sometimes long for the streets of San Francisco, the West Coast, and a partner. My life seems almost whole now. The absence of someone to share it with is difficult at times, especially during Vermont's long, cold winters. Throughout my life, I have had many boyfriends, but I was never ready for anything serious. Today, as an older and wiser man with a stable job, I would like to have a serious relationship.

I also would like to adopt an African American son—someone with whom I can share my life and legacy. I know there are many black children in the childcare system who could benefit from the loving environment I, and maybe someday a partner, could provide. I would love to adopt one or two of these children, kids who might otherwise never find good parents to raise them into adulthood.

A few months ago my mother passed. I loved her very much and she was the only family member who took me for who I am. I am pleased knowing I came out to her a few years ago and that she said she loved me anyway. As I said earlier, my father and I are still not good friends; I doubt we ever will be. I have gradually grown to accept my father as he is and I'm fine with that. My brother and I struggle to have a relationship. He never left the Bronx and never attended college. Despite our differences, I am thankful he has been a part of my life. I am fine with our situation as well.

It has been a long journey, from growing up effeminate in the Bronx, being taunted by other African Americans because of my sexuality, and even being blackballed from a fraternity, an organization that later elected me alumni chapter president. Today, in my early forties, I feel peace. I have long since abandoned the Apostolic faith of my youth. I found true spiritual happiness through the Glide Memorial Church in San Francisco. The people there affirmed my gay self. They taught me that God will love and guide me, whatever my sexual orientation. I know, as the Bible promises, I was made in God's image. Today I attend the Unitarian Church of Burlington, which also affirms me for who I am. The minister of our congregation marched in the 2006 Burlington Gay Pride Parade. One day I plan to have my civil union performed in this church. It is a wonderful goal.

I did not turn out to be a drag queen, nor do I aspire to be female. My interest in running from being a working-class, black, gay man has ended. I use the knowledge I gained through having these attributes to make myself a better teacher, scholar, and human being. I am still astonished I am living this amazing life and that I can help make higher education a more inviting place for those it previously excluded. I will always be thankful for the opportunity to make this journey, one that started in the Bronx so many years ago.

NOTE

1. It is Devine Nine now, but it was the Elite Eight when I pledged. Later, another fraternity was added to the list.

REFERENCES

Graham, Lawrence Otis (2000). *Our Kind of People*. New York: Harper/Perennial, 71–92.
Ross, Lawrence C., Jr. (2000). *The Devine Nine: The History of African-American Fraternities and Sororities*. New York: Kensington Books.

NINE

My First Closet Was the Class Closet

FELICE YESKEL

THE FEELING WAS FAMILIAR BUT THE ISSUE WAS DIFFERENT.
THE SENSE OF PERSISTENT PRETENSE WAS GONE. I FELT AT HOME.
I WAS COMFORTABLE.

About four years ago, I attended my first Working Class Studies Conference in Youngstown, Ohio. I was in a room with a few hundred other academics from working-class backgrounds. Most, like me, were the first in their families to attend college. I heard story after story of folks transitioning from their working-class worlds to college. (In my current situation, "transitioning" has a totally different meaning, since I'm more often around trans folks than conscious working-class ones, not that a person couldn't be both.) People's class transitions came with a range of attendant emotions: dislocation, feeling different, excitement, feeling isolated, culture shock, and so on. That common bond allowed me to imagine I was with people who "got it." No need for lots of explanations here. They had "been there, done that." It reminded me of the first time I walked into a lesbian bar over thirty years ago, as well as the subsequent Womyn's Music Festivals and Gay and Lesbian Liberation marches. In these experiences I found release from my long years of hiding and passing.

I've had lots of practice hiding and passing. My first closet was the "class closet." I was five. Do you know how little five is? My daughter is seven. She regularly sucks her thumb, she has rarely spent the night somewhere without one of her parents, needs her love-worn "blankie" to sleep, and is often too shy to talk to strangers. I was only five years old, forty-seven years ago, when I got on John DiMaggio's bus and traveled across New York City to attend Hunter College Elementary School (HCES), a place for "intellectually gifted children." I lived downtown, while Hunter was "uptown" on 68th Street and

Park Avenue. The bus trip took forty-five minutes or more, depending on the day's traffic. When I began third grade I started taking public transportation; that meant two busses in each direction.

How did I come to make this trek across the miles, the neighborhoods, and the cultures? It's hard to remember for sure, partially because it was a long time ago, but mostly because I needed to forget. To succeed, I needed to forget where I came from. I thought I needed to forget my past to embrace my future. I made that decision before I could read or write, before I could understand what "the future" was. Today, I pick through my tattered memories looking for clues to some essential part of myself. I remember fragments and, from those fragments, I try delicately to assemble the picture.

I remember my mom dragging me around to be "tested" in the tidy offices of various child psychologists. They gave me little tasks to do, problems to solve, questions to answer. I guess I must have answered the "right" way because I made the cut. Hunter College Elementary School was a public institution, but also highly selective and elite. Thousands apply for the fifty or so spots each year. The current brochure states:

> In general, the children who attend Hunter College Elementary School are self-motivated, independent, and inventive. They tend to be curious, persistent and questioning youngsters who love the challenge of learning new concepts. They often have artistic/creative talents in addition to their strengths in school tasks. Most of the students have outstanding verbal skills and have developed large vocabularies. The children are also characterized by having good memories and exceptional critical thinking skills.

In other words, I tested "smart." I was five, inspected, and selected. Being identified as "gifted" meant leaving my family, my neighbors, and my friends to go to a different school across town. Although it wasn't part of the official curriculum, I also learned to be ashamed of where I came from and to think of myself as one of the best and brightest, all the while wondering, "Who the hell am I fooling?" In short, I felt at home nowhere—not on my neighborhood streets or in my school classrooms. I felt alone and scared, never really being myself, constantly "passing," or pretending to be like the kids from upper-middle-class homes. I forgot how to talk as I typically talked or behave as I usually behaved. The worst part was nobody noticed, and no one ever acknowledged my dual reality.

I remember teachers and administrators asking me, "Father's occupation?" I asked my daddy what to say and he replied, "Say 'bagman.' " He drove around in this big red truck, stopping at bagel and bialy (a flat breakfast roll usually covered with onion flakes) bakeries all over the Lower East Side of Manhattan and Brooklyn, picking up the used cotton and burlap bags that flour came in. Every Friday he would take his full load to a recycling center and unload it, receiving about half a cent more per bag than he paid for them. He would come home daily, caked in flour and sweat. Even at five, I knew "bagman," was not the right answer, so I asked him what else I might say. He suggested "peddler" and I knew that wasn't any better. How did I know, how had I already learned to be ashamed of my father's occupation?

I recall going home with a school friend to her Park Avenue penthouse. I remember my surprise when the elevator stopped and the whole floor was her apartment. My entire apartment would have fit into her front entrance hall. All the furniture in her place was white, as were the rug and walls. I was worried. I feared my very presence might dirty something. That was the day I unconsciously resolved never to bring anyone home from school with me to see where I lived. For my entire six years of elementary education I never did.

Hunter was totally my mom's idea. She passed away a few years ago so I can't ask her how she even heard about the school. For work my mother sold advertising, over the telephone, for the *New York Telephone Directory*. My mom was very well read and knowledgeable about history, literature, and art. She enjoyed the enormous free cultural opportunities New York City had to offer. She longed for my father to care more about these things as well.

From my mom, and from society, I learned to be ashamed of my father, who answered the door in his underwear. My dad loved me just as I was, no matter what, and he only wanted my happiness, nothing more. I allied with my upwardly mobile mother, who needed me to "make it." I internalized her values of success. My mom was very critical; she pushed and pushed and made me feel like nothing was ever quite good enough. Yet she held out the possibilities of a wider world to me—with my mom came more choices. There I was, caught between love and power, and I didn't want to choose.

Although no one told me the result of going to Hunter College Elementary School would be that I would never feel at home anywhere again, I sensed I was fulfilling my mother's dream. Her dream was for me to "get out," go to college, associate with "better" people, and have "nice" things.

Sometime over the summer when I was eleven years old, I walked over to my local public junior high school and asked if I could register for classes. The officials looked at me as if I were crazy. They said I couldn't just register—I needed to bring a parent and show my birth certificate. Somewhat discouraged I went home and had it out with my mother. I had already gotten a full scholarship (school uniform and other essentials) to attend a "good" local private school. If I hadn't gotten the full scholarship, attending a private prep school would never have even been a possibility. But I was tired of passing. Back then I called it "being different." I longed to be just like all the other kids in my neighborhood; I wanted, finally, to be "normal." I'm not sure which of my arguments worked, but I won the fight and got to go to my neighborhood public junior high school, Junior High School 104.

MY NEXT CLOSET: EGAD, I'M A LESBIAN!

Besides changing schools, another interesting thing happened when I was eleven. I found the word "lesbian" in the dictionary. I'm not sure where I first heard the term, or why I was looking it up. I do know when I read the definition, I immediately felt sick to my stomach, and I certainly recognized it was describing me. I had barely escaped one closet before I found myself deep inside another one.

My self-realization happened years before Stonewall, and I told no one. At least I finally felt less alone class-wise at my neighborhood school. I had friends I could bring home, make brownies with, go bike riding with, and with whom I could have sleepover dates, go to the movies, and have slumber parties. Unlike at Hunter, many others at my neighborhood schools had parents who never went to college and who did manual labor. Finally, in one sense, I felt like everyone else—except for my newfound and shameful secret, a secret that made me feel unbelievably different and alone.

I was an only child, and thus all my mother's hopes and dreams centered on me. Part of the class transition expected of me was an "upward" marriage to some "professional" man. Realizing I was a lesbian certainly threw a wrench into that part of my mother's carefully constructed plan for me. I wonder if my mom's class aspirations had been less, or our class position higher, whether I might have had an easier time coming out as a lesbian. If either of my parents had attended college, would this have made them more tolerant of my sexual orientation? Possibly. Here was another advantage flowing (or not) from one's social class origins. Oh well. As it was, with the weight of needing to "succeed" and fulfill my mother's dreams, coming out felt like too much of a challenge. Every day I thought about killing myself. Today, I know there are lots of kids who weren't as lucky as I; I survived adolescence. Interestingly, and unlike many other lesbians at the time, I never worried about being disowned. That thought never really crossed my mind. I worried about hurting my parents and letting them down, but not about losing them. Since I knew how much they'd invested in me and how totally they loved me, I didn't want them to feel they'd made a bad choice. So, for the next ten years, I told no one about my feelings.

Like many of my generation, I became politicized through the anti-Vietnam War movement when I was in high school in the late 1960s. My personal politics, however, were much more involved with students' rights and the struggle to wear pants to school and keep my butch integrity. The struggle over my body and what clothes I could wear was intense, and I have vivid memories of my mother calling me a "transvestite" for wanting to shop and dress exclusively in army-navy store clothes. Though I lived only a few blocks from Greenwich Village and the Stonewall riots, I knew nothing about them. That part of my politicization had yet to happen.

High school was hard socially, too. Most of my friends started dating, and heterosexual dating was the only visible option. I hid out with the politicos organizing moratoriums against the war in Vietnam and the artistic types working on school plays. This gave me a purpose and focus as other friends started going to frat parties at NYU and City College. Despite drugs, "free love," and the open attitudes of the late 1960s, as I left New York City for college, part of me was still certain I was the only one who felt as I did. The only lesbian.

OFF TO COLLEGE

I received a scholarship-financed education at a "good" private college, the University of Rochester. I encountered kids who had spent as much on their bicycles as I eventually spent on my first car. My roommate had a convertible sports car and a kidney-shaped swimming pool in the backyard of her suburban New Jersey home. When I visited her home and those of other college friends, once again, I found myself standing in white rooms seeing white rugs, white walls, and white furniture. And I still felt like I could make it all dirty.

Getting good grades was something I could give to my parents, and I did well academically. In my senior year, I was elected into Phi Beta Kappa. My parents came up for my induction into this honor society. They could scarcely hide their pride. At the U of R, I also encountered the women's liberation movement and became chair of the Women's Caucus, our campus feminist organization. I was involved in advocacy, and I organized anti-rape campaigns and events like "Women's Weekend." This put me in contact with leading feminists of the day, including Robin Morgan and Flo Kennedy. I will never forget sitting in the faculty club with Flo Kennedy. She passed out song-sheets and led us in a rousing version of "I'm Tired of Fuckers Fucking Over Me" and "Move on Over or We'll Move on Over You" (sung to the tune of the "Battle Hymn of the Republic"). I was bold in many respects, but when it came to leaving the closet, I kept that door locked tight.

While each event I organized had the requisite lesbian workshop, my palms sweated as I quickly passed the room where they were meeting. I went to none of these sessions. It wasn't until my senior year in college that I fell in love and became involved with a woman. Still not ready to come out, our furtive meetings and total isolation doomed the relationship. In the aftermath of the breakup, I finally started to deal with being a lesbian. My progress was slow. The year after I graduated, I stayed in Rochester. I got a job working as a researcher on a study of schizophrenia for the Department of Psychiatry at the U of R med school. My real work was coming out of the closet, and I spent many nights sitting in my car across the street from the Riverview, Rochester's lesbian bar. I stared at the door for many months before I ever walked through.

Not long after, wanting to fulfill my mom's expectations and desires for upward mobility, I headed off to a doctoral program in counseling psychology at the University of Florida, in Gainesville. A good friend had preceded me to this program, but by the time I started, he had dropped out. Gainesville was even more conservative than Rochester. For me it was not the best place to come out as a lesbian. I lasted at the University of Florida for less than a year. My sexual desire trumped my class obligations. I followed someone out to the West Coast, to Berkeley, California, and luckily found myself at the epicenter of 1970s-style lesbian feminism.

COMING OUT OF ONE CLOSET: I'M A DYKE

California was just what I needed. Through three braless years of separatism, I developed intense pride in my lesbian self. I lived in an apartment building filled with other lesbian and gay people. I worked at a social service center for "sexual minorities" and did political work in the lesbian and gay community. All the women's bookstores, coffeehouses, restaurants, bars, garages, and the *Women's Yellow Pages* assured I would rarely have to interact with anyone who wasn't a dyke.

In 1978, when John Briggs, the ultraconservative state senator from Orange County, placed an anti-gay initiative (Proposition 6) on the California ballot, I came out even more publicly. The failed initiative would have banned gays and lesbians, or anyone supporting gay and lesbian rights, from teaching in California's public schools. I worked to defeat Prop 6 through EBACABI (East Bay Area Coalition against the Briggs Initiative). I coordinated a speakers bureau and addressed many community groups. I also spoke at rallies and on television and radio. It was weird to be so out publicly, but not out to my family.

Finally coming out to my mother (who claimed to already know) was the release from fear and guilt I needed, and I haven't been in that closet since. No longer needing to put 3,000 miles between my family and me, I left Berkeley and followed my lover, who was going to finish college at Swarthmore, back east. After three years of not knowing anyone who was straight, I wanted to take the healing and pride I got from living in the "lesbian and gay ghetto" of the Bay area and give it to the "real" world. Not having any plan for what to do, two weeks before school started I applied to a little known graduate program, pinned down financial support, packed up, and drove across country. That's how I found myself, by chance, back in the academy—at Swarthmore College getting my master's degree in psychology.

My California years were consumed with being part of a womyn's/ wimmin's/women's/dyke/lesbian/lesbian and gay community. Class issues had receded into the background. Except for tending to work many hours, saving lots of money, and financially bailing out my friends (who usually came from upper-middle-class backgrounds), class didn't seem a major force in my life.

CLASS CLOSET REDUX: MY CLASS CONSCIOUSNESS REAWAKENS

Swarthmore College is in a suburb of Philadelphia, adjacent to Philadelphia's elite Main Line. The Main Line is a collection of affluent suburban towns (some of the wealthiest suburbs in the United States) west of Philadelphia named after the Main Line of the Pennsylvania Railroad. I was one of only a handful of graduate students at Swarthmore. For me, going to graduate school was like a job, but one that provided considerable flexibility. Between outright grants, on-campus teaching assistant-type work, and collecting unemployment insurance based on my last job, I did okay. I especially liked the autonomy and control over my time the academy afforded.

It was ironic that I landed at Swarthmore. When I was in high school trying to figure out where to apply to college, I had visited Swarthmore, on the way to another school, and fell in love with the intensity and commitment to learning I saw there. I wandered past faculty sitting with small groups of students under trees. Everyone in each group was absorbed in rigorous academic debate. That was my idea of learning. Unfortunately for me, the guidance counselor in my 4,000+ New York City high school strongly discouraged me from applying to Swarthmore. His reasoning: We each received only three high school transcripts so I didn't want to waste any by applying to places likely to reject me. It seemed no one from my Lower East Side high school had ever gotten into Swarthmore. Thus, he figured, there was no chance I would either. Of course, it wasn't clear if anyone from my high school had ever *applied* to Swarthmore and, with that kind of administrative support, I doubt anyone had.

My experience at Swarthmore was close to what I had anticipated, but with a bit of an edge. The campus was beautiful, with a gorgeous rose garden right outside the library. I enjoyed my courses; my mind felt really worked out. Faculty and students truly engaged, and classes were small. However, I would go from standing on the unemployment line in Chester, Pennsylvania, a mostly black, burned out city (the closest city to the pristine Swarthmore campus), back to school, where I would listen to young Marxist-inspired students theorizing about the working class. I wanted to dynamite the stately Swarthmore build-ings. The theorizing seemed mostly disconnected from the realities of life just down the road. I felt angry at these overprivileged students, whose parents were funding their educations, and who were so cut off from real life. Yet, I too had fled the real world for the ease of contemplative living.

One year later, after getting my master's degree, I moved into a political community of nonviolent activists in west Philadelphia. Although the harshness of daily life confronted me each time I opened the door to leave my collective house, I was emotionally buoyed from my involvement with an intentionally political community called Movement for a New Society (MNS). MNS was trying to "live the revolution now." In practical terms in the late 1970s that meant several things, including anticonsumerist simple living in collective houses, working at a job only long enough to support "real" unpaid politi-cal work, sharing childraising responsibilities, communal financing, consensus decision-making, and examining every facet of life through a political lens. Part of the MNS ethos was "bread labor," meaning you worked only because you needed money, and you did as little work as possible. We assumed the important task of transforming society would be, of necessity, unpaid. The system we were challenging would not finance its own demolition.

My "bread labor" job was different from my comrades' minimum wage jobs as prep cooks or dishwashers. I put my job skills to use by working in the academy—first as assistant director of women's studies at the University of Pennsylvania and then as co-director of Common Woman, a feminist peace and justice center on the Penn campus. These were *just* jobs. My *real* work happened on my own time, as an activist. My MNS connection separated me from most folks I met at Penn. The people on campus seemed to think what they were doing in academia was their real political work. My association with MNS helped insulate me from the class and status-conscious environ-ment an Ivy League campus oozes.

WHERE DO I FIT IN?: FINDING A CLASS IDENTITY

Once again, I was shuttling between the privileged life of the campus and the harsh realities of my neighborhood. Being a lesbian, even being a dyke, in MNS was a non-issue. Besides lots of sexual experimentation on many peoples' parts, there had already been significant consciousness-raising about heterosexism and homophobia in MNS. This meant my sexual identity faded into the background and class orientation took center stage again.

Shortly before I joined MNS, there had been a class revolution in the organization. Folks from poor and working-class backgrounds started speaking up about the classism they experienced in MNS. They thought classism was endemic to the largely middle-class, progressive left in general. This led to everyone in the MNS community being part of class identity groups and to a heightened consciousness about how class operates in organizations.

I had always considered myself middle class. Although I was the first in my family to attend college, I had the "privilege" of an elite education. However, when I checked out the MNS middle-class support groups, I felt completely out of place. I tried the working-class support group as well, and I couldn't really relate to most of the struggles they were discussing. Many in the working-class group grew up Catholic and working class, and the main issue they struggled with was feeling stupid. Because I'd been labeled "intellectually gifted" and told I was among the best and brightest since I was age five, feeling stupid was not my issue. Later, a Jewish, working-class community member approached me and said, "Felice, you didn't grow up middle class, you come from the working class." After she shared her experiences with me, I felt for the first time I had finally found a home, class-wise.

Over the years, I have come to understand I feel the strongest class affinity when I am with other Jews from working-class backgrounds. Jewish culture strongly emphasizes education. Although neither of my parents went to college, they always held out college as an expectation for me. I wasn't sure who would pay for it, but I always knew I would attend college. My mom was born in New York City; her parents ran a small luncheonette and candy store. My grandfather, my grandmother, and my grandfather's sister were the workers. The store was open from early morning until late at night seven days a week. Until they stopped working, my grandparents never took a vacation together. My father was born in 1919 in Chechanovitzer, Poland, and immigrated to the United States with his parents while he was a child. I followed a common second-generation, Jewish pattern of education as the road to upward mobility. From my current vantage point, I realize I grew up bicultural with respect to class, able to negotiate very different class worlds, but not exactly at home in any one. I describe my class identity as "straddler," having a foot in different class worlds. I am from the working class and now live in the "professional middle class." My MNS discussions helped me understand this. Certainly, nothing in my formal education ever prompted me to think about these issues, or provided any clarity.

During my years in Philadelphia and time with Movement for a New Society, I had countless conversations about class and money. We developed a process of paying for events called "cost sharing." This involved figuring out the appropriate percentage of the total costs based on your resources relative to others in the group—your "fair share." Of course, this required that we disclose our individual financial situations. Not surprisingly, this made most people uncomfortable, given mainstream Americans' reluctance to discuss class and money, other than in general terms. The first time I participated in the cost sharing process, I threw up because I was scared and ashamed. I feared being evaluated by others, as well as my own self-judgments. Then I was angry. The cost sharing discussions were my first exposure to the notion of "trust funds." I had no idea some people my age didn't *have* to work to survive. It was the first time I heard such intimate details about other peoples' financial lives—their incomes, assets, debts, likely future inheritances, and so on. It was eye opening; we were breaking *the* big taboo.

There were clear class patterns to how people viewed "fair share." Those of us from poor and working-class backgrounds had to stretch much further to pay our part than did those of middle- and upper-class origins. Years later, I introduced cost sharing to a Jewish feminist community I had just joined. We have been using this approach to pay for our yearly retreats ever since. I even wrote an article detailing how our process works (see www. classactionnet.org).

CLASS AND THE ACADEMY: "PROFESSIONAL" CLASS

From Philadelphia in the early 1980s, I again followed my heart and a girl-friend, and landed in Amherst, Massachusetts. Not wanting to move without a job (a practical consequence of growing up working class), I found employment at the University of Massachusetts. I lived in a dorm as a residence director, a position that simultaneously solved my income and housing problems. The two things that most surprised me about my new situation were: (1) how much drinking went on (UMass is often called "Zoo Mass," and if the behavior of the students in my dorm was an indication of what was typical, it was a well-deserved reputation), and (2) the lack of a visible gay and lesbian community among the UMass staff. Here, my class-based concerns and my sexuality clashed. To keep my job meant I might have to retreat into the closet. Although there were many lesbians (far fewer gay men), only a handful of students were out on campus. Since going back in the closet was not an option for me, I started helping organize the lesbian and gay community on campus.

I worked with a group that included allies and closeted folks to get the UMass antidiscrimination policy expanded to include "sexual orientation" as a protected category. This provided enough safety for other staff and faculty to begin inching out of the closet. In 1984, I organized the first Lesbian and Gay Awareness Week on campus, which provoked a strong reaction. Confronted with the first visible demonstration of gay pride seen on campus, a group of homophobic students began reacting. They orchestrated a "Heterosexuals Fight Back March and Rally." Homophobic posters and graffiti appeared all over campus and they threatened to "hang a homosexual in effigy."

In response, students and progressive allies on campus engineered a counterdemonstration. About three hundred of us marched on the administration building, presenting a list of fifteen demands. Due to the effective media work we did, all our activities unfolded before three different televison news crews. Most of the school's administrators had never weighed lesbian and gay concerns, so they did not know how to respond to the students' demands. The campus administration asked me, as the most out, nonstudent on campus, to help them figure out what to do. They hired me to assess the situation on campus for lesbian and gay students and advise the administration on how most effectively to address this community's concerns.

After a semester conducting research, I published a report, *The Consequences of Being Gay: A Report on the Quality of Life for Lesbian, Gay, and Bisexual Students at the University of Massachusetts, Amherst.* In this commentary, I made several recommendations (remarkably similar to the students' demands presented eight months earlier) to improve the campus situation. One suggestion was to establish a staffed center specifically focusing on lesbian, gay, and bisexual concerns. The following year, in 1985, the Center for Lesbian, Gay, and Bisexual Concerns came into being, and campus administrators appointed me its first director. A number of years after that founding, we added transgender concerns to our mission and changed the name to the Stonewall Center: A Lesbian, Gay, Bisexual and Transgender Educational Resource Center.

Somewhere near the beginning of my twenty years at the Stonewall Center (I left about a year ago) and twenty-three years at UMass, I started taking courses. The main reason I enrolled in these classes? They were free, and I had learned early to never look a gift horse in the mouth. I didn't have to pay for the classes because I was a "professional" employee. I took courses in the School of Education, in the psychological education program. Its mission was to develop curricula and pedagogy relevant to people's lives. The courses focused on issues of identity, relationship, and power. After a few classes, I formally applied to a program so my work would count toward a degree. Otherwise, I felt my labors would be wasted. Before I knew it, and without much stress or effort, I had accumulated enough credits for a doctorate. The only problem—I needed to write a comprehensive paper (essentially a literature review), and then a dissertation. Having no real need for a doctorate, and not liking to write, I put finishing my degree on hold. Instead, I focused on directing the Stonewall Center, fostering campus activism, participating in the international, feminist, antimilitarist movement, and organizing actions at army bases and at the stock exchange on Wall Street.

Besides my job and activism, I started focusing on classism issues. The academy mostly ignores social class concerns. There had been three failed attempts to organize "professional" staff on campus. That's actually what an entire class of workers is called, "professional staff." (A digression: Why is some work considered "professional"? If someone gets paid for doing something, isn't that being a "professional"? Thus, if a person earns a living as a plumber, then that person is a "professional" plumber. If I make my living as a lawyer, I am a "professional" lawyer. Right? Has "professional" somehow taken on the meaning of being higher class?)

On campus, there is a clear classification system. Different parts of the workforce are categorized into "classified workers," "professional staff," "faculty," and "administrators," creating an unnecessarily hierarchical and divisive culture. Different unions represented classified workers, professional staff, and faculty, making solidarity in contract and funding negotiations difficult. Such is the classist nature of the academy that some workers, especially faculty, are expected to work not for money, but mostly for the pure love of the job. They receive a salary year round, whether they teach or not; the salary provides funding for their life of scholarship. Similarly, "professional staff" aren't supposed to watch the clock, but to feel a particular ownership of their work and therefore labor until the job is done. They are on salary. The "classified staff," on the other hand, must be watched at all times, punch the clock, and be closely supervised. There is no expectation that their work be fulfilling in and of itself. These are the "hourly workers."

There are also different benefits (i.e., vacation time, health care, tuition remission) and different amounts of control and autonomy for each job classification. Another manifestation of campus classism is how much office space different campus groups command: the "higher" in the hierarchy, the larger the office. Parking spaces closer to their offices are given to faculty who aren't even on campus every day. Meanwhile, secretaries, who work daily, must walk farther from their parking spaces to their offices.

As director of the Stonewall Center, my position was "professional staff." When the next attempt to form a union for those in the "professional" category happened, I spoke out and got involved in the coordinating drive. This time we succeeded in organizing the professional staff and I became a member of SEIU, part of the Service Employees International Union.

I also raised the classism issue in the School of Education. At this point, my program in the School of Education offered courses on various "isms," including racism, sexism, anti-Semitism, heterosexism, and ableism. These were grouped into a Social Issues Training Project, where graduate students learned to teach the courses and undergrads took them. Students studying to be teachers or counselors had to take two "ism" classes for their degree programs.

As a graduate student, I taught many "ism" courses. I started to question why we taught nothing on classism. Faculty in the program were confused—what did I mean by classism? What did I mean by class? We started a study group. We read the classics—*Worlds of Pain* by Lillian Rubin, *The Hidden Injuries of Class* by Sennet and Cobb, and a favorite of mine, *Equality* by William Ryan. After a while, faculty members became convinced there really was such a thing as class and classism. They gave me the go-ahead to develop a classism curriculum. I was part of a team that taught the first course on classism. This was in the late 1980s. Reagan's trickle-down policies were doing their damage and class issues were becoming harder to ignore. It was exciting to watch the lightbulbs going on for students as the importance of class in their lives was validated.

Some years later, I decided to finish my doctorate. I realized I wouldn't let myself take on another significant project while an unfinished degree was hanging over my head. A part of me always felt I was "supposed" to be working on my dissertation. I decided I needed to make a real decision. I should either abandon all hopes of finishing my degree, thus freeing my energies for other obligations, or fully commit to completing the degree as fast as possible and then getting on with my life. Since I couldn't simply ditch the degree, I chose the second option. Years later, I realized I got my doctorate for my mother, to fulfill her dreams for me. It was my mother's voice inside my head insisting I not "waste" all the time I'd already invested. I could imagine her saying, "Get your doctorate."

At first, I tried to make the dissertation process meaningful. I wanted to focus on training and educating people about class and classism issues. At my committee's insistence, I spent over six months trying to define "class." The trials and tribulations my committee subjected me to might just have been the typical hoops graduate students must jump through. But I couldn't seem to shake the thought that this was also evidence of their personal, social-class prejudice. They were uncomfortable and unfamiliar with the concept of classism. I sensed they felt uneasy due to the inherent contradictions between their own current class positions and their commitment to social justice. Whatever their reasons, it seemed my committee resisted my dissertation efforts at every turn and I gave up on my original idea. I concluded that addressing class issues would be my life's work. Meanwhile, for my dissertation, I needed an easily doable topic so I could finish the degree and return to my organizing and reform efforts. I picked another subject, a case study of campus change on LBGT issues. I finished the dissertation in less than a year during 1991. My work at the Stonewall Center certainly helped, but so did the fact that heterosexism was legit in a way that classism wasn't.

After taking the PhD, I became an adjunct faculty member in the Social Justice Education Program at UMass. I continued teaching both graduate and undergraduate courses about classism and other "isms." From all my years of such teaching, I've found classism provokes the strongest reactions of all the isms. It meets the toughest resistance and causes students the greatest confusion.

I remember one time asking students to get in small groups and envision a nonclassist society. Most of them assembled and quickly engaged the assignment. One group was sitting in silence. I checked with them and asked if they had any questions. Their response was surprising. They said, "We believe in democracy!" I replied I did too, and I wondered what that had to do with envisioning a nonclassist society. For them, evidently: democracy = capitalism, nonclassist = communism, and, therefore, communism = antidemocracy. Hence, they couldn't engage in the assignment because they believed in democracy, the "American way." This incident reminded me of how hard it is sometimes to get students to question the values they gather, almost by osmosis, from the surrounding culture.

I did not get my doctorate for any reason I could ultimately respect—I did it to make my mother proud, to repay her and father for their fierce love, and to compensate for what they didn't get to do. I got my doctorate for reasons of class. I now have an ambivalent relationship with the academy and intellectualism. Part of me feels embarrassed to have gotten a doctorate, yet I love ideas and thinking. The doctorate, as a status marker, moved me even further from the working class. I didn't really want to join the ranks of the ivory tower eggheads, spending their days manipulating words. I have lots of confidence in my mind (thanks to those early messages), but I feel superior to the academic enterprise. Yet the campus environment was a workplace that tolerated my propensity for casual dress (read: jeans) and radical ideas. While I love to teach, I had no desire to engage in scholarship; I have a more activist bent. These days I mostly view the academy as a site for organizing and a place for doing social change work.

My hunch had been correct. Getting my doctorate freed up my energy. Ironically, the anti-gay backlash led me deeper into class issues. We were fighting one regressive affront after another, working hard to defend the few gains we'd managed to achieve. Gays and lesbians were being blamed for destroying the nuclear family. We were right up there with feminism and Murphy Brown on the list of evildoers. The right wing was using wedge issues like abortion, welfare, gay rights, immigrant rights, and so on to divert people's attention from what was really happening—America's widening economic inequality. The rules of our economy were being systematically rewritten to benefit the superrich at everyone else's expense.

This analysis led some of us, in 1994, to form a nonprofit organization initially called "Share the Wealth." After about a year, we convened a few focus groups to get reactions from ordinary people about different ways of discussing our work. We wanted to talk with folks who weren't already convinced, so we changed the name of the organization to United for a Fair Economy (UFE). UFE works to raise consciousness and activism directed toward the country's growing economic inequality. We focused on rule changes, including tax policies, trade policies, Federal Reserve policies, and the stagnant minimum wage. These factors and others, combined, had tilted the economy dramatically in favor of the wealthy.

At the same time, a friend and I started a cross-class dialogue group to have a laboratory for a more personal exploration of class issues. Our group started with eight people. Four of us were from poor and working-class backgrounds. The other four were from owning-class backgrounds, people with at least a million dollars in assets. The range of resources in our group went from $60,000 of debt to $14 million in assets. We met monthly for six hours in each others' homes. We analyzed everything, ranging from the potluck contribution we brought for dinner, to where we vacationed, to how much we spent on haircuts and new cars. We shared our fears, our judgments of each other, and our projections. We started unpacking the societal and familial messages that helped maintain the class system. The group was transformational for me. It became clear that just altering the rules or structures of our class system was not enough. We needed consciousness-raising to change peoples' thinking about class issues.

Jenny Ladd (who comes from generations of wealth) and I had started the cross-class dialogue group. After six or seven years, our dialogue ensemble ended and the two of us started Class Action, a nonprofit organization, which raises consciousness about class and classism and its impact on our lives, organizations, and cultures. Class Action promotes heightened class consciousness as well as cross-class alliances. College campuses and the K–12 educational system are a primary focus of Class Action's efforts. We hope to help higher education become more welcoming toward first-generation college students as well as faculty and staff of poverty and working-class origins. Class Action helps campuses examine their policies and practices through a socioeconomic lens and to develop strategies and practices to lessen class inequities. Campuses routinely have women's centers, along with centers for students of color and those with disabilities. These days, more and more campuses also feature centers or programs for lesbian, gay, bisexual, and transgender students. Unfortunately, campuses have not applied the same rationale to create programs or centers for poor and working-class students. These students, if they have somehow managed to get themselves to campus, must fend for themselves.

PILLOW TALK: CLASS IN THE BEDROOM

Another place I've learned a lot about class has been in my intimate associations. Most women with whom I've been in serious relationships have come from the upper-middle class. They have been both WASP and Jewish. In daily living, over time, class differences can become visible. When is food "too old" and "needs" thrown out? What after-school activities does our daughter need to attend? Do we buy clothes not on sale? How much to work, how much free time? Which are idiosyncratic personality differences versus those that are the products of coming from different class cultures?

In one relationship our communication styles were different: she was calm and reasoned; I, on the other hand, was emotional and impassioned. The more intense I got emotionally, the calmer and more rational she became. I needed to know what she was feeling. The way she responded to me seemed detached, not engaged. I felt abandoned. To her, I seemed out of control. She relied on her class conditioning, which was "born to manage." I became another problem she had to take care of. I didn't want to be managed; I wanted to be met. She viewed me as abusive when I raised my voice. I wanted her to yell back. Perhaps WASP versus Jewish style differences played a part, but so did class. She grew up in a large house that had different wings. When there was conflict, her parents and siblings retreated to their own space. I grew up in a small apartment and the only door that really closed and locked was the bathroom. Going to your own space wasn't really an option. I could tell you what our upstairs and downstairs neighbors fought about.

There are exceptions to every generalization, but I believe there are different class cultures that significantly affect our sense of self, our choices, our expectations, and our values. I've also had close friends who come from working-class backgrounds—Ashkenazy Jews, Irish, Italian, and German Catholics. I've felt an immediate sense of comfort and camaraderie with sister "straddlers" who were college-educated but who felt like they were from my old neighborhood. If more of us talked out loud about the similarities and differences we experience in our relationships and friendships, we'd know more about class.

WHAT GOES 'ROUND COMES 'ROUND

In many ways, the work I've done around LGBT issues on campus has been good preparation for addressing class issues. Developing educational curricula, organizing support and study groups, arranging speak-outs, and confronting the administration were some strategies we used. Once invisible on campus, the needs of LGBT students have, in recent years, made it onto many administrative radar screens. The proliferation of offices like the Stonewall Center at UMass evidences this point. I hope my work on social class issues, including addressing the needs of first-generation college students and staff/faculty from poor and working-class backgrounds, will help members of these groups leave the closet and start demanding their full and equal rights.

Class Action provides consulting, training, and technical assistance to various groups, including: schools, colleges, and universities; community-based and grassroots organizations; direct service providers and advocates; and social change groups. The overriding goal in every instance is showing these various constituencies how to effectively integrate a class analysis and approach into their efforts at addressing environmental, social, and economic justice issues.

My coworkers and I hope the work we do will contribute to the emergence of a broad-based, cross-class, multiracial, economic justice movement. Class Action is working to transform "class" and "classism" into household words. Perhaps readers of this text will join us in our efforts. We guarantee that you will find the work rewarding, for there is no better way to achieve socioeconomic justice than by acting to make our nation's promise of "equal opportunity" a reality. Contrary to what my students thought, democracy in America has little meaning when there are such wide and growing disparities in the distribution of wealth among our people. Together and through Class Action we can help remedy this problem.

TEN

One Bad Lecture Away from Guarding a Bank

Identity as a Process

MICHALLENE McDANIEL

Academics with something less than middle- or upper-class backgrounds come to their profession through various routes. The career paths become even more diverse if we also consider these faculty's sexual orientation. Exploring how those who are LGBTQ (lesbian, gay, bisexual, transgender, questioning) and of poverty and working-class backgrounds and who later become academics is a valuable experience, not only for the personal perspective it gives those who did the traveling, but also for those who have yet to make the journey.

What follows is a more or less chronological account of my identity formation, focusing on three criteria. These are: my original socioeconomic class, my educational attainment level, and my sexual orientation. Rather than claiming to be a fully formed adult, I present myself as a work in progress. In telling my story, I feel awkward speaking of childhood memories in formal academic writing. Thus, my tone will be informal throughout.

The experiences recounted from my childhood derive from my memory, which is legendary among those who know me, but close family members have confirmed my recollections. Two of these relatives appear throughout this chapter, as they have in my life. These are Bette McDaniel, my mom, and Raymond McDaniel, my brother.

1969

I was three years old. I was a white girl, living in Jacksonville, Florida, at-tending Methodist Sunday School with my grandmother. We went to church every weekend. Dad was a self-taught (unlicensed) mechanical engineer.

Mom stayed home and cared for me. She had just given birth to my little brother, Ray. We lived in one side of a duplex townhouse, renting from a gay couple living next door. I didn't learn about their sexual orientation until I was much older, but it never seemed an issue with my parents. My older sister and brother had moved out of our house by 1969. They were children born to my dad and his first wife. He had married his first wife right after returning from serving in the Marines during World War II.

These were happy times. I read a lot and was very close to my parents. Dad always brought home educational toys for me. Once, he bought my older brother a map puzzle, where all fifty states were pieces that had to be fit in the outline of the United States. I don't know if my brother ever used the puzzle, but one of my earliest tricks was assembling the thing for surprised visitors. This feat might not have seemed quite as impressive had they known I had renamed many of the states after characters on Sesame Street. Michigan looked like Oscar to me.

I assumed we were just like all the other neighborhood families. Our home looked the same as theirs. Their dads, like mine, went to work every day, as far as I could tell. My family had everything it needed, as far as I could tell.

1972

I was six. I had just started first grade. Jacksonville had integrated its public schools a few years back, and, despite being shy, I made friends with white and black kids. This was my first year in school because I was too young to attend kindergarten when the last school year started. I had the pleasure of staying at home with Mom for another year. I don't know whether skipping kindergarten affected my social development, but I still haven't learned to nap publicly or to color within the lines.

Before starting first grade, I played school all the time at home. I loved to sit in my room and write in a spiral-bound composition book, copying words out of our ancient encyclopedias. By the time I started school, Mom and Dad made sure I knew the alphabet, could write, and count. My grandmother taught me to spell my entire first name in one weekend. I am convinced this gave me an advantage over other first graders. I mean, after all, my first name is ten letters long! I was always very curious, and drove my parents crazy with questions. Sometimes they had to be very creative to give me age-appropriate answers. At home, I do not remember anyone in my family ever talking down to or ridiculing me for my intellectual curiosity.

I loved school from day one. Well, I should say I loved the academic aspects of school. I was deathly afraid of the cafeteria, due to something traumatic that happened within the first two weeks of school. I had finished my lunch and had packed up my lunchbox. I took my tray to the disposal area and threw away my trash. I went outside and stood where we were supposed to line up to go back to class. I figured I would be the first in line. The principal came out, grabbed my ear, pulled me back into the cafeteria with the admonition, "You don't leave this cafeteria until you are dismissed with your class! Do you hear me, young lady?" Not only did I hear her, I had nightmares about her for months afterward. To this day, the smell of peanut butter in an institutionalized setting gives me flashbacks to this early lesson in conformity. Senseless conformity, it seemed to me. Still does.

The irony of this episode is that I was an extremely well-behaved kid. I hated getting into trouble. Self-control was a big theme in my family. I wasn't going to run off from the cafeteria. I was going to stand outside and wait for my classmates. I always did what my teachers told me, to the extent I was the geek who was given the task of taking names when the teacher left the room. If I was being rambunctious, all the teacher had to do was look at me to guilt me back to behaving.

Toward the end of first grade, I started my first romantic relationship. It was with a cute, red-haired boy named Aaron. We were still together at the beginning of second grade and eventually I went on to go with several boys at a time. Thus began my early career as a heterosexual. I was unaware there were any other options.

I also learned around this time that my mom, Bette, wasn't my birth mom. My grandmother had driven me over to play at my cousin's house one afternoon. My older cousin, Amy, ran up and said "Michallene, Aunt Bette isn't your real mother! Your real mother died!" To my knowledge, Amy is still in trouble for having transmitted this newfound piece of family lore. After asking my parents about this, though, I was fine. My birth mother, Dad's second wife, had died of complications from a rapid-onset neurological disease when I was two months old. I was old enough to understand, cognitively, what Amy said, but young enough not to really care. I knew who my mom was.

1975

I was nine and in fourth grade. It was my first year in the gifted program. Every Friday I spent the day in a special classroom with some of my best friends. We did fun, creative things, like designing our own board games and making a model Statue of Liberty out of chicken wire and papier-mâché. We talked of things we did not consider in regular classes. We discussed issues. We talked of how we felt about the world. We explored our emotions through art (after all, it *was* the 1970s). I felt a sense of belonging with these kids, I loved our cool, young teacher, and I could not wait for Fridays.

I knew all the regular teachers resented that about ten of us were missing class once a week. It was mostly the older teachers who were not thrilled to cooperate when we had to complete missed classes assignments or go on special field trips. All of this latent turmoil only solidified my notion that school is what I did best. We must be special, I thought, or people would not be so mad at us.

Several boys in my gifted class became my boyfriends. I made a boy's participation in "gifted" a criterion for considering a nine-year-old's equivalent of "a relationship." I liked boys who planned to grow up to become scientists. I went to the boys' houses to play Star Trek and, occasionally, kiss. I felt I belonged.

Certain things had begun to concern me. One night I was assigned to write a report on John F. Kennedy. I tried gathering information about Kennedy from the ancient encyclopedias we had at home, but I could not find anything, so I finally asked Mom for help. She explained that our encyclopedia was published in 1946 and the world did not yet know who Kennedy was. She apologized and said I would have to look up information about him in the *World Book* at school the next day. From then on, ownership of a current *World Book* signified that a family must be better-off than we. The cracks in my social class foundation were appearing, right in time for the Bicentennial.

1977

I was eleven, in sixth grade and entering the quagmire of adolescence. This is the year I really started paying attention to what was happening at home, which didn't improve my attitude. Dad went through a couple of different jobs during this period. His not having an engineering license was taking its toll. Occasionally, one of his friends, a well-intentioned licensed colleague, offered to help Dad prepare for the licensing exam. Certainly, he was smart and experienced enough to pass it. However, I think our financial situation probably prevented him from having the time and energy to prepare for the test.

By now, I knew our family's situation was not like those of my friends' families. I had always identified with the kids at school and in my neighborhood. Now I was growing up and realizing we were the only renters in our middle-class suburban neighborhood. We lived there because my parents were particular about which public schools we attended. I am eternally grateful for their wisdom. But we were different. Our landlords had possessed, at best, an insouciant attitude toward home maintenance. Not only were they reluctant to repair anything, they were not too keen on my dad doing it, either.

Adding to my growing class awareness was the fact on a few occasions we clearly were not covering our basic needs. My parents were good about stretching the budget or timing out bill payments so Ray and I would not detect any financial shortfalls. When you run out of fuel oil, however, and the outside temperature falls into the low thirties, even the most preoccupied child notices. I remember this happening, and my mom asking our neighbors if we could borrow firewood. All four of us walked a couple of houses down the street to help carry the wood back to our place. When we returned, I wrote a letter to God. I was not a religious child, and wasn't even attending Sunday School at this point, but I felt desperate. I put the letter in the top of my closet, thinking it would be more noticeable the higher up I placed it. This appeal to the supernatural certainly indicates my childhood level of concern for my family's well-being.

This tendency to worry also revealed itself in my absolute refusal to ask for anything I did not feel I needed. I took this to ridiculous extremes, and the result was that I mostly lived in a single pair of blue corduroy pants the entire school year. Mom regularly washed them at the laundromat, and even suggested I might get a new pair. My worry and guilt prevented this.

Meanwhile, I began living a double existence at school. I was still one of the smart kids, still in gifted, and I won some minor poetry competitions. However, I was also the kid with the blue pants. One day when I wore something else, everyone noticed and commented. They did so out of surprise, rather than malice, but I wanted to fade into the bulletin board. After the holidays, my friends would talk about what gifts their family members exchanged. They talked about expensive tracksuits, televisions, and vacations. While my parents always gave us a wonderful holiday, the disparity between what I bought as gifts and what my friends could afford made a strong impression on me.

During this year, two other changes occurred. First, I had no boyfriend. I held highly public crushes on unattainable boys, which was to become a pattern I would maintain through the early years of college. At this age, calling people gay became a very amusing insult for kids at school. I do not remember anyone calling me names, but by this time I was strictly forbidden to use such epithets at home. Dad explained, after I called someone on television a fag, it was not a nice name and I could hurt someone's feelings by using it. That sunk in.

The other major change involved a bit of information Bette (Mom) told me about my birth mother. She was Jewish. Her father was from Austria and her mother was from Romania. They fled the Nazis, came to the United States, and had four children. My birth mother, Gloria, was the youngest of the four. She was raised in the Bronx. Few people were thrilled when she married my dad, the Methodist from Georgia. I was supposed to be raised Jewish and receive a Hebrew name. When the only person in my family with any immediate knowledge of Judaism died, so did my Jewish upbringing.

When Mom told me about my ethnicity, I went back to my room and stared at myself in the mirror for a long time. I had a few Jewish friends at school and I knew they did not put up a tree at Christmas. Instead, they received presents for eight nights. I knew their beliefs were somehow different from the Christians'. That is all I knew then. What did this new information mean to me? I felt I was staring at a stranger. My Jewish friends assured me in the days following this revelation that because my mother was Jewish, I was not half-Jewish, as I thought. I was fully Jewish. If only it were that simple.

So I was different from where my life began. Now I saw myself as lower class, Jewish, and, at least I thought, straight. The main constant in my identity was my performance as a student. I wholeheartedly poured myself into that status in the upcoming junior high years.

1980

I turned fourteen shortly after starting ninth grade. At the beginning of first semester, things were normal. I was starting my third year at a junior high school I really loved. Academically, I was a constant performer: I got all As except in math. I was in advanced classes and by eighth grade some kids were calling me "the Encyclopedia." I was section leader in band. I could pursue this activity because my best friends did too. I could ride with them. Still, I always knew we didn't have the same financial stability as the other neighborhood families. For example, I started obsessing about not having a college fund. At the same time, I knew we were doing okay compared to some of the less fortunate kids at school.

About a month into ninth grade, Dad entered the hospital for eye surgery. During his pre-operative exams, his doctors detected a spot on his lung. They canceled his eye surgery and scheduled an operation for the next week to remove part of his lung. There was a good chance of his having a favorable outcome, but I knew my parents were worried. I tried to focus on school and spending time with my little brother.

During surgery, the extent of the cancer in Dad's lung required removing the whole organ. While this was a major operation, his prognosis for improvement should have been very good. However, he developed a raging staph infection in his lung cavity while recovering in the hospital. For about nine months, Dad mostly lived in the hospital while doctors tried experimental procedures to cure the infection that was killing him. Eventually, some version of my dad came home to us. Given the infection's toll on his body, Dad was physically quite different. In reconciling himself to his disabled status, his personality changed. This was a longer process.

During the many months of my father's acute illness, my entire family's class status changed. We became a charity case. Churches we didn't go to prayed for us and brought us food. Family friends gave us money. Relatives sent us old clothing. I still have an old flannel shirt we received during this time. Things only got worse.

Another change happened. With my dad in the hospital, or quite infirm when he was home, I was physically the strongest one in our house. I had always been a tomboy and my parents did nothing to discourage my somewhat nontraditional gender behavior. Dad had always encouraged both Ray and me to be strong and healthy. At fourteen, I was stronger than my mom and certainly larger than my eleven-year-old brother. I became the "heavy lifter" in our family. When someone donated large bottles of drinking water, I carried them around. I remember this clearly. While it didn't seem particularly odd to me, this certainly wasn't what girls I was friends with were doing in their homes.

Unfortunately, during this same year I had a dispute with a school friend. As can only occur among power-mad middle schoolers, rumors about my family's medical and financial predicament spread. Moreover, a former friend employed that reliable means of hurting another adolescent: gay rumors. On the school bus I started hearing speculation about my sexual orientation. I didn't get too upset about it because I knew these rumors were unfounded. After all, I had boyfriends. Nice ones. So nice I rarely had to defend my virtue. So, no, I didn't seem gay.

This was probably the most life-altering year of my youth. My class position, my social status at school, and even my sexual orientation were either altered or questioned. Ironically, this was one of my best years academically. I edited the school newspaper, took a project to the regional science fair, won numerous medals at band competitions, and brought home the year-end trophies in English, biology, band, and all-around academics. Looking back, clearly I was channeling my energy into the one aspect of my life that had never betrayed me: being a good student. By the end of ninth grade, this was about the only stable identity remaining.

1982

I was fifteen at the end of tenth grade. I was finishing my first year in high school. Dad was classified as permanently disabled. His struggle with the staph infection had aggravated his rheumatoid arthritis sufficiently to preclude him from continuing his drafting career. As he dealt with no longer being the breadwinner, we all adjusted to the incredible changes that had occurred in our family structure. Mom was at home caring for Dad, we lived on Social Security disability, and Ray and I continued attending school.

In general, my new school was more affluent than the junior high I attended. The kids in my advanced classes certainly seemed far better-off than my family. This was the height of the preppie trend; Topsiders and polo shirts were everywhere. Sometime during this year, the preppie girls in my physical education class began wearing several polo shirts layered over each other. I remember thinking how nice it would be even to have one polo shirt. If I did, I knew I wouldn't mess it up by wearing it at PE class. I did the best I could to fit in, even buying no-brand preppie-looking clothes when I could.

This year the shock of the previous one caught up with me. Now that Dad's condition was stable, I did not have the daily worry of whether he was going to live through next week. I relaxed enough that the changes in our family began really hurting me. Between our shaky financial situation and the typical mood shifts of adolescence, I was a very depressed kid. That same year, the Reagan administration intensified my dour mood by cutting certain Social Security benefits. The reductions meant that when I turned eighteen, right after starting college, my part of our family's income would end. The only option I had to avoid this eventuality was enrolling in college part-time at age fifteen. This was impossible in terms of time, transportation, and tuition. I took this federal action change personally and it marked the beginning of my deep concern with the effects of public policy on American families.

While my financial world was shaky at this time, my romantic life was nonexistent. I developed a large crush on a young man who was a senior. He was nice to me, but unattainable. This crush became well known and in retrospect insulated me from having to pursue real relationships with guys.

One morning a girl in my homeroom told me I had a nice smile. Since this was the only positive thing that happened all day, I told Mom about it when I got home. She said to be careful when girls gave me such compliments. I asked why. She said, "Because of the way you are, some people might get the wrong idea." What did she mean, *the way I am*? "Well, you know, you've always been a tomboy, and because of some of your interests, you just aren't the typical girl. Some young woman might make a pass at you," she explained. I asked what I should do if that happened. Mom's sage advice: Say you are flattered, but not interested. Being a good daughter, I followed her recommendation for way too long and probably missed having a much more interesting social life. Thanks, Mom.

During this same period, I went on a few overnight trips with the school band. I have never been fond of expeditions where I have no control over the itinerary. This made me very anxious about traveling. Also, having grown up with my own bedroom, I wasn't used to sleeping among other people. To allay my travel angst, I asked a good friend if I could room with her. I knew she was looking for a fourth person and this seemed an obvious solution to my problem. Without hesitating, she said no. I asked why, but she refused to explain. This frustrated me so much I harassed her until she finally said why. She confessed she was afraid I was gay and therefore she didn't want me in the room with her. This was a girl I'd grown up with! I thought of her as a role model because she read *Seventeen* and knew how to apply eye shadow. To have this embodiment of teenage girlhood say what she did meant not only did I not measure up, I was somehow a threat to her. I was devastated. Besides, didn't she know about my very public crush on Mr. Senior?

With no financial stability and no typical high school dating life, I focused on academics. Unfortunately, that aspect of my life somewhat fell apart in tenth grade. Algebra II vexed me. I went from getting all As to having to come in early a few days a week for extra tutoring. This failure to excel shook my confidence and some of my other classes suffered, as well. By year's end, I had earned three Ds on my report card. Because academics was my last defense against feeling like a total loser, I did not end tenth grade on good terms with myself.

1984

I was seventeen and about to graduate high school. Eleventh and twelfth grades were a slow recovery from tenth. My grades improved, I made some good friends, and I looked forward to college, thanks to grants and loans. We still had barely enough money to make ends meet. I had a limited social life, but I was back in the honor society.

By the middle of my senior year, I wanted to pursue a career in film. I thought it would be great to make movies that addressed important social issues. Of course, my family couldn't afford a VCR, much less any camera equipment, so that career aspiration, while genuine, was impractical. That's one of the good things about not having your parents pay for college, though. They can't exert much influence over your choice of major. I just remember being very eager to get out of high school and on with life. I wanted to be in control of my own bank account and be surrounded by people who thought about important things and had artistic vision. I wished I could push the fast-forward button to the extent that I told many people I wished I were thirty-five and had a career. In the back of my head, I think I knew the road to thirty-five was going to be bumpy, but I'd be happier when I got there.

I also decided to explore religion during my senior year of high school. I had received some pressure from a couple of Christian friends to attend church with them. However, during this period I really felt a need to connect in some manner to the birth mother I hadn't known. One way I did this was by learning about Judaism. I studied on my own, asked my Jewish friends all sorts of pesky questions, and attended a conversion class at the local synagogue. Technically, I did not have to convert, having been born to a Jewish mother. I was a big hit with the parents of my Jewish friends, though. While many of my friends were moving away from their religious backgrounds, I was trying to embrace mine to establish my identity.

I took Advanced Placement English that year. I remember noticing that of all the kids in my class, I was one of only two who had gone all the way through public school. I found that amazing, but it also made me proud. I had made the most of my education, without costing my parents thousands of tuition dollars. This appealed to my inner contrarian. The kids in this class were also my best friends in school by this time and we talked about college a lot. Most of my friends were going to Ivy League schools, or at least expensive private institutions. For their families, money for college was not an issue. I was just happy knowing I was going to a good state school and had enough financial aid to get there. One reason for this was Mom's decision not to work during my senior year. While this hurt our family financially, it enabled me to qualify for more aid.

By the time prom rolled around, I had yet another crush on a nice guy. I thought I truly loved him, despite not knowing him well. About two weeks before the prom, he asked me, as a friend, to attend with him. Some mutual friends had encouraged me to accept because they wanted us to go, and neither of us had a date. I floated for about a week after he asked me out. Then I had to face the reality of finding an affordable gown at the last minute. Somehow, I did and we went. It was fun and friendly. We shared a polite kiss at the end of the evening and in my mind I built this up as the beginning of a lovely relationship. Conveniently, he was headed for the Ivy League and I was on my way to Florida State.

1985

I started college as a working-class, Jewish, heterosexual woman (for all I knew). My first year at FSU was enlightening. I was in an all-girls dorm because this was where the high school friend I had planned to room with had already been living for a year. There was considerable economic diversity on our hall. One young woman from south Florida grew up in a house with its own private airstrip. For Christmas that year, she received a pony. I couldn't relate to this, but I got along with her. I remember most of the women looked forward to going home over break because they would get more money and take long showers, as there would be plenty of hot water, which wasn't the case in our dorm, where hot water was at a premium. My experience was the opposite. While I very much looked forward to spending time with family, I was better off in my dorm, so I stayed there over part of the break. Rather than worrying about running up my parents' utility bill at home, I enjoyed the long, hot showers at school. If I wanted entertainment,

I could see cheap movies on campus. I could afford the occasional bit of high culture, as well, and take advantage of student discounts to the ballet, plays, and choral groups. While I still worried about my family, I was feeling more optimistic about my future.

Socially, however, things weren't so bright. I maintained my crush on Prom Date and told all my college friends how much I loved him. This allowed me the public dignity of missing him and the private advantage of not having to date. Occasionally, I would attract male attention, but it was usually men significantly older, from another country, or someone involved with drugs. While I never had relationships with any of these men, I was confused as to why they were the only guys interested in me. Later, I decided it was probably because I didn't view them as obvious romantic possibilities, so I was relaxed and more myself around them. In a way, they were the only men who saw who I really was then. However, I clung to the idea of my unattainable Ivy League prom date.

In the middle of my first year at FSU, I moved to a single room around the corner on the same floor of my dorm. I had wanted more privacy than I had had with my roommate. I was really excited about the move. When I got back to school, several friends helped carry my belongings into my new room. As was the norm, I affixed a Ziggy dry-erase memo board to my door. When my moving crew and I were down the hall retrieving the final load, one of my friendly new hallmates scrawled the welcoming word "Lezzie!!!" on my memo board. My friends and I all saw this as we brought in the last load and I went out and calmly erased the board. I came back in and my friends all looked horrified. One asked, "Aren't you mad?" I said I wasn't thrilled, but because it wasn't true, I wasn't going to get upset about it. Another friend announced, "If that happened to me, I would just cry." Blame it on the power of suggestion, but that's exactly what I began doing. I did so because this was an unpleasant way to start the year, not because I had any inkling the epithet was true.

At the beginning of my fourth semester, I was living in an off-campus apartment with a friend and had started taking classes in my major. Each semester my grades had dropped a bit more. I wasn't sleeping and I couldn't concentrate. I had come clean with Prom Date about my unrequited feelings for him. He was great about it and said he was flattered but had no idea I felt that way. In telling him I loved him, I realized I didn't. He was a wonderful guy and a great friend, but this love idea was fantasy on my part. It was incredibly freeing to get that in the open, and we continued as friends. However, now I had no convenient immunization from a dating life. All these issues, coupled with a pretty serious chemical imbalance, led my parents to encourage me to drive home one weekend. I went to my family doctor, who diagnosed me with clinical depression. I went back to school long enough to withdraw for the semester. I intended to return in the fall. After all, who was I without a school connection?

After I dropped out of college, part of my medical recovery involved weekly visits with a psychologist. The beginning of my therapy involved dealing with childhood issues. Because I didn't really have a social life then, my doctor suggested we deal with social relationships as they occurred. We talked about my lack of serious relationships with guys. I just hadn't developed the feelings my friends seemed to have about intimacy with men. I always figured this would happen later. My doctor had the prescience to suggest some people were perfectly happy in gay or lesbian relationships. Great. Now a "professional" was suggesting this to me. I said I didn't even want to think about that, and went back to discussing my childhood.

Although I didn't dislike gay people, I just didn't think I was one. I didn't seem to fit whatever stereotypical notions of lesbians I carried. I liked men. Some of my closest and most important friendships had been and were with men. Nobody abused me. I got along with my family. Unfortunately, even as late as the mid-1980s, there were very few positive, public gay or lesbian role models in our culture to help dispel my stereotypical notions. The lesbians I recognized were usually famous tennis players.

1987

I was twenty-one and hadn't returned to school as planned. I was a happy college dropout, working as a racquet stringer and general flunky at a local tennis center. I had become obsessed with tennis while working through my medical problems. I started playing, and began reading everything I could about the sport. Without school in my life, my brain was eager to absorb something. I inadvertently grasped a great deal of technical information about tennis equipment. My dad suggested my interest in tennis, combined with the technical abilities he had passed down genetically and had taught me to value, could lead me to an enjoyable job. For my birthday that year, he bought me membership in the USRSA, the professional racquet technicians' organization. As membership cost over $100 annually, this was an indulgent gift. However, I studied all the technical information I received and with help from a woman who would become a very influential friend, I learned to string racquets. I passed the national certification test less than a year after beginning to string.

I loved the physical aspects of my job at the tennis center. I strung racquets and helped care for seven clay courts. I hit with anybody who needed a partner. It was a wonderful experience and completely removed from anything I thought my life would involve at that age. I didn't miss college. I was earning a living through manual labor and technical skills. This was quite a change after all my years as a brain and a band geek.

Working at the tennis center raised some old issues for me, though. While I worked there, I could take free clinics and participate on a city league team without paying club fees. This was wonderful in terms of playing competitive tennis. However, it also thrust me into an environment where I was surrounded by people who could pay for their leisure pursuits. They had money for recreation, meaning they had far more earnings than I did. I felt I was in high school again. I reacted by trying hard to beat these people. Usually, this showed in a healthy manner, but I struggled with resentment whenever I played in country clubs. Not only could I not afford to join these clubs, I knew several of them still didn't admit Jews as members. It was very important I beat these people on the court, and sometimes my strategy worked. I had used the same compensational strategies in school; I may not have as much money as you, but I'll try my best to outperform you.

Through my interest in sports, I made friends with a young woman who greatly influenced my identity development in my early twenties. While we got to know each other through mutual interests in tennis and literature, she became my social mentor as well. Although she never acknowledged it during our first year of friendship, she was a lesbian. She separated that aspect of her life from our affiliation. She was a few years older and later said she wanted to protect me from the rougher people she knew. She probably meant the bar crowd who couldn't discuss literature with me. This friend was important in several ways. She was an excellent athlete and therefore fit my stereotype of lesbians. She was funny, warm, bright, and very popular. She had wonderful relationships with her parents and didn't dislike men in the least. I eventually noticed even people who knew she was gay didn't focus on that aspect of her life. They just liked her, lesbian or not. Our friendship went a long way toward dispelling many of my archaic misconceptions about lesbians. The more time I spent with her and some of her other friends the more I realized I was comfortable socially with them, relaxed unlike anytime before. I wasn't romantically involved with any of them. I simply recognized a large piece of my identity puzzle was falling in place.

My close relatives and friends noticed I was becoming more comfortable with myself and obviously happier. During one week in the early summer of 1988, a high school friend, my sister, and my mom all mentioned how well I got along with lesbians. This began my process of coming out to my family and close friends. I didn't really have to do this with my younger brother. For many years, he had been telling me I was probably gay. Ray simply enjoyed seeing his theory verified. Mom told Dad of the situation. After a few years of hoping this was a phase, he accepted me as I am. Given the rough time I experienced in college and after I dropped out, the people who loved me were ready to support anything that made me happy and healthy. They knew I was the same person as always, but with a greater peace. I will always appreciate the support and love those closest to me showed during this time.

Now that I had settled the issue of my sexuality, I started longing for school. I enrolled in some classes at the local community college to finish my associate of arts degree. Having my diploma would make it easier to transfer to a new school. I was nervous about returning to college, but I felt my brain rotting. I started a new job at the same time I returned to school. The tennis club fell on hard financial times and my friend Brian suggested I do what he had been doing for a living. I became Security Officer McDaniel, guarding a savings and loan center at night.

Security work was great for a night owl with lots of homework. The job included bad HMO coverage, which is more health insurance than I had enjoyed since childhood. I also got a one-week annual vacation. My work exposed me to an interesting intersection of social classes. My fellow security guards ranged from young people just starting their working lives to older people with dodgy pasts. I got along with everyone, although they generally didn't understand why I was in school. After all, the security company kept offering me dispatcher positions so why did I need a college degree? The same people who saw me as having a bright future in security work got their news from supermarket tabloids. And not the fancy ones, either.

On the other end of the class and education spectrum were employees of the financial institution we guarded. When they bothered to talk to me, these clerks and analysts said I was different from the other guards. One day, while at my lobby security desk, a banker stopped and said, "You're the only one who ever looks like you are really guarding us." This was funny and frightening, as I was reading my anthropology textbook when she said this.

I kept my security job for three years and it definitely spurred me on to bigger things. I certainly didn't want to spend the rest of my working life guarding banks.

I finished my AA and spent the next year working full time. I continued my security career, but began stringing racquets as an outside contractor for a large sporting goods chain. I loved the work. Being paid per racquet strung was highly motivating and I loved the other young people I worked with. Most were in school and, like me, just passing through this segment of the job market. Occasionally my class issues surfaced. Sometimes customers from the country club set would come in and try to order me around. They were the exception, though. Mostly, I enjoyed interacting with the wide variety of customers. It was a nice counterpoint to the solitary hours I spent working security.

As much as I loved my stringing job, two factors pushed me back to school. First, I knew I had more in common intellectually with some customers who were professionals than I had with the store management. The myopic vision of the retail industry disturbed me in light of what I considered the world's real problems. As our nation built up to the Gulf War, I kept thinking, "I know there's more to life than sporting goods. Shouldn't we acknowledge that?" My heart was not in retail.

The second factor that pushed me back toward formal education involved how I performed my stringing job. I was very good at it and developed a solid customer base. As I brought in more stringing business to the store, management noticed and speculated how much more money the company would make if they didn't have to pay me. They considered having on-the-clock employees do my work. It seemed the better I did my job, the less job security I had. This recurring threat told me I had to make some changes.

By the end of 1990, I was living with my parents, who kept encouraging me to return to school. Since this was a last-minute decision for me, I didn't know how to get enough money for tuition for the upcoming semester. I applied for a personal loan at my bank, but to no avail. I was at a loss. I went to see a movie with my former prom date shortly before the holidays and afterward I was in his front yard talking to his father. I told him I wanted to go back to school, something he had encouraged me to do for years. I told him about my tuition problem and, knowing he was a retired accountant, I sought his advice. He asked me how much I would need for the semester. I told him and he said he'd loan it to me. After so many years of being the poorest kid among my friends, I had developed a serious reluctance to ask for help. Here was a man offering assistance I hadn't even requested. He said, "Michallene, that amount of money is nothing to me, but it's everything to you right now. Please let me help you." He was right: It was everything to me. He paid for the rest of my BA education and then forgave the loan. This was one of the most stunning acts of generosity I've ever experienced. It changed the direction of my life.

1991

I returned to college at the University of North Florida in Jacksonville. It was a very good school academically and allowed me to live at home and remain a racquet-stringing, security guard. I had long ago abandoned my filmmaking plans. I realized it wasn't the art of film that interested me as much as the messages films can convey. In choosing an academic major this time, I was extraordinarily practical. I looked through the descriptions of all the majors in the college catalogue and found one that encompassed topics I most cared about. Due to my life experiences, I was obsessed with social inequality in all its guises and how it affected individuals. I found everything I was looking for under the sociology description. I had taken an introductory sociology course at the community college and had done well. Besides, in looking through my textbook for that class, I noticed I had made more notes

of outrage in the margins than I had in any of my other texts. This showed
I cared about these issues.

So I returned to school as a twenty-four-year-old, working-class, lesbian,
nonreligious, racquet-stringing security guard and sociology major and women's
studies minor. When I was a child, I could have never imagined my identity
would have so many facets. From my first class on the first day back at UNF
I felt at home. I never wanted to be out of a classroom again. At least people
here were trying to understand things that mattered to me, unlike my bosses
at the sporting goods store or my fellow security officers. I felt so much more
comfortable in college this time because my life experiences gave context to
the new things I was learning. School is much easier when you know who
you are, even if you aren't totally satisfied with it.

After so many years away, I was apprehensive about my first exam. When
I walked out of class, opened the test, and I saw an "A," I burst into tears.
I was finally back doing what I had always done best: school. I wanted a
career centered on formal education.

I also found a wonderful community of feminists at UNF. This was an
enormous relief to me. Although I had been friends with lesbians before returning to college, I would not classify those women as feminists. Not when
they attended wet T-shirt contests and generally objectified women as much
as the most chauvinistic men. I hoped to find people at school who shared
my political sensibilities, and I did. Not all my friends were gay, but all were
bright and concerned about the same things that interested me.

I also entered into my first real relationship. It was with a woman eight
years my senior whom I had met at school. Having failed to heed the portents
of potential doom that hovered over this romance (for instance, we met in
Introduction to Social Problems), I plunged into what I now refer to as the
Learning Experience. While this relationship did have some fine moments, its
dynamics were based in part on my being the "young one." As I started to
grow up, I apparently just was not that interesting anymore. I gladly accept
the heartache I suffered in exchange for the lessons I learned about what I
did and did not want in a relationship.

I kept working two jobs while I finished school. I generally loved my
classes and had some wonderful professors. I noticed how my professors lived.
They seemed happy. They taught, were involved in community service, and
did research. They got paid to be at school. Sweet! I saw academia as a vi-
able career. This meant I would have to go to graduate school, which would
mean leaving home.

1993

I graduated magna cum laude from UNF and moved to Athens to attend
the University of Georgia's graduate program in sociology. I adjusted to my

classes well and really enjoyed the environment. I became friends with several sociology graduate students, and some remain my best friends today. I was comfortable in this environment because my fellow students came from varied class backgrounds. None had been terribly wealthy and we were all working to make the world a better place. I assumed loans to cover living expenses my assistantship wouldn't pay for. This was an unfortunate necessity that will haunt me for a good thirty years. My brother Ray started graduate school on a fellowship at the University of Michigan that same year, so we both sensed our lives could only improve.

In the middle of our first year of graduate school, Dad died suddenly. One reason I had applied only to graduate schools near Florida was so I could be close if something happened to my father. Not only did he die, it happened before I could get back to see him one last time. I drove home that same day to be with Mom. The next day I picked up my devastated brother at the airport. Living with a disabled person, in this case my father, is like waiting for the other shoe to drop. You never know when things might turn bad again. After fourteen years of holding our collective breath, Dad succumbed to congestive heart failure. Mom and I were somewhat relieved by Dad's death, knowing he would suffer no more. He wasn't bedridden at the end and never faced the indignity of a nursing home, something he deeply feared. Conversely, everything about our family structure changed.

Mom could no longer afford to live in the apartment she shared with Dad, so within two weeks of his death she moved in with her sisters who were living nearby. Fortunately, she had this option, but visiting her certainly didn't feel like "going home" anymore. Her entire life was disrupted in ways that mine, now being conducted away at school, was not. Her circumstances show how few options we have when we don't have enough money. Mom's financial condition had a powerful effect on my brother Ray. He became Mr. Responsibility. He displayed a much stronger work ethic than he'd ever had before. He vowed to never die poor.

My brother and I reacted very differently to Dad's death. I had always thought my high self-motivation explained my school accomplishments. My parents never pushed or threatened me into applying myself in school. They just supported me and were interested in my work. Or so I thought. It wasn't until after Dad died that I realized how much he had motivated me to work. He always asked detailed questions about what I was studying. He read all my college papers. Only months before he died, he sat patiently as I explained the wonders of statistical data analysis software. I realized after his death that he was the audience I had always carried in my head. As self-aware and reflective as I thought I was, it stuns me I never understood this until my dad was gone. While Ray's motivation level kicked up several notches, mine dropped considerably. This was somewhat healthy because I no longer panicked over small details or deadlines. However, graduate school is mostly about details and deadlines.

I had the added concern of worrying about Mom and our family's finances. No other members of my graduate school class had to use financial aid money to pay off the balance of their father's cremation bill. As much as I tried to escape into the wonderful world of books and papers, real life kept rearing its ugly, insatiable head.

One very positive aspect of graduate school, though, was that I was surrounded by educated, open-minded people with progressive political viewpoints. It was no big deal to anyone that I was gay. Graduate students and professors alike treated sexual orientation as just another part of who I was, which is how I wanted it. Because most people close to me had been so accepting during my coming-out process, I assimilated my sexual orientation quite easily. It was no big deal and I was grateful all my friends felt the same way. This is one advantage of being surrounded by people who are academic sociologists. Despite the traumatic breakup of my first serious relationship shortly after Dad's death, I felt at home among my bright, supportive, mostly heterosexual friends who nurtured me emotionally. As would become my pattern, I bonded with people who have similar hearts and minds as mine, rather than similar sexual orientations.

At the end of my second year of graduate school, I took a road trip to visit Mom in Florida. While there, I went to a movie with my ex, and then she dragged me to a bar to meet up with some friends of hers. As the engine block in my car had cracked a few days before, I was at her mercy as far as transportation. Otherwise, I would never have gone to that bar. As it turned out, I am forever grateful I did.

That evening I met the woman I have been with ever since. She was in the bar at the invitation of a mutual acquaintance, and early in our conversation realized there was an easy rapport between us. At one point she looked at me and asked very seriously "Now, what is your connection to these people?," gesturing to the group of acquaintances. I pointed to my ex and said, "I'm broken up with her." She then asked "How's that going?," to which I replied "Much better now, thank you." We just "got" each other on a much deeper level than we had with others. We ran into each other at an event two days later, and the easy/exciting rapport was still there. About a week after that, at the urging of mutual friends, I invited this new friend out for dinner. That date led to a great summer, during which she met and received the approval of my family. Mom even suggested she move to Athens to live with me. After selling her house and preparing to relocate her business, that is just what she did.

I finished my MA and immediately began working on my PhD at Georgia. I started teaching my own classes, which I loved. This experience absolutely validated my career choice. I had come to graduate school to become a teacher. Despite considerable pressure from well-meaning professors to strive for employment at research-one institutions, I was experienced enough to know that quality of life is very important to me. Just as I knew life wasn't only about sporting goods, I knew it wasn't only about getting a job at a research-one university.

2001

True to the wishes of my seventeen-year-old self, this was the year I turned thirty-five and had a career. I had a tenure-track position at a good two-year transfer institution in the North Georgia foothills. My partner and I bought a house this year. Since childhood, I didn't think people in my family were allowed to buy houses. Every day, I appreciate having a solid relationship with my family and friends, a house with my own grass and trees, and a nice office on a pretty little college campus. None of these eventual outcomes seemed possible earlier in my life. Medical problems and earning a living have hampered progress on my long-suffering dissertation. Although it has taken a long time and some friends have either left graduate school or chosen nonacademic careers, I have never once considered not finishing my degree.

In class my first year of grad school we were talking about social class issues and I was asked why I wanted a PhD. Without hesitation, or really even much forethought, I said, "Because once I have it, no one can take it away, and it will obscure the social class behind it." I was voicing the sentiments I had been carrying from sixth grade: Perhaps with good enough grades, people wouldn't notice my old clothes. I was still in high school hoping that if I could discuss the same cultural references as my rich friends, they wouldn't notice I couldn't afford to attend grad night with them. I was still playing tennis at the country club, hoping that if I beat someone soundly, she would overlook my 1967 Dodge, inherited from my grandmother, parked next to her Jaguar in the parking lot. Always hide the financial inadequacies behind a big vocabulary. It's a magic act. I wonder how much better the energy behind it could be used if I didn't feel obligated to perform the act so often.

TODAY

My workplace is making the transition to a state college with a few four-year degrees. This will allow me to work with advanced undergraduates again. I am scheduled to complete my PhD in the next year, and then I will go up for tenure. Although I look forward to graduation for personal and professional reasons, financially I'm in for a lot of loans coming due. After many years of patience, I know my partner is ready for me to finish my dissertation.

I'm very happy with the learning environment at my school. I teach a number of first-generation college students. Many are from humble backgrounds. They have real family problems and don't exude the air of entitlement students have at other institutions where I've taught. Importantly, I love my colleagues. Not only are they some of the brightest people I've met in academia, they have lives outside work. They could be publishing regularly, but they care more about teaching, service, and family life. While most of them are happily married heterosexuals, they treat my family and me like everyone else. Academia has been a very comfortable, welcoming place for my sexuality.

Interacting with students is usually the highlight of my day. My teaching load is heavy and my office is usually filled with students between classes. Sometimes I can't believe someone as shy as I was in school, someone traumatized by a cafeteria incident and scared of other children, now has trouble finding time away from people to complete my work. As a teacher, I use all my life's experiences and all stages of my identity formation to meet my students at whatever developmental level they occupy. I know my experiences as a lower-class person, as a lesbian, and even as someone with a complicated family and religious background, give me an empathy that helps me connect with a great variety of people. I can relate to gay students because I've been one. I was a straight student, too. Methodist? Yes, I've done that, but I can relate to students even if they're Jewish, or agnostic, or whatever. Work a manual labor job? My calluses have finally healed. Have no health insurance? I know what that's like. Just be careful. Failing math? I've been there, too. I am now grateful for all these experiences—they make me a better teacher.

It isn't all perfect. Although my colleagues and my school's administrators support my relationship, I generally don't mention it to students. I've never brought it up in the classroom. Most of my students are very conservative Christians, with even stronger negative stereotypes of gays and lesbians than I had growing up. I want to reach them and not alienate them, so I talk around this part of my identity. Sometimes it is painful because I want to say, "You know, one of the main things that makes me the person you feel so comfortable with is the one reason you would condemn me." A few summers ago I guest lectured in a class a friend was teaching on another campus. I was a visual aid: here's a lesbian, ask her some questions. It was an amazing experience to be out to a classroom of students, even if they weren't mine. I felt whole in a way I do not with my own students. It gave me a small taste of what my work could be like one day, if attitudes continue changing, I get tenure, or both.

My current class, educational attainment level, and sexual orientation are aspects of identity I've had to grow into. These variables live in a complex intersection within me, and it's an intersection with a past. Along the way, I've tried other identities on for size. I know I'm still evolving. However, largely because of my education, I've changed social classes and better accepted my sexual orientation. One day I hope to feel more comfortable living in the middle class and ideally have my students accept me for *everything* I am.

When I leave work, my sexuality is not an ongoing, problematic issue for me personally. Class, however, haunts me. When I started working on this chapter, I tried writing about my class issues as if they were forever in the past. However, I still worry about my mom's finances, as does my brother. I worry about the massive student loans I'll be repaying longer than my mortgage. I often sacrifice research time to teach an extra class, so I'll have a small cushion in the bank. If I were from a wealthy family, perhaps I would have had enough financial support from them to finish my dissertation earlier. While outwardly I have a middle-class life, it doesn't feel like it on the inside. In my head, I'm one bad lecture away from guarding a bank.

ELEVEN

Becoming (Almost) One of Those "Damn, New York, Pinko Intellectuals"

DONALD C. BARRETT

Long before I thought I might be gay (homosexually active, to be more accurate), I got the message very clearly that I was going in the "wrong" direction. Bookish and curious, daydreaming and shy, sneaking peeks at *The New Yorker* at my uncle's house (the one who never acknowledged he was a faggot), labeled "nigger-lover" in high school for questioning "separate but equal," it sure looked like I was headed toward being what was widely disliked in the South of the 1950s—one of those "damn, New York, pinko intellectuals" who was coming down and "ruining everything."

Getting close to that ignoble status required many years of meandering down two paths definitely not on the road map for a blue-collar kid: the path of becoming an activist intellectual[1] ("New York" was a code word for "interfering, busybody, liberal, snooty intellectual") and the path of becoming a pinko queer.[2] The paths seemed very separate for a long time, but looking back over the past fifty years, their interconnectedness is clear. The map presented next is thus filled in by historical retrospection and of course sullied somewhat by the hazards of recall. Still, I believe it an accurate analysis of my development and the eventual intersection of the two paths.

One important point before telling you about my travels down these paths: as I've interviewed men over the years and looked at the existing research, I've come to strongly believe that our life course is very heavily influenced by what happens to us as children, thus I'm focusing fairly heavily on my childhood and early adult years with much less detail about my adult life. By the end of this chapter, my reasons for choosing this approach will be evident.

GROWING UP JUST SOUTH OF THE GEORGIA LINE

Whenever I mention growing up in Florida, I get arguments that Florida isn't the South. Well, Jacksonville is only thirty miles from the Georgia border, southern food and a southern drawl are standard, we had to stand for "Dixie" at some school functions, even grammar school kids joked about "getting points" for "killing niggers," and everyone talked about "those damn New York Jews" who were taking over south Florida. So, given these facts, how did I become an academic, an activist, and a relatively happy queer?

From one perspective, the makings were there for *not* becoming intellectual (or academic). The man (technically speaking, my father) who lived in the house (most of the time) until I was about twelve was a plumber (when he worked). Mother, who had pretensions of being middle class, had hoped to find a man to take her there, but hadn't. Where I went to high school, the topic of "going to college" never came up—none of my friends was going, and the teachers never mentioned the possibility to us. Of course, it didn't help that my high school had lost its accreditation the year I graduated, or that I had spent the last two years of high school in Diversified Cooperative Training (DCT)—a program purportedly designed for teens with no college aspirations (or who needed to work to support the family—my situation) where you went to school half a day and worked half a day at a job that was supposed to teach you good work skills (like sorting mail).

Looking back, though, there were a few things that at least helped set me on course to becoming an academic. For one, both my parents were surprisingly bookish considering their backgrounds and the anti-intellectual attitudes they publicly espoused. We had a full bookcase in the living room (including an encyclopedia), both parents read the newspaper regularly and rigorously, Mother subscribed to three magazines (*Look* or *Life*—never both, *Saturday Evening Post*, and *Reader's Digest*), there was a subscription to *Popular Mechanics* for us boys, family trips to the library were frequent, and reading was encouraged. We did watch or listen to popular television shows and radio dramas, but we also listened to news and commentary shows that were probably not typical fare for young, working-class children—including the 1952 political conventions (Mother was a Republican, Father a Democrat). Probably most important, afterward we talked about what we had heard or seen—it wasn't just passive entertainment.

It helped, too, that both parents were good models for being unconventionally masculine. Father, though generally passive or absent in much of my childhood, was also not a stereotypical blue-collar male—there was no push for involvement in sports or other "masculine" activities, and when he was around the house, he spent much of his time reading classical literature or technical books and listening to music (including classical). Mother, though she kept hoping my father would be the white knight who would take her away from her white-trash background, wasn't willing to sit by idly waiting until that happened. Assertive, surprisingly well read, active in PTA and volunteer work, athletic (a good swimmer), openly sexual in dress and demeanor, and frequently "inappropriately" demanding, she wasn't exactly a stereotypical 1950s feminine, working-class housewife.

Our nonconventional family life wasn't the only factor in encouraging my curiosity. In a perverse way, my stature and health also aided the path to intellectualism. As a family, we were shorter than average—in that part of the South most whites were very Anglo-Saxon with plenty of six footers, but my father was (I think) only about five four and my mother was five two. Not only did I inherit their shortness, I was slower growing than average (I grew after high school) and was very sick for most of third grade and well into fourth grade. Being short and sickly, there was only one way to avoid the typical public school harassment—withdraw. One place to withdraw, of course, was into books and intellectual games,[3] which fit perfectly with life in my family. (A favorite picture from that period is one in which Mother and I are playing Chinese checkers at a card table set up in front of my father's workbench.)

Mother's desire for a middle-class life also, perversely again, helped push me toward intellectualism. Her strong desire to be seen as middle class meant that much of the family social life in our childhood was centered around a Methodist church where the congregation was primarily middle class or above. Mother somehow never understood the strain this put on her children, since we were never invited to social events with other kids in the congregation. I suspect we were excluded because of, among other things, my father's work, we always drove old cars, we wore secondhand clothes, we couldn't talk about the latest movies, and just generally didn't know how to act middle class. This exclusion pushed me further into books and into a rudimentary form of sociological analysis, including trying to determine what was different about us that resulted in our not being liked.

Besides these family dynamics, several adults nurtured my confidence and intellect in important ways. I particularly remember my third grade teacher (I think her name was Mrs. Glick) and how much help she gave me in keeping up my schoolwork through the time of my sickness—and how she discouraged my mother from holding me back a year. Later, in my last two years of high school, the director of the DCT program for working teens somehow managed to give to me a sense I was someone with something to say. He encouraged me in my first "activist" task of being on the board of the student association for DCT. I don't know exactly why he was supportive—other than possibly because he was dating my mother.

There were a number of supportive grown men with whom my relationship seemed to go beyond the standard model of adult male/child interaction.

It may be that some of these men were acting out of homoeroticism, or simply out of recognition of "difference" and an implicit sense of mentoring me into feeling that being "different" was okay. My Uncle Wally was a key figure in suggesting that "different" was acceptable. Wally never married (and never admitted to being gay), liked musicals, and his best friend was an airline steward. Wally was sort of a substitute father (since my own wasn't around much). I somehow felt very comfortable with him—he accepted me for who I was and I could talk with him about family problems. Besides, he left good reading material around the house. Most readily available was *The New Yorker*, but some surreptitious searching would turn up good fantasy material such as *After Dark*. *After Dark* was purportedly a magazine about modern dance—but it sure had many wonderful pictures of almost nude men in all sorts of positions and poses.

Homoerotic relationships with three other men similarly stand out as telling me my nontraditional boyhood was okay. One was the education minister at the church. Most of my memories of him involve when he was running the Friday afternoon church swimming party. I got to know him fairly well because I helped with readying the pool and then closing it (later in life I learned that because we were among the poorer members in the church, we frequently ended up helping with the church in exchange for not paying/ donating our way). While I suspect I've mixed my later erotic fantasies with my recollections of him, I have very clear memories of the comfort I felt at the swim party when he would put his hands on my shoulders (probably because he was one of the few adult males I knew who was comfortable with touching). I clearly felt a sense of acceptance from him. Interestingly, he suddenly disappeared from the church at the end of one summer, with no formal farewell—I've often wondered if he was pushed out for being too close to the boys (he was unmarried).

Another man whose image has stuck with me throughout my life was Mike,[4] who worked at the same company as my mother (Uncle Wally managed the company). Well before I was old enough to work, I went out with the crews to help them (I realize now this was a form of childcare). Often the workers would get angry because I was in the way, but Mike never did—he never shouted (as Father frequently did) that I brought the wrong tool. He would instead assign me to a task I could actually do, and would thank me with a warm smile when I completed the task. Though there was no hint of a homoerotic undertone between Mike and me, many of the men I've found sexually interesting are reminders of him (an image similar to the early Bruce Springsteen, if my recall is correct).

Then there was Lee, an outside auditor at a company where I was working when I was in twelfth grade. Somehow, Lee and I frequently ended up in the office when no one else was there. We would spend long periods talking about life, my schooling, and things at the company. There was a fairly clear sexual component in this relationship. One Saturday we went to the beach together and then back to his motel—where he was clearly frustrated because I was too naïve to understand what was supposed to happen.

This just-mentioned episode brings up the question of my teenage sexual naïveté, which was surprising considering my sexual experience had started early. Some of my earliest sexual memories are from before entering grammar school, when one of my friends (Sam) would get upset because I got sexually aroused when we would run around the yard in our underwear (kids did that in the Florida summer heat). Later in grammar school, his mother got very angry when she caught him trying to teach me to dance. (I suspect that anger was based partly on her probably having seen oddly intimate cowboy/Indian wrestling matches between Sam and me.)

Near the end of grammar school (at about the time Sam got sent off to military school to learn discipline), Jimmy and I became friends. My four-year friendship with Jimmy was clearly heavily laced with sexual exploration (involving lots of swimming naked and discovering body parts)—though labeling anything that pre-adolescent boys do as erotic sounds odd. Jimmy's family didn't seem concerned about what we were doing on sleepovers—I suspect they just laughed, saying "boys will be boys." Unfortunately, my mother mandated I stop hanging out with "that sort of people"—his family was "farm folk" from rural Georgia (a social negative for those wanting to be middle class). Luckily, Mother had to work during the day so Jimmy and I kept doing things together—though I knew not to tell her (and thus learned to hide behavior and feelings). His family moved back to Georgia when I was in about ninth grade and Jimmy and I lost contact—I still wonder what happened to him. Writing about Jimmy now, I realize I had sort of a crush on him—though I wouldn't have put it in those words back then.

After Jimmy, and throughout high school, my closest male friend was Rick. Interestingly, Rick was much more middle class than Jimmy, and, looking back, I see my relationship with him was never as close. I suspect it was one of the first (and few) instances when I used my blue-collar demeanor rather manipulatively to get something I wanted. His family had a cabin on a lake in central Florida and they'd let Rick and me go down alone to the cabin—which was a great escape from my own house. He was amazingly shy (it took several trips to convince him to skinny-dip in the lake), and I suspect my somewhat more crude behavior was appealing in a way.

Besides these close, intimate, primary friends, there were always other working-class teens I regularly lusted after (though I didn't know what "lust" meant then). Though never friends, it somehow worked out that tall and lanky Dick (whose family lived in a rundown cabin at the end of a dirt road) and I ended up skinny-dipping at the same time in the swimming holes in the neighborhood, with no one else around. Then there was Butch (his first name was actually Sharon), who couldn't form a reasonable sentence and drove a green 1957 Pontiac Bonneville (considered to be a very "hot" car in those days)—but looked very good driving to the beach in one of those tight, square-cut, stretch bathing suits popular in the early 1960s.

Looking back over these friends and other guys, I think I learned in the relationships with Sam and Rick about the shame others (including parents) attach to sex. With Jimmy, I most clearly learned that sexual play can be fun—and probably also learned that treating sex as "fun" was considered "lower class." With the other guys, I just developed a rich fantasy life.

And girlfriends—how could I forget? Maybe it's because I can't remember any of their names or what they looked like. I did, however, spend a lot of time trying to conform—dating and heavy necking started early (about sixth grade) and continued through high school. Luckily, "necking" was exactly the right term—above the neck and thus no resulting pregnancies—unlike the experience of many of my high school classmates.

SUMMING UP CHILDHOOD

The first steps to becoming a "damn" intellectual:　How then, did these childhood experiences influence my activist intellectual development? Though the overall cultural environment of my school and neighborhood was fairly negative about intellectual activity, there was just enough room in my relatively immediate environment to get around this negativity—and future sexuality played a part in this. At home, the acceptance of reading and encouragement of discussion helped build the basic skills for intellectual development, while the lack of pressure to conform to conventional activity-oriented masculinity made it okay to be a "bookworm." Outside the family, the presence of a few adults who seemed accepting (or even supportive) of me and my "difference" helped create the confidence to be myself, while the ostracism we encountered in an institution very important to my mother (the church) motivated me to search for answers as to why we were excluded.

The basics for becoming a "pinko" queer:　Tracing my sexual development in my childhood is not so easily packaged. Just based on critical use of the label "queer" in high school and by many adult males, it was easy to learn that interests like mine were not necessarily shared by other boys or men, and thus sexuality was to be hidden. At the same time, my experiences with close friends and others taught me there were people who shared my sexual interests. Interestingly, though I had childhood friends I was sexually active with, we never actually acknowledged we were being sexual, nor did we label what we were doing. Thus, as a child and teen, I never thought of myself as gay or queer—though I was sometimes anxious about my lack of interest in girls.

THE MILITARY AS A RADICALIZING INSTITUTION (AGES EIGHTEEN TO TWENTY-TWO)

Although I received no encouragement to continue my education, I applied for college after high school. I suspect it was just an excuse to leave home. Unfortunately (which turned out to be fortunate), I had to work full-time to cover my living expenses while going to school. In December 1966, eighteen months out of high school, I was finding myself utterly exhausted by trying to go to school full time (to avoid the draft) while also working full time. I was also feeling directionless in general, not having any good sense of what I wanted to do in life. I quit college and, to avoid being drafted, joined the military. Looking back, I credit the military with having been a significant factor in my intellectual, social, and emotional maturation—an effect that started very quickly.

In April 1967, Mother (who disapproved of my joining) drove me to Naval Air Station Jacksonville, where they processed everyone entering any of the military branches. The morning started with a fairly simple test of reading, writing, math, and work skills. The rest of the morning was my first exposure to the military's efforts to break recruits of their teenage self-centeredness. New recruits spent three hours standing in various lines with one hundred other guys (stripped to their underwear and carrying their clothes in their hands much of the time) to get through what was really only a twenty-minute medical exam, all of which was conducted in a much gruffer voice than most of us had ever experienced from our own doctors. (Yes, I was asked if I was a homosexual—I remember briefly hesitating before answering, "No.")

My first experience of being in charge of others happened later in the day. After a box lunch we were shuttled off in school buses to a processing point for sending us to basic training. At the processing point I was told, based on my test scores, I was in charge of getting the other ten guys to Lackland Air Force Base in San Antonio. I had never supervised anyone, been on a plane, dealt with making connections in strange terminals, or been more than four hundred miles from home—and I was going to lead ten guys on a trip that required three flight changes (Jacksonville to Atlanta to Houston to San Antonio)! I was panicky I'd muck up and we wouldn't get there on time—but we made it (partly because some of the other guys had flown before).

The next six weeks of basic training were just a blur and there's no need to recount them in detail—other than how efforts to break one down oddly increase self-confidence. A purported main goal of basic training is to remove your feelings of self-importance and increase your sense of commitment to working as a unit. Stripping away your sense of self-importance seems to be the whole point of shaving heads, requiring ill-fitting uniforms, denying sleep, being shouted at a lot, and being assigned senseless tasks. Unit cohesion is expected to occur because the unit (usually twenty to thirty guys), and not the individual, is punished if the group fails a task (e.g., cleaning the barracks), even if the breakdown was due to one person not performing his assignments. While I don't recall gaining any sense of cohesion with my unit out of this silliness, just getting through it contributed to my self-confidence and helped make the next three years manageable.

One of the most important factors in redirecting my life toward intellectual activity and academia happened in basic training. When I enlisted, I had requested to be sent to electronics school because I thought it might be something I would find interesting. However, during basic training I was asked to take an exam that tests ability to learn foreign languages. I did well on the exam and was assigned to start eleven months of intensive training in Russian at the Defense Language Institute in Monterey, California.

Monterey was the start of a long process of opening new worlds of intellectual activity to me, while challenging all my basic assumptions about life. The institute was housed at the Presidio of Monterey, which is a small military base nestled between Monterey and Pacific Grove, about a fifteen-minute walk from Fisherman's Wharf. At the Presidio we spent seven and a half hours a day in intensive Russian classes, had to devote two to four hours each night in labs or studying, and otherwise had quite a bit of free time. With weekends free there was plenty of opportunity to explore the mind-boggling (for me) wonders of the mountains, deep woods, and rugged coasts of the Monterey area—and to spend afternoons wandering the bookstores and artists' galleries common to Carmel and Pacific Grove.

After finishing Monterey and a short assignment to central Texas for schooling on intelligence-gathering techniques, the real adventure and growth began. In November 1968, I flew by military charter to Frankfurt, Germany, and then was taken by military bus, in the dead of a very cold night, to my barracks in Darmstadt, Germany. Darmstadt was my first real assignment, where my task was to intercept radio communications. For the rest of my military career, I worked on a schedule of four evening shifts, a day off, four day shifts, a day off, four night shifts, and then three full days off. This worked out so that if you could stay awake enough for touring, you had four and a half days of travel time between the end of your last night shift and the start of your first evening shift. Because Darmstadt is in a fairly central location and had very good train service, I traveled quite a bit around the Rhine and Mosel valleys, made a number of trips to Amsterdam and northern Switzerland, and longer trips (one time each) to Austria, London, Paris, and Scandinavia. For an American kid from the South, Europe was simply amazing—the sense of ancient history, the different organization of cities and transportation, the openness of sexuality, the foods and music, the politics—it was all one, vast educational experience. But it turned out to be relatively minor compared to what was next.

In the fall of 1969, I was reassigned to Sinop, Turkey. The assignment involved going back to the states and then, on Christmas Eve, flying from Jacksonville to New York City and then transferring to other flights destined for Paris, Istanbul, and then Ankara. The intercontinental flight itself was quite a learning experience—going to and from Germany had been on military charter flights, but this was a conventional Pan Am flight with businessmen, tourists, and others traveling on Christmas day to the Middle East. The concept of "world traveler" was beginning to take on meaning. I got off the Pan Am flight in Ankara, found the American military attaché desk in the airport, and was sent to a downtown airport. Because of fog for my connecting flight to Samsun, Turkey, I had to layover in Ankara for several nights. Those first days in Ankara were a letdown—I had not expected Ankara to be just a poorer version of a Western city, but that is what it was then. Luckily, that changed. On New Year's Eve, I flew to Samsun, and then caught the military shuttle to the base in Sinop.

Sinop is a small town on the Black Sea originally settled in about the seventh century B.C. It is directly across the sea from the Crimean peninsula, then part of the Soviet Union (which is why the United States had a listening post in Sinop). In 1970, the town seemed quite primitive compared to what I had experienced so far. There were few cars in Sinop. Horses and donkeys were common forms of transportation. The conveniences (e.g., well-lit streets) of more Western cities were not existent. Sanitation standards (e.g., food handling, cleanliness of restrooms) were very different and, to the untrained, seemed backward. In squares and other public places, men and women never interacted. Minarets loudly broadcast the call to prayers every day. In 1970, the town was isolated, with no paved roads or railroads to other parts of Turkey. Luckily, there was an older sergeant who liked to organize tours around the area and he could get a base van for those of us who liked to explore. Together with a regular group of about six other guys (one of whom I had an unfulfilled crush on), we saw quite a bit of coastal rural Turkey on short, one-day trips. We made a four-day trip to historic Amasya in north central Turkey. Our travels also included a very memorable five-day trip by coastal steamer to Istanbul. The year exploring Turkey and encountering a culture that was radically different from the United States was one of the most profound experiences in my life.

The day after Christmas 1970, I began the trip back to the states, now feeling like a "world traveler"—two days by bus to Ankara; two nights in Ankara; New Year's Eve on a Pan Am flight from Ankara to Istanbul to Rome; transferring in Rome to a Pan Am 747 (a new plane then) to Paris and New York; and then subway, train, bus, and motel stopover from New York City to Fort Dix, New Jersey. I was discharged (groggy from traveling) from the air force on January 2, 1971.

SUMMING THE MILITARY YEARS

Getting closer to becoming a "damn" intellectual: If it hadn't been for my time in the military, I would have probably never left Jacksonville, ending up with a very limited worldview. My military experiences showed me another way to see and approach life, a way far beyond the path laid out by my cultural background. Of course it is impossible to separate how much the military influenced that versus where my basic personality would have taken me even without those experiences, but I think my military years had a number of important effects on my life (though many of these weren't the effects the military would have wanted).

In particular, I credit the military with having contributed to my intellectual life by creating a sense of wonder that was good for both my confidence and curiosity. Part of the "wonder" is just amazement at what I did. When I entered the military, I was a shy, insecure, immature southern boy who had never dealt with the world of travel and was somewhat fearful of the world "out there." I am amazed I so quickly became accustomed to flying alone across the country and across the Atlantic. I quickly learned to negotiate foreign airports, train stations, trolley systems, rental cars, and hotels, and to explore the cultures and streets of places where I didn't speak the language. All of this may not seem like much to the modern worldwise young adult, but in the provincialism of my lower-class southern upbringing in the 1960s, it was a startling change.

A different sense of "wonder" was the feeling of being amazed at how the world really didn't work as I was raised to assume. Learning Russian taught me that language (and thought) structures don't follow a common pattern. Traveling abroad gave me knowledge that made American history look trivial (e.g., living in and visiting towns with artifacts dating back two millennia). Negotiating daily life challenged my sense of how even the most common tasks were performed (e.g., seeing skinned carcasses of lambs hanging outside butcher shops for inspection by passersby in Turkey).

Combining these two senses of wonder, it seems the military gave me willingness and courage to explore strange things and to be curious about how those things shaped the lives of the people immersed in them. The military affected my self-confidence in other ways as well. Completing Russian language school and being on a fast track for promotions gave me some sense of my abilities. But, there was also an effect on self-confidence from just getting through the harsh and frequently very nasty circumstances of military life (e.g., nonsensical rules and men with exaggerated needs to prove their masculinity).

My military experiences helped radicalize me politically. Being in Monterey in the late 1960s, with the hippie and antiwar culture all around, helped me develop my own feelings against the Vietnam War. My politics continued to move left as I was in European countries where there was less economic disparity than in the United States (and less consumerism). The strongest effect on my politics, however, was due to my experiences in Turkey. Sinop's economy seemed to be primarily based on three activities: serving nearby agricultural villages; being a port and processing point for Black Sea fishermen; and supporting our base. Sinop was thus a fairly quiet and friendly village. Though many things about the local Turkish culture in 1970 were radically different from American standards (particularly the treatment of women), the local populace seemed quite happy with their rather uncomplicated (by American standards) lives. Seeing such a culture made me seriously question certain American values. Moreover, the imperialist nature of our military presence (there was no effort to encourage an interest in Turkish culture among our troops), combined with the fact I felt I was representing a superpower wrongly involved in a war (Vietnam), made even clearer the need to question U.S. principles.

Unfortunately (or fortunately, depending on your perspective), I learned early in the military to distrust parts of the political left. One particularly memorable example happened at Monterey. Many other servicemen in the language school were against the war, and it was not unusual to hear antiwar music playing rather loudly in the barracks. There was one instance, however, that led me to question the ethics of some other antiwar servicemen. One Saturday, outside our barracks, there was a very large formation of Marines who had finished language school and were about to be shipped off to Vietnam/Southeast Asia. One man in my barracks turned his stereo on very loud (clearly audible to those in formation), playing a *Country Joe and the Fish* song with the lyrics "be the first on your block to have your son come home in a box." Many in the barracks thought this funny, but I was already beginning to understand that enlistees were simply pawns in a larger political chess game. Thus I felt that haranguing the Marines about their possible death was immoral.

Putting the brakes on becoming a "pinko" queer: The effects of those military years on my sexuality were generally negative. Though I didn't consciously know or sense I was gay, I knew I wasn't interested in what most men around me were interested in—and I was frequently harassed for that. Starting in basic training and lasting through all four years of service, I would frequently get hassled about "looking" at guys in the showers or restrooms—though I never understood this charge because I didn't realize I was doing it. This hassling, however, was almost always done in a semi-joking manner and thus wasn't too harmful. The first inkling of the more serious difficulties that were to come happened during my brief assignment in central Texas. The Mexican border cities were known for their prostitution, and there was constant pressure to join in on a weekend sex "tour"—my consistent refusal to go did not result in any actual harassment, but it did isolate me somewhat. Later in Germany, when fellow servicemen went to Amsterdam to visit the red-light district, there was again some isolation due to my not joining in the activities and not talking about exploits with women, but there were no real problems. Turkey, however, was a different story. Being in a remote location where there was little potential sexual outlet for the average young servicemen, there were frequent difficulties. In my barracks, there were about three of us who did not spend long hours with others talking about our heterosexual exploits. We thus experienced multiple instances of being shouted at as "you fags" by drunken servicemen, and even a couple of episodes of having to barricade ourselves in rooms with chairs propped against the door as drunken comrades pounded on it, screaming, "I'm going to kill you, you fag." Of course you had to ignore this since reporting it to superiors would have only drawn more attention to us. Besides, the next day you were likely to be working with, or even supervising, the men who had threatened to kill you the night before.

My experiences in the military may have been atypical. In interviews I have conducted over the past few years, many men in the military in the late 1960s had sexual affairs with other military men. The fact that my position required a high security clearance may have had an effect, but many men I've interviewed have also been in positions requiring such authorization. One Korean War–era veteran I've interviewed was at a very high security base but shared a room (and was sexually active) with his lover in the barracks. Only one man I've interviewed got into trouble for his homosexual behavior, though I've known many men over the years who were dishonorably discharged due to sexual activity. Unfortunately, if anyone around me was homosexually active when I was in the air force, I didn't know it.

SEARCHING FOR DIRECTION (AGES TWENTY-THREE TO FIFTY-THREE)

Despite the intellectual curiosity and political awareness sparked by my military experiences, I still felt aimless when I got out. A good part of my direction-lessness probably stemmed from lacking a "map" of my interests. The absence of family curiosity about my life may have played a part in my sense of aim-lessness, but it also played a part in my finally moving on. When I returned to Jacksonville after being discharged, there was very little interest by family or friends in what I had seen or experienced in the previous four years of world travel—or in what I thought about it. There was no discussion of my future—other than assuming I would settle in Jacksonville. It may have been this last part that spurred my returning to college—somehow I sensed I would never have a life of my own if I stayed in Jacksonville. Going away to college (luckily Jacksonville did not have a state-supported university then) was, again, a good excuse for breaking the family tradition of living near home.

My first college after the military, the University of West Florida (Pensacola), was where I got my BA—but that was only the beginning of thirty years (until about 2001) of searching for some way to assemble my life. Over those thirty years I:

- Moved in and out (sometimes more than once) of ten metropolitan areas: Berkeley, California; Binghamton, New York; Bloomington, Indiana; Boston, Massachusetts; Buffalo, New York; Jacksonville, Florida; Los Angeles, California; Pensacola, Florida; San Diego, California; and San Francisco, California,

- Lived in too many different apartments and trailers (seldom for more than a year) to even begin to count—and owned (not simultaneously) two houses and two condominiums,

- Attempted five different college degrees and completed three (BA, Master's in Computer Science, PhD in Sociology),

- Worked for (or consulted with) numerous research companies, commercial businesses, city governments, individual researchers, universities, and the IRS—seldom for more than a year of employment,

- Was an officer or key participant in gay groups in almost every city I lived (except those in Florida),

- Lost contact with my father, had a three-year period of no contact with my mother or brothers, and then returned to a distant but friendly relationship with them,

- Had, depending on how one counts, three or eight lovers,

- Explored public parks, bathhouses, and other gay cruising areas in forty-nine states, four Canadian provinces, and seven other foreign countries.

When looking at this history, I'm very conscious that others might say I was simply restless, lacked direction, or was irresponsible. My own perspective, however, is that much of this movement was due to always having trouble finding a sense of fit, a sense of belongingness—to the problems of a working-class person trying to fit both class and sexuality into a middle- to upper-middle class, overtly heterosexual academic world.

Since covering all the changes I experienced during these thirty years would be a needlessly long task, the rest of this chapter summarizes my sexual and intellectual development during these years. Looking back, finding a place sexually was the main factor through much of that time, so I will start there.

Defining the "pinko" queer inside: I often say it took moving out of the South for me to discover my sexuality. When I returned to Florida after the military, it had been only a year since the Stonewall riots, which are credited with starting the modern gay movement. North Florida, where I lived, had always seemed to have more in common culturally with Georgia and Alabama—areas where gay liberation, or homosexuality at all, was not something talked about in the 1970s. Also, what there was of visible gay life in those days in north Florida was mostly related to drag, and I found men who acted exaggeratedly feminine off-putting. Combined with this conservative environment, I was still somewhat attached to my family (visiting them once a month or more when I lived in Pensacola) and thus I felt uncomfortable doing anything I would have to hide or that would embarrass them (homosexuality was illegal and people did get arrested for it in those days).

It was when I made my first attempt at graduate school, in Binghamton, New York, that I began to get the basic skills needed for integrating my sexuality with the rest of my life. At Binghamton, I tried dating women, but luckily fairly quickly met Garry. Garry somehow managed to get me to try sex with him (November 1973) and we had something of an affair for about four months. As was typical of many men in those days, I first insisted I was just experimenting and possibly bisexual—but gave up that pretense after a couple of months. A fellow graduate student (who was straight) also helped me through coming out—he took me to the one Binghamton gay bar in those days, the "Cadillac Bar and Grill." Quickly the Cadillac became a community center and sort of home for me. It was where I felt comfortable, where I could commiserate with other gay graduate students and campus staff, could begin to know the local community, and meet people further to explore my own sexuality—I still view bars as community centers. I also met (and had a short affair with) Bill, an openly gay faculty member who was only a couple of years older. Besides living in Binghamton, Bill had an apartment in Manhattan and I spent considerable time there learning to negotiate the city, cruise bars, enjoy the baths, and have sex in the abandoned wharfs off the West Side highway. In Binghamton and New York City, I found, among other things, ordinarily masculine men of my own age who were sexually adventurous and intellectually interesting, a broader culture less conservative than Florida, and a long enough distance between my family and me to no longer fear accidental discovery. (Besides, I had entered "alien"—New York—territory, by their standards.)

After Binghamton, I moved around the country many times. Part of the reason for all the geographical movement was a continued seeking of some sort of "gay space" where I was comfortable. The exploration, however, was always intermingled with trying to find an environment that provided meaningful work and educational opportunities. Having been exposed to California in the military, I was particularly drawn to the open spaces of the West and the freedom of gay life in San Francisco. I quickly discovered, though, I couldn't live (emotionally or financially) in the West if I couldn't find meaningful work, and San Francisco was always a difficult place to find employment. Thus, the mid-1970s to the mid-1980s involved a lot of movement trying to find a "gay space" that worked both emotionally and financially for me. During this time, I found the urban leather component of gay life was most comfortable, a discovery that helped in figuring out places I could tolerate living. I made my final move to California in 1984, from Boston. Though Boston had been a better place for me economically, the continued greater openness of gay culture in San Francisco compared to the East, even at the height of the AIDS scare, was a strong part of the attraction of the West Coast.

Distancing myself from my family was also an important component of coming to accept my sexuality. Through my teenage years, the military, and even my time at UWF in Pensacola, I had stayed relatively close with my mother and my brothers.[5] Coming to terms with my sexuality and my intellectualism required not only escaping from the culture of the South, but also from the culture of my family. Being "little brother" (I was the youngest) had never allowed for the independence needed to develop my own life, and any regular contact with my mother always felt like my life was being sucked into her need for someone to give her status. The total lack of interest in my life meant any contact with them was an emotional drain, so it became easiest to put as much distance as possible between them and me. From about 1974 to about 1977, I had no contact with family and they didn't know where I lived, even though I moved across country and back. In about 1977, feeling confident about my sexuality and work, I made contact with the family and slowly developed a level of conversation. Mother was accepting of my sexuality if I had a partner to talk about and introduce her to, but my brothers did not want to hear about my life. Through the 1980s and early 1990s, Mother and I talked about once a month on the phone, and once a year either I would fly to Jacksonville or fly her out to see me—never being able to tolerate visiting for more than four days.

Though I use the term "partner" in talking about negotiating my sexuality with my mother, I was never particularly good at having only one partner. Depending on your definition, I had several "lovers" over the years. Though there were many good times in those relationships and they helped me work through many issues, the relationships were always somewhat problematic for me (and one was tortuous) because I always valued the freedom to explore the world and men around me. Only in my forties did I realize the best situation for me was not having a lover (at least as typically defined). Instead, I was happiest having a small number of close friends to share life's turmoil (and maybe sex once in awhile). This need for a small and intimate, but nontraditional "family" made it quite clear that life worked best for me when I lived in a heavily populated urban setting where alternative lifestyles are easier to maintain. My continued need for the gay environment of very large urban areas became very clear when I moved from San Francisco to San Diego in 1996 for my current teaching position. Though San Diego is a major urban area and has an apparently large, open, and politically involved gay community, the city just wasn't urban enough. In 2000, I moved to Los Angeles (while continuing to teach in San Diego County[6]) and have since developed an open, very extended gay "family" that works best for me.

The "real world" side of becoming a damn intellectual (Part 1):   Finding a fit between my intellectual self and the world in terms of education and employment wasn't much easier than finding my sexuality, and was confounded by a growing interest in intellectual work that could incorporate political activism with my sexuality. During much of the thirty years covered here, activism and "work" were two different tracks, and thus I'll cover them in different sections. In this section I focus on work.

In 1971, when I started on my BA at the University of West Florida (Pensacola), I first majored in accounting. This seemed a logical choice because I had done bookkeeping-related work in my senior year of high school—an accounting degree would lead to a job. Though I made good grades in accounting, I was often depressed[7] and somehow could not see accounting as my future. Fortunately, UWF had a good counseling department and I spent many sessions with them sorting through depression and life choices. Since I had liked a sociology course I took in the military, I decided to try that as a major. I generally enjoyed it, but couldn't fully settle on it and took many courses in my other fields of interests (psychology and philosophy). Luckily, veterans' benefits were enough in those days that I could get by with working part-time, spending time exploring courses, being involved in antiwar activities on campus, and living a more or less "hippie" lifestyle. Since I had taken some college courses in the military and received credit for my language school classes, I finished a BA in May 1972.

In my last semester at UWF, the Internal Revenue Service contacted me about working for them. They were looking for social science majors who had some human-relations skills, and my accounting background and veteran's status gave me a high rank on the civil service test. I started that summer and was sent to a government school in Atlanta to learn the tax code. I started auditing taxpayers in September or so.

I was a good auditor, but quickly became disheartened by a government policy of going after taxpayers who were easiest to audit: those who couldn't afford lawyers. Though the clients I was auditing had technically cheated, most had been misled by corrupt tax preparers. We were picking on struggling people who didn't understand the system and were just trying to get by. The whole process felt immoral. Despite making a very comfortable salary and having good career possibilities, I quit after six months as an auditor—having gained, again, valuable insights into class dynamics.

The experiences with academic exploration at UWF and the disappointment at IRS were symptomatic of the next twenty years. I spent much of the 1980s and 1990s wandering across the country trying different jobs. After I grew frustrated with each one, I would return to school. When I got frustrated with school, I would go back to work. Part of my wandering was due to continued disappointments with finding that institutional goals (like at the IRS) did not match the work actually performed. Part also was because I really wanted to work in an academic setting but my background (the wrong colleges, no connections, poor interpersonal skills) made it difficult to get such jobs. Of course, a major part of this wandering involved finding a place where I was comfortable with my sexuality. This explains the constant shopping for graduate schools, work, and cities.

There were, however, four different changes in that period that affected my life course. The first was in 1976, when after several false starts in various cities, I landed a position as a statistical programmer on a Section 8 housing evaluation project in Boston. Though I had trouble staying with that or any job, statistical and related programming were my main sources of income for the next twenty years. The statistical work typically involved public policy evaluation in some way and thus felt meaningful. It was also mentally challenging and rewarding. My coworkers were always interesting and politically involved people and I typically had considerable flexibility in my work schedule and location. I've never been good at working 9–5, Monday–Friday (a working-class trait?). I'd rather be outside when the sun's up and then work in the evening and into the night.

One reason I had trouble keeping the Boston job (and many other jobs thereafter) was probably my always feeling like an "outsider." A good part of the outsider status came from commonly hearing very educated, intellectual colleagues make broad, gross assumptions about the conservativeness and simplicity of southerners or about the gung-ho patriotism of the military. When I would mention that they were talking about me, many would then conclude I must therefore be sexist and gung-ho militaristic. Another part of the discomfort (and thus outsider status) was simply the presence of relatively subtle class differences in the workplace—disparities when talking about past experiences, an inability to afford a similar lifestyle, and unfamiliarity with the presentation skills required for both work and socializing (I was frequently described as being too abrupt). Of course, there was also the minor problem of sexuality. Though most places I've worked have been supportive of gay men, the expectation that anyone of my professional status would be coupled (or want to be coupled) was obvious (e.g., "bring your partner," "are you seeing anyone?")—somehow it became quite clear "I had a hot time with a couple of guys at the baths" would not be accepted as an appropriate answer to "What did you do last weekend?"

A second key change during those years was my decision in 1980 to go to Indiana University for a PhD in sociology. Though that choice, like many others, was hard to stick with, I eventually finished my IU degree in 1993. It took so long to get the degree because, yet again, I felt out of place in terms of both class and sexuality. When I started IU, I was already in my mid-thirtie's and had experienced big city gay life. At Indiana I quickly became a key person in the gay student group, but secretly felt my own sexuality was being suppressed by having to be a "respectable" gay leader. It was also very difficult in those days to assert that gay topics were intellectually valid—I consistently felt pressure to do more "mainstream" topics.[8] The competition among PhDs in those days made it clear that it would be virtually impossible to obtain a teaching position in a city where I could tolerate living as a mature gay man. When the extent of the AIDS crisis became evident in 1983, I felt both isolated at IU and the need to do something worthwhile for gays in general. Having been sexually active everywhere AIDS was hitting hard, I assumed (this was before the HIV test existed) I had the disease and probably would die early. If that were going to happen, at least it should occur in the sort of urban gay space where I felt at home. So, I left IU after three years of taking classes and, after a short period of working in Boston, moved back to San Francisco.

The third point in my intellectual development was when I landed a position at Stanford as a statistical programmer. This was in 1986. The job was with the Stanford Heart Disease Prevention Program, where I analyzed data evaluating a community-based heart-disease risk intervention. The position was ideal in many ways because it helped me develop my statistical abilities, gave me very strong and direct experience with the processes of conducting large-scale research projects, provided both the work and working environment I like, and allowed me to live in San Francisco in a community of like-minded gay men.

Another benefit of working at Stanford was that I finally found a way academically to combine some of my interests. Health research broadened the number of future job options in general and allowed me to connect my interest in the lives of working-class people to the consequences of the class structure. Realizing I now had something intellectual that worked for me and met my interests in social justice, I contacted faculty at Indiana. I told them about my work at Stanford and my interest in completing my PhD while living in California. I received a positive reply from IU encouraging me to finish the degree. The Stanford position was very helpful in allowing flexibility in my schedule so I could take some necessary courses at Berkeley (for my minor) and complete some papers many years past due at IU.

Though the flexibility at Stanford was helpful for working toward the PhD, I was not comfortable there due to the elitism in the overall campus atmosphere. I left and went to work in research at UC San Francisco. After a yearlong detour due to a tumultuous affair, I completed my dissertation in December 1992 using data on AIDS risk behaviors among gay men that the San Francisco Department of Public Health had gathered.

I enjoyed the research work and my colleagues at UCSF, but I was frustrated with the theoretical approaches used in many of the disease prevention studies I worked on. I generally felt they lacked insight into the breadth of difficulties social class placed on changing behavior. I wanted to be in a teaching position where I could write more freely and be a stronger agent for social change. Unfortunately, as I looked for academic jobs, the problem I encountered at IU was still there—the most promising jobs were usually in small towns where I knew I would be unhappy as an open and sexually active gay male.

The fourth, and final, turning point in this thirty-year odyssey was when a position came open in 1995 in San Diego County at CSU San Marcos. The job was an ideal fit and I applied. I was offered the position and moved to San Diego in July 1996. As many an academic would testify, what seemed like an ideal fit wasn't and the first four years were among the most stressful, in terms of work, I've ever had. But, as I told friends back at UCSF, I also felt I was getting the most respect I have ever received for my work. In the end, the respect and opportunity outweighed the stress and I still hold that position, and will most likely be working there till retirement—though, as noted earlier, I realized my sexuality didn't fit in San Diego and thus moved to Los Angeles to live.

Activism—starting to integrate the "damn intellectual," the "pinko," and the real world (Part 2): It was in this over thirty-year period that my involvement really developed and I could, eventually, connect this activism to my intellectual interests. Making such a union was not easy. Just as in my job world, I saw that even within activists there was a divide between middle-class and working-class standards.

The middle-class nature of activism first became evident to me in the antiwar movement when I was at UWF in Pensacola in the early 1970s. When I tried to become involved in the antiwar movement, I quickly discovered that many campus antiwar activists did not understand the class structure that resulted in some of us becoming veterans. A distrust of veterans combined with a failure to realize the class biases in their organizational efforts meant antiwar activities were not very welcoming for people of lower-class backgrounds, like me. After a few meetings, I dropped out of active participation in the group and simply attended public events.

My early involvement in Gay Liberation activities, in the mid-1970s, worked out much better. When I became involved in the Binghamton Gay

Liberation Front, there was such a dearth of people willing to be out and open that it was easy to be an active member in the organization and feel camaraderie with the core group members. A few years later, working on the San Francisco Gay Pride parade and then Boston Gay Liberation marches, this same egalitarian sense among activists was present. Unfortunately, though I didn't understand it at the time, by the later 1970s there was a growing conflict between the open, egalitarian, and loosely organized Gay Liberation movement and the more structured and conventionally political Gay Pride[9] movement. The first time I became aware of this conflict was when I was living in Boston and working on the committee for the annual march. The 1977 Boston march was primarily a loosely structured gay liberation demonstration with thousands of shouting participants. But, in 1978 and later, there were more debates about what the parade should look like and what types of organizations to include. This stress between liberation and assimilation was surfacing regularly and everywhere in the late 1970s. Even at the *Gay Community News* (where I volunteered and occasionally wrote), there was a frequent but half-hidden argument between presenting and defending what we did versus presenting a more "white bread" portrait of us as "good gays" (e.g., should we write articles protesting police entrapment in the parks?). The early stages of the AIDS epidemic, particularly on the East Coast, saw even more shifting in gay politics away from sexual liberation and toward a more restricted definition of community.

In Boston, I learned my lesson—the characteristics of gay and AIDS organizations were changing in a way that did not fit with my sexuality or my social class. When I moved back to San Francisco, I became involved in AIDS organizations, but I stayed away from any leadership roles that might create conflict between the organization's goals and mine. It wasn't until getting a faculty job at CSU that I found a way again to affect class and sexuality issues. Through teaching, community service, working with gay groups, writing what I wanted, and participating in gay issues in the professional associations (American Sociological Association and Pacific Sociological Association), I could finally integrate work with social change.

ALMOST "PINKO," ALMOST INTELLECTUAL, ALMOST DAMNED

So, after fifty plus years (getting close to sixty!), where am I? In many ways things have settled out well. I've come to accept the reality that my sexuality and my class background are going to frequently leave me feeling like an outsider. More important, I have reached a point where, instead of fretting anxiously over not fitting in with the rest of the world, I use my outside status as a topic of intellectual pursuit and scholarly activism. Part of the reason I can do this is that there is an increasing interest in sociology in the intersection of class and sexual orientation, and thus writing in this area is more accepted. Finding a spot in the California State University system was also a tremendous help—as one of a small number of openly gay faculty on campus, I can bring my own perspective on class and orientation into discussions of sexuality and curriculum. And, because many of my students are first-generation college, I can use my "outside" status to help them think critically about inequality.

Since I present my current situation so positively, why the "almost" in the heading? For one, by the academic standards of many, I'm not quite an intellectual: (1) I'm teaching (and enjoying it) in a university system that is not top ranked, (2) I didn't become a faculty member until age forty-nine, (3) my publications do not appear in the top-ranked journals (and I don't care about that), and (4) I'm not one of the names that's on the tip of everyone's tongue when thinking of gay scholars (I like it that way). My "pinko" (gay political activist) status is questionable as well. As contemporary gay politics moves increasingly toward an assimilationist stance that we're "just like you" (meaning just like straights),[10] I'm finding myself outside what has become the contemporary gay movement (and I prefer to stay on that edge). So, "almost damned" may fit. By stressing that gay sexuality is not quite like it is typically depicted, and by writing and speaking about that, there's a fair chance of my disagreeing with a wide mix of gays, academics, and everyone who has accepted gays because "they're just like us." There's a chance, even, that I'm providing fuel for those who call gays "perverts" (a title I embrace for myself). Am I, then, a gay political activist (a "pinko")? The answer depends on what part of the label one focuses on. If one focuses on "gay," then I'm no longer an activist, since I don't support the current gay political movement. Instead, by continuing to publicly push an agenda of sexual liberation, I've become one of a small number of sex-positive activists who have yet to form into any sort of movement.

Before closing, three important clarifications should be included in the story presented here. One is that it hasn't been as easy a ride through life as it may sound. Having reached a fairly comfortable position *and* having reached an age and security where I don't let things stress me out as much as they used to, it is possible to write this in a fairly positive tone that suggests a life of relative easygoing wandering that eventually fell together. Things have not been that simple. Like all lesbians and gays, I experienced plenty of homophobic verbal and physical threats in high school, in the military, and subsequently as an adult—including having guns pulled on me and having a concussion and a year of inability to work from what was probably a homophobic attack (the concussion left me with no memory of what happened).

In many ways far more difficult, however, was the complete lack of interest and even hostility by family regarding my intellectual and personal development. I was never asked about my studies and thus never went to any of my own graduation ceremonies since no family members would come (which sometimes makes attending my students' ceremonies emotionally difficult). And, of course, the complete lack of interest by family in my personal life was disheartening for many years. Thankfully, with the death of my mother in 2002, all stressful pressures to maintain connections with the rest of the family have ended and we haven't spoken since just after her funeral. It is occasionally stressing to think that relatives may have died without my knowing it, and that my own death would go unnoticed by family. But that's not unusual for many working-class gays I have known.

Adding to the stresses faced by many gays, my wandering from job to job also took its toll, causing frequent periods of anxiety as to whether I would ever have financial stability or find a niche in life. The sense of not fitting in with the gay community made developing friendship networks more difficult and resulted in long periods of feeling alone. Luckily, all of that started resolving in my late forties.

A second clarification is that, though I stress the importance of leaving the South as part of coming out intellectually and sexually, I've not elaborated on the extent the South has remained a part of me. The fatalism of blue-collar southern culture has always been a part of me and clearly has been both an obstacle in finding direction and a benefit in dealing with life's blows. Clearly too, the lazy, fluid, sweaty, sensuality of the South (before air-conditioning) is an integral part of my own sexuality. These charms of southern culture have clearly been a detriment as well. I've a habit in both academic and activist circles of coming out not only as gay, but also as blue-collar background, a military veteran, and as a native southerner. The combination clearly sets people off into a collection of assumptions that I'm racist, right-wing patriotic, and sexually irresponsible. I try to use such responses as teachable moments to talk about how stereotypes are used to obscure the rich variety behind labels such as "southerner," but it's often difficult to move people away from putting those categories into their perception of who I am.

The third clarification is that the story I've presented could be taken as assuming an essentialist perspective on becoming homosexual:[11] the supposition that I believe I was born a homosexual and that homosexuality's effects on the rest of my life were unavoidable. This is not true; I don't think people are born homosexual and I don't find the scientific evidence on this point very convincing. However, I do believe various environmental, social, emotional, and biological factors interact in such a way, frequently very early in childhood but sometimes later in life, to cause a very strong desire for same-sex emotional and sexual relations. Thus, I don't think homosexuality was something that existed in me at birth and affected my life course. Instead, I feel the various factors described in this chapter, plus some not described, fell together in such a way as to affect my orientation toward same sex partners.

EPILOGUE: "IT'S NOT ALL ABOUT ME"

One thing that both working-class people and many gays learn to do when in a room of strangers is avoid drawing attention to themselves. Why then go out on a limb and put my own personal history up for public view?

Though the very notion of working-class gay *academics* suggests that it is possible to rise above class and sexual stigma into middle-class academia, I hope my own story (which is similar to the stories of many other men and women I've known) illustrates that it is relatively rare for all the circumstances of life to fall into place and make such success possible—and even then it can take many, many years to achieve this end. Thus, I feel personal stories, such as my own, are important in illustrating how class and sexual stigma (including from one's own sexual community) operate. Ideally, out of such stories, there will be more concern for resolving the systemic cultural, sexual, and economic inequities of society.

NOTES

1. Due to the history of anti-intellectualism in my background, I'm treating the words "intellectual" and "academic" as relatively equal—though it is easy to argue that many academics are not intellectuals (and vice versa).

2. In the 1950s South, being called "pinko" could be labeling you as a Communist/ Socialist ("Commie") or a homosexual. Since one way to make "Commies" seem completely detestable was to label them queer, the double meaning was more effective.

3. There's a theory that gays are more likely to turn to books and the arts due either to curiosity about their sense of difference or as a need to escape from pushes to conform (see Barrett, Pollack, and Tilden 2002).

4. All nonfamily names are pseudonyms.

5. My father and I exchanged letters when I was in high school and in the military. I saw him a couple of times in the early 1970s and then did not see him again except once in about 1980. In that meeting, I tried to come out to him, but he did not seem to hear me. I never spoke to him again and did not attend his funeral.

6. Many openly gay faculty members I know report living far from their campuses.

7. Clearly, some of the depression was due to my suppressed sexuality, but much of it was also caused by feeling adrift in general.

8. A late 1990s survey of LGBT Sociology PhD students found that many still felt their faculty viewed "gay topics" as not quite real subjects.

9. The change in language from calling it "gay liberation" to "gay pride" is itself an interesting question, apparently reflecting the shift from demanding acceptance for who we are, to demanding acceptance that we're not really different except in the sex of our partners.

10. The term "heteronormative" is frequently used to define this movement toward promoting the image of gay relationships as similar to nongay relationships in structure (i.e., dyadic and monogamous).

11. I use the term "homosexual" here instead of "gay" to denote relatively base-level sexual and emotional needs. "Gay" refers more to how we organize our lives to meet those needs.

REFERENCE

Barrett, Donald C., Lance M. Pollack and Mary L. Tilden (2002). "Teenage Sexual Orientation, Adult Openness, and Status Attainment in Gay Males." *Sociological Perspectives,* 45(2): 163–182.

TWELVE

Weaving the Self with Gender

Uniting Race, Sexual Orientation, and Social Class

TERELL P. LASANE

When I broach the idea of "self-concept" to students in my Introductory social psychology class, I use a popular exercise called the *Twenty Statements Test*. Students are asked to reflect on the question, "Who Am I" and complete the statement: "I am _____" with twenty self-descriptive statements. This exercise invariably generates considerable discussion about aspects of personal identities most salient to individuals. Although the *Twenty Statements Test* is widely used in classroom demonstrations, I did not complete this exercise when I began studying social psychology. When I started writing this chapter, I guessed at how I might have approached my self-description at age twenty-one, when I took my first social psychology class. I decided my self-descriptors would have included the following: "I am black, gay, and financially challenged." These dimensions of my self-concept have been salient for much of my life. As I write my reflections, I revisit scattered recollections from the 1980s. In the fall of 1980, I was entering my final year of middle school. The pejorative din of my classmates still rings in my head and reminds me of the multiple identities that shape my life:

"*Faggot! Sissy! He walks like a girl. He talks like a girl. They say he is funny.*"
"*He thinks he's white. He talks white, acts white, he even dresses white.*"
"*Look at how he dresses. Can't your mother afford real clothes?*"

THE FABRIC OF MY LIFE

I am the third of four children born to a family in which my father was a noncommissioned diesel mechanic in the air force. My mother was a housewife who entered the food service industry and later the hotel service industry when my three siblings and I were preteens. I was proud of my father and my family's history. My parents encouraged me to believe I could do anything I wanted. My mother's emotional support and spiritual inspiration were especially instrumental to my academic success, including being the first college graduate in my family. My family was poor. I didn't feel poor given my parents' and siblings' love, support, and encouragement.

My parents separated in early 1980. Later that year, my siblings and I lived with my mother in my parents' hometown of Plantersville, South Carolina, a rural, racially segregated section of Georgetown, South Carolina. As a "military brat," I was accustomed to being a racial minority in the multicultural communities where we lived. My siblings and I were usually the "only person of color" in our classes at school. This changed dramatically in Plantersville. The segregated community where my parents were reared was unaffected by the racial integration of the previous three decades. Even today the community's racial lines are clearly drawn. The unspoken message is clear: "Blacks and whites do not belong together." It was the loudest unspoken message I had ever heard. My entrance into an all-black school for the last five years of my secondary education made my race, social class, and sexual orientation of paramount importance in my adolescent development.

Adolescence is confusing for most people. According to the stage theories proposed by developmental psychologists, the bridge between childhood and adulthood is characterized by psychosocial steps one must negotiate in establishing "Who am I?" Most youngsters successfully establish their sexual orientation, personal value systems, and career/occupational goals during these years. I had to resolve these dilemmas within the hostile framework of a gender-biased world. Because I was feminine, I suffered dearly for violating a societal script that defined expectations regarding how boys *should* behave. I was called names: faggot, sissy, funny, white acting, stuck-up, a nerd, a bookworm, a teacher's pet, a brainiac, and exceptional, just to name a few. In sum, I was made to feel very different. The whole time I lived in South Carolina and for most of my time at Howard University, I knew I was very different, and I wondered where I belonged. I was a profoundly lonely youth. Adolescence is marked by perceptions of being misunderstood, but somehow I realized I far transcended the term's usual parameters. I knew by virtue of my immutable social identities (race, sexual orientation, and social class) I would somehow always feel on the edge: different and alone. Revisiting that difficult period of my life has reawakened anxieties, pain, and feelings of despair that seem as raw today as they were twenty years ago. Examining these issues as a social psychologist, human rights activist, feminist, and avid multiculturalist has allowed me to reexamine this part of my life in a way that brings rhyme and reason to it. Still, it does not dilute the deep pain I experienced then. The social rejection I felt during those years has made me who I am today. But now I better understand what was happening to me in my adolescence.

The self is a tapestry of various textures and colors woven from social experience. In my life, gender has been the defining thread for integrating who I am, the person I celebrate and share today. To grow up poor, of color, and nonheterosexual in our society makes assembling my tapestry a little more difficult. Gender, I submit, provides a framework to appreciate the inextricable linkages among the various aspects of my identity.

GENDER AND RACIAL IDENTITY

My racial identity happened without dramatic existential contemplation. I did not experience what many racial identity theorists describe as the *encounter* stage of development. This encounter stage means someone recognizes for the first time "I am black and this is a socially meaningful dimension in my life." My parents socialized us with a strong pride in our African American heritage. I did not have to discover through some horrific incident at school that being black denoted some meaningful social difference in my life. My parents gave us a spirit of racial pride and helped us appreciate the diversity of human ethnic experience. I was taught to make social decisions based on values transcending race. My siblings and I always had a diverse group of peers. We celebrated these differences and did not rank people by their ethnicity. In seventh grade, a white boy called me *nigger*. I was shocked because I had only heard this word used as a playful term among relatives or as a pejorative epithet in past historical periods on a television documentary or docudrama. Before I could respond, my white peers in this Michigan junior high school were openly chastising my assailant. My offender became a temporary pariah at school. White classmates' words of support were overwhelming. They gave me optimism about the possibilities of harmonious race relations.

Ironically, a heightened awareness of my racial identity was imparted to me in a "trial by fire" episode during my years at the all-black high school I attended for grades eight through twelve. From my first day on campus, I felt like an outsider. Before that first day, I was giddy with excitement about the prospect of *not* being the only black in the classroom. My excitement was short-lived. From the first time I spoke, my peers showered me with barbs. They saw me as an outsider who wanted to be "white." Most other students spoke a strong southern dialect, which I appreciated. My mother and father retained many elements of this dialect, even after over twenty years of traveling abroad. So I welcomed the familiar, comfortable, and beautiful speech of my peers. When I spoke at school, however, I was marked as an "Oreo": black on the outside and white within. Other students would say,

"He talks so white." They would say, "He thinks he's better than us. He is always trying to be something he is not."

This rejection was painful. My family had taught me to accept differences. I was shocked at how much other students disliked my speech pattern. I knew none of the various peer groups would accept me simply because I "acted white." A few years ago, I was paradoxically comforted and distressed when my good friend, a cultural educational anthropologist, Signithia Fordham, coined the term "racelessnenss" to describe the widespread phenomenon in the educational experiences of African Americans whose educational attainment (speech style, enthusiasm for learning, high academic achievement, investment in educational outcomes) moves them toward "acting white." Had I known this at age fourteen, I might have better handled being ostracized.

During that time, I *really* wanted to belong to a social group. I did have many acquaintances. I was outgoing, affable, and accepting, so my experience was not as difficult as it could have been. When I discuss this period of my life with other gay male African Americans who also grew up in rural, segregated environments, I know how lucky I was. Unlike them, I had a solid support group. Fortunately, because of my large, stocky frame, I did not experience much physical intimidation or physical aggression. Given my academic performance and outgoing personality, I had earned the support, admiration, and respect of many wonderful teachers.

Not surprisingly, my friendly relationship with the school's teachers and administrators did not endear me with my peers. The county where I resided was near the bottom of educational achievement in South Carolina, which was near the bottom of national achievement indices. I defied every stereotype many of my teachers (black and white) had about black males. I was soft-spoken, non-athletic, emotionally expressive, and naturally interpersonally sensitive. I was feminine.

During this time, most of my friends were females, and so were my teachers, who often called me a "sweet, nice young man." Of course, this further alienated me from my peers, who considered me "not black enough" for their tastes. Every day in school, I was reminded I was not black enough. My peers ridiculed my vocabulary, how I responded to literature I read in English class, and my soft-spoken, nurturing, and interpersonal style. I was mocked whenever I said, "You guys. . . ." To make matters worse, my teachers further alienated me from other students by saying these very traits made me exemplary.

Clearly, my socialization in multicultural environments led to my black peers rejecting me outright and with hostility. Had I followed the standard expectations of how black men are supposed to behave, my life would have been much easier. My brother, who is one year younger, was also a high-achieving student, but did not experience the rejection I did, probably because he was much more masculine and less emotionally expressive.

I am sure my racial identity was intimately linked to my gendered behavior. My female friends would refer to me by the wrong pronoun. They would say things like, "Girl . . . I mean boy . . . you know what I mean." These errors never offended me. I felt a kinship with women I rarely experienced with men.

In African American communities, the prescriptions for masculine behavior may be more pronounced than among other ethnic groups due to the historical emasculation of black males through various forms of disenfranchisement. My mannerisms deviated sharply from these traditional notions of blackness. "Cool Pose Theory" (Majors and Billison 1992) describes the importance of masculinity in African American culture. That so many people have questioned my racial identity is testimony to this theory.

Recently, I was talking with an African American male teacher. He interrupted me mid-sentence and said, "Why don't you stop talking so white and can you even try to sound more butch?" It was not coincidental that he paired my racial identity with gender identity and found them annoying. I said I was not trying to sound one way or another. I was just being me. This incident reminded me how my gendered speech defies stereotyped images of black men and how I have suffered and benefited from these assumptions. I have come to expect the looks of shock, surprise, and embarrassment when someone I have spoken to on the phone sees me in person for the first time. There I am: A large-framed, dark-skinned African American man, not the white person they expected. Many of these people, both black and white, have said, in poor taste, "Oh my goodness. You sound so white on the phone. I didn't expect you to be black." I usually reply with, sarcastic levity, "But I am black. That is all I have ever been, or want to be."

The fact so many people interpret my feminine behavior as "white" is curious. Conversations with various white people help me understand how this schema might affect social perception. Often someone will say a black person is too "aggressive" or "not very warm." This comment reveals a lot about the speaker. Such gender bias is at the center of prejudice against members of certain ethnic groups. African American men and women are called "too direct" or not "soft enough." Conversely, when other races enter the African American community they are described as "fake" or "too soft." Ironically, given my personality and manner of speaking, my experiences in the African American community have given me a feeling of "black deficiency." Still, I will welcome the day when I do not have to defend my genuine racial pride against the narrow view of how all black men are supposed to act. I will relish the time when everyone can express themselves in ways that provide optimal personal growth and development.

GENDER AND SOCIAL CLASS

While racial identity has affected much of my life, social class has too. In our society, social class as a facet of identity is paradoxically ubiquitous and invisible. I sometimes regard the discussion of class consciousness as "the elephant in the living room." The sanctions against class prejudice are not as defined in our culture as are race, ethnic, or gender prejudice, although we cannot disentangle social class from these dimensions of our self. Accordingly, my sense of my social class was not a salient aspect of my identity. I did not recognize I was economically disadvantaged. I was never hungry or without shelter or clothing. I was happy as a nonmaterialistic person and I did not experience perceptions of relative deprivation.

My social class awareness started flowering in 1985 when I enrolled as an undergraduate at Howard University, the well-regarded historically black school in Washington, D.C. Social class identity was quite different from racial identity awareness. Race is a physical, visible characteristic that is clear in our society. Class and sexual orientation are not. There I was attending classes with students who were third- or fourth-generation college graduates, often the sons and daughters of doctors, lawyers, and other highly paid professionals. I began to appreciate the benefits of being born to economic privilege. At Howard, I was discriminated against because of my social class origin, not my race. I was on the periphery of a privileged class of black students who had fancy cars, expensive clothes, private school educations, and lots of money. I remember one especially painful episode that exposed the difference between our two worlds: It was when I went to Western Union to send my mother scholarship money to pay her high phone bill. I had been very homesick and had "reached out and touched" too often. While in line to send money, I saw several of my classmates were there to receive their monthly parent-sent rewards. Not only was it shocking to see all these students lining up to collect their family allotments, the amounts surprised me. They were getting as much money as my mother got each month from my father's military pay.

Many people at Howard assumed I was from a privileged class simply because of my manner of speaking. The same style of speaking that had previously led to accusations of "acting white" was now, ironically, the same cue that led to my being allowed to mingle with the many elite social class students at Howard. When they asked what my mother and father did for a living, I told them matter-of-factly that my mother worked in the hotel service industry and my father was a mechanic in the military. I was proud of what my parents had accomplished and the sacrifices they made to support my personal and academic development. My peers were uncomfortable with my personal revelations. Their conspicuous consumption suddenly aroused my sense of how class privilege is an invisible marker but one with *significant* social force. Until I witnessed the carefree financial lifestyle my Howard peers enjoyed, I never realized I had such humble origins.

During my first year at college, I learned that one of my closer friend's parents were of the same socioeconomic stratum as mine. I was appalled when I heard that he had fabricated a middle-class identity that tripled his family income. I didn't understand why someone would feel obligated to misrepresent himself this way, especially when the differences were based on accident of birth. My friend was equally appalled I was so naïve about the importance of class.

I was particularly struck by the conspicuous consumption that characterized the life of the Howard coeds. I walked along the campus grounds seeing women headed to class dressed as if they were going to Fortune 500 company interviews. Likewise, my peers drove cars that were usually fancier than the nicest one my wealthiest relative drove. My peers would often run up restaurant bills for one person that would readily feed my entire family at the places they usually went.

The same social class theme persisted beyond graduate school. The hotel chain I was working for while I was a graduate student opened a property in the town where I currently live and teach. I was interested in making extra money on weekends, plus there were the added benefits of discounted hotel rates, which would have helped a lot when I traveled to professional conferences. I applied and was hired to be the weekend breakfast attendant for this local hotel's complimentary continental breakfast. Perhaps not surprisingly, more than a few colleagues and administrators raised their eyebrows when I took this position. This episode profoundly affected my understanding of social class bias. To patrons, I was just a black man in food service, a common stereotype of who works as a breakfast attendant. My role rendered me invisible to most patrons. Most guests would not even look me in the eye when saying the coffee was low or the buffet did not have enough cinnamon-raisin bagels. However, when someone staying at the hotel asked questions about the college, the front desk personnel would send the person to me, a professor at that school! Respect, admiration, and even humility in some cases, replaced my invisibility as a breakfast host. West (1993) is right to say "race matters." But so is hooks (2000) who says "class matters." Class is at least as important as race. In some instances, such as the hotel episode, class transcends race, since many patrons who changed their ways toward me were black.

Let me give another example of class trumping race. When I moved to the integrated (65 percent white, 35 percent nonwhite) town where I now reside, I was regarded as a black man who often walked his miniature pinscher, "Peanut." In those first days in my new community, my fellow dog-walkers were often distant and aloof when I spoke to them in the mornings. Later a white woman I had seen for nearly three months overheard a conversation I was having with a friend. She inferred that I was a professor at the Public Honors College of Maryland. Her demeanor toward me changed instantaneously. Ever since, she talks to me every time I see her. Before, she never spoke to me and didn't respond to my greetings and pleasantries. I had moved from being a black male who probably worked in a low-status job to a neighbor of high occupational prestige. Moreover, she now felt comfortable talking to me about the "ghetto-, poor white-, or welfare-trash" driving down our property values. Every time I heard one of her classist tirades, I realized sometimes class transcends race. She is ostensibly not bothered by my blackness, or my gayness. I am okay in her eyes because I have a PhD and my salary exceeds hers. I want to tell her the people she calls trash are the same folks I grew up with. Some are family members who are responsible for my success. Instead, I allow myself to listen and learn about the enormous impact of social class.

As a college student, the nation's progressive, economically vibrant capital taught me one had to play the part to reap the social rewards of the American social caste-like system. The friend who felt his parents' modest social station required that he overstate their socioeconomic status would take me shopping for new clothes. He said my present wardrobe was inadequate. After we had become closer friends, he intimated that my apparel was downright hideous and needed serious overhauling. He said my penchant for intellectualism gave me an edge over other socially mobile recruits to the privileged class, the one he aspired to. Still, he said I needed an "extreme makeover" on the outside if I were really to join this group.

After two semesters of my friend's "finishing school," I was ready for my high-society debut. I disappointed my mentor. As he was leading me through this Pygmalion transformation, I started exploring philosophy and sociology. I began rejecting our society's narcissism and conspicuous consumption. The suggestion I needed to hide any aspect of myself was unsettling. I was gaining pride in my less privileged economic background. It was becoming a conscious part of my identity. Further, I was growing to dislike the accoutrements of upper-middle-class society. After three years of friendship, he and I parted ways. He could not convince me I should suppress the details of my social origins (or, later, my sexuality). I would no longer accept his intolerance for difference in this world. The dissolution of our friendship was one of the saddest events in my life, as this happened on the eve of my coming out as a gay male. It was not the last friendship I would lose. My insights as an educator help me again to appreciate the contributions of gender in this process.

Gender roles are also implicated in the social classes individuals are linked to. Masculinity is marked by instrumentality, competence, and agency. Men can use powerful speech, powerful dress, self-promotion, intimidation, and competition to obtain their ends. My college friend was training me toward a more masculine interpersonal style. He often said my sensitivity, communalism, and passivity would thwart my opportunities. He and I reached an impasse. Although I do not have a problem with the behavioral tendencies associated with masculine socialization, I again decided to behave in ways I was most comfortable.

Just as I would not change my speech, to downplay my interest in academics, or act more masculine and thus become more popular, a "more black" male in school, I would not change my self-concept just to gain more economic rewards. I kept being myself. I knew I was violating gender norms and this would probably limit my opportunities, but I was also preserving and affirming my own identity. I had shown my true personality when I sent my mother some of my scholarship money versus buying a $40 tie and $95 shoes. Although I knew it would come at a price, I decided just to be myself. This would make me unique and comfortable and that was good enough for me.

I know our world rewards masculinity. In the movie, *Dolores Claiborne*, based on the Stephen King novel of the same name, principal character Vera Donovan tells her devoted companion, "Dolores, it's a depressingly masculine world we live in." Each day I see the link between gender and social class (wealth, power, and prestige). Vera is right. I am comfortable as an academic and thus I do not need all these values of the masculine world. Although I could make a much higher salary and have greater social power working for a corporation, I want to teach a liberal arts curriculum. My profession allows me to instruct the same leaders who may change the world so that ethnic minorities, sexual minorities, and economic underclass members are not rendered invisible, as happened to me when I was viewed as just a "breakfast host" versus a "college professor." My family members and professional friends marvel that I would squander my education on a job paying so little. Few understood why someone with a doctorate in social psychology would not want more wealth. If I worked for a corporation, I would have *both* wealth and a prestigious job.

One of the most satisfying aspects of academic life has been my same-sex friendships with men. In academics, men are not as restrained by gender role expectations. I have had close friendships with other academic men of various ethnic backgrounds, sexual orientations, and social classes. Higher education allows its members to express themselves more freely without regard to ethnic or sexual stereotypes. My colleagues are also not as preoccupied with the usual symbols that would show their wealth and power. Many friends from college have jobs paying more than I make, but they seem obsessed with material objects, such as cars, homes, clothing, and so forth. To me, these things say nothing about the person's real value. I feel distant from these once close friends. They don't understand my value system and I don't understand theirs. I know my views on class put me in the minority. I'm accustomed to being in the minority.

GENDER AND SEXUAL ORIENTATION

In our society, homosexuals, as a minority group, have had an arduous time finding self-acceptance. Being a gay male is an essential part of my personality. More than any other aspect of my self-concept, my sexual orientation has been an obstacle to achieving a well-integrated self.

For most of my life, I have been castigated for being feminine. Being feminine is considered especially inappropriate for black males in our society. I knew my detractors' criticisms masked something more insidious than femiphobia, or a disdain for feminine behavior. I knew from seeing the shame and embarrassment in their eyes that my parents, siblings, and close friends feared I was homosexual. For much of my life, I had the same phobia. I came out as a gay male two weeks shy of my twenty-first birthday. I was a college junior and a close friend helped me realize I was never going to find the right girl. Obviously, he was right, as I had never dated or had any genuine interest in women. When I was forced to confront my sexual attraction to men, I knew this was not just a phase I was going through. When I acknowledged these facts, in turn, I thought my life was over. More important, I *wanted* my life to end.

Until then, I had been taunted and teased with the insinuation of my homosexuality. Although I did not have a homosexual experience until I was twenty-one, this prospect humiliated me for as long as I could remember. Finally acknowledging my sexual orientation seemed a fate worse than death to me.

For years, family members, my friends, and people on television had spoken ill of homosexuals. These speakers were cruel and relentless. Even my dear mother, who loved and accepted everyone, or so I thought, had little tolerance for homosexuals. She, like most of my family, considered homosexuality a disease, or, in religious terms, a "demon spirit." I vividly recall the disdaining scowl my oldest sister registered upon hearing someone might be homosexual. In high school, somebody began a rumor that I might be gay. My brother confronted me after hearing the rumor. His obvious anxiety told me he would not accept my coming out. I listened with great interest one day when some of my college roommate's friends came into our room and discussed all the disgusting prospects for "queers and queens" in our local residential community. I was silent, scared, and ashamed.

I had no model for a healthy coming out. I was alone. I was afraid. Still, there was no denying I was gay. When I came out to my family, my brother cried. He acted as if I had contracted a rare, incurable, and terminal illness. In many people's minds, I suppose, I had. I knew my family loved me and would not stop loving me. But I wanted more than their love and tolerance. I deserved more. I wanted acceptance. I wanted the freedom to be myself. I wanted to talk about my sexuality as easily as they discussed their hetero-sexuality. They could not understand that. They were fine with "it" as long as I suppressed it and did not flaunt it. It was as if my family had instituted a "Don't Ask, Don't Tell" policy.

My family never did understand how humiliating it was/is to be treated this way—as a second-class citizen. Heterosexism is rendering all other forms of sexual behavior invisible and inferior. The degree to which heterosexism is ingrained in our culture sometimes shows itself through hostile, overt means. My heterosexist family members are not overly antagonistic to me. Many of my friends are not as fortunate. They must deal with outright hostility and rejection from their families. When I had a lover several years ago, I knew not to bring him home to a family gathering or to have a picture of him in my house. I waited for years for my mother to invite my partner and me home to Thanksgiving dinner. She knew I had spent several previous Thanksgivings with his family. Each time I spoke to my family I longed for them to ask about him. I wanted them to acknowledge the gifts he gave them or his concern for their welfare. This validation never came. Long after we broke up and he died of AIDS, I wanted my family to send a card to his family. I wanted them to offer condolences or ask how this was affecting me. Eventually, I came to understand their heterosexism would always make this aspect of my life invisible. I admitted their support would never come. When my little niece comes to visit my house, my family had made it clear I must put gay literature and gay-themed pictures away, lest she realize her uncle is gay.

There were many other gay men at Howard. Several had girlfriends and were leading what novelist E. Lynn Harris called "an invisible life." Those who were exclusively gay could only be that way in the so-called safety of underground communities of gay clubs and nightlife, where alcohol abuse, drug abuse, and unsafe, random sexual encounters abound. I internalized my hatred of homosexuals. I am ashamed to say I refused to befriend any gay person who might betray my "dirty secret." The underground gay community had a code: (1) Only come out to other gay men, (2) Don't sleep with flaming queens, (3) Never go to gay bars near the campus or where heterosexuals might see you, (4) Always act butch, and (5) Never call yourself gay. Today, in African American communities these rules are called being "on the down-low." Until then, I had never discriminated against anyone because of gender mannerisms, nor did I try to suppress my own naturally feminine tendencies. Suddenly, however, I was afraid of being exposed, so I followed these rules.

This was when a spiral of self-hatred and self-destruction began. When I was coming out, gay men had sex in the most humiliating ways and places. There was always the fear of being exposed. We lusted after one another, but we did not mention our sexual intimacies. Because we were not really gay and not really having sex, we did not discuss safe sex in the early days of the AIDS pandemic. When I came out, I was unhappy with my life—more so than I had ever been. The sexual self I had ignored throughout my adolescence was suddenly awakened in my young adulthood. Still, I never felt more empty or alone. My intimate encounters were filled with game-playing rituals that made me feel like the "man" in the relationship. I needed something dramatic and powerful to save me from my ever-increasing unhappiness. I found the answer in two simple words: so what?

Many factors converged to lead me to this new self-awareness, including my philosophical questioning of the meaning of sexuality, an interest in prejudice and discrimination derived from social psychology literature, my deep reserves of inner strength and resiliency, and the love and support of phenomenal gay friends who provided the models I so desperately needed. I started evolving into a person who could view his sexuality as one of his immutable aspects, just like his social class, race, and shoe size. My sexual orientation is part of me, nothing to be ashamed of. So what if I'm gay? So what if I desire romantic intimacy with men? So what if I'm a minority? I had been a minority all my life and I am none the worse for wear. So what! So what! So what! Those two words changed my life in ways I cannot explain.

I read books that said anti-gay bigotry had the same structural elements as other familiar prejudices. My self-hatred and self-pity had blinded me to this until I said "So what?" With this new awareness, I decided to no longer fall prey to the age-old brainwashing tactic of telling people from oppressed groups they are inherently deficient and responsible for their own plight; the majority is right to hate *them*! Those in power were the problem. I was not. I began finding solace in being me, as I had done so many times before. I would be myself and be proud of who I am. This straightforward idea has sustained me. It has helped me acknowledge the self I always was. Accepting my homosexuality, a characteristic my gender mannerisms had predicted, made me free in virtually every aspect of life. I no longer had to feel ashamed of how I spoke, behaved, laughed, cried, or dressed. I no longer had to apologize for the books I read, the movies I enjoyed, the music I listened to, or the celebrities and protagonists I admired. I did not have to be ashamed of who I am.

My coming out was not easy. It was distressing and happened painstakingly gradually. There were bumps in the road, as well as setbacks. There were casualties along the way. I lost many close friends and even former partners to AIDS. Some other close friends and family decided the only way to deal with me was *not* to deal with my sexuality. One of my closest college friends said my coming out meant I would never ascend to high society. He never accepted my sexuality. Many gay friends quit talking to me, fearing I might "out" them. All these losses saddened, hurt, angered, and demoralized me. Nevertheless, by coming out I recaptured something that had guided me through my adolescence and still charts my course: by being true to myself without apology, regret, or conditions, I was loving myself unconditionally. This was my curse and blessing all at once. I have been rebelling against a power structure that pigeonholes people based on some normative gender standard. I have become a proud black, gay male educator who is of humble socioeconomic origins.

TYING IT ALL TOGETHER

Gender roles are a prison warden presiding over ethnic minorities, the economically disenfranchised, and sexual minorities. These overseers restrict our freedom of expression. My sense of self has revolted against these tyrannical power mongers. I have mostly escaped their shackles. I avoid associating with anyone who makes me feel self-conscious or ashamed of any aspect of my gendered self. I mostly avoid friends or family who request I behave in certain ways while I am with particular groups or who deem certain aspects of my life "off limits." I now embrace my sexuality, a sexuality that was once the source of so much humiliation and shame. I had no alternative when enduring these insults as a child. As an adult, I have a choice. Today, I surround myself with those who only expect me to be myself. I had no clear sense of my sexuality when my youthful peers were taunting me. Back then, more than anything I feared their accusations were true. I was labeled gay because of my feminine ways. My society taught me being gay was horrible. I ran from this fate till I finally realized I could not run from myself. As the song says, "There is no place to hide." When I accepted my true self, I found peace. I discovered new and real friends. I sometimes found romance. But I realized the most important thing of all: self-love. Of course, I also encountered rejection, hatred, closed-mindedness, hostile exclusion, and social distancing. I endured these things simply by looking at my own androgyny, my ability to show masculine and feminine elements irrespective of biological designations these gender dimensions supposedly signify.

As a man, I have always felt comfortable showing my expressiveness and my instrumentality, corresponding respectively to feminine and masculine gender role orientations. I found my home in higher education. The academy released me from gender conformity. Most of my college colleagues are open to diversity, including sexual orientation. This empowered me to be me. I do not worry that someone will think I sound too white, or I want to be something I am not, or I think I am better than someone else. I do not have to impress people with my knowledge of upper-class customs and tastes. Most of my colleagues do not care about the car I drive, the type of home I own, or whether I have designer shoes, slacks, or curtains. I can speak freely about my sexuality, about my partner. I can do these things in the spirit of genuine acceptance, not mere tolerance. At the academy, I do not have to suppress any of my identity. Most colleagues embrace the diversity of the human experience. They do not stand behind religious, political, or social ideology to defend their prejudice and bias against members of one or more groups. In higher education, I can be what I have always wanted to be: *me.*

I know academia is often considered an abstract place that holds little promise for practical good and bettering the human condition. I lament this. One of my most passionate causes as a professor of social psychology is making the disciplines we teach more practical. Academic life saved me. I would not have continued writing books and articles without the benefit of knowing about a wide array of subjects ranging from social psychology, to feminist theory, to political theory, to sociological theory, to biology, and so forth. The knowledge I have gained from these fields has saved me from a self-loathing I was falling into several years earlier. My scholarly experiences have further enhanced my appreciation for the beauty of diversity everywhere. My research has helped me understand my shame and my prejudice. I have learned "Different is not deficient." My students say I help them see and appreciate the importance of social justice and proactive leadership on political questions.

I am lucky. Every day I appreciate my education. I thank my parents for helping instill a passion for learning that has, ironically, sometimes distanced me from them and others who have not been educated toward introspection and philosophical inquiry. Consequently, they suffocate in a space that prohibits the inhalation of self-acceptance and acceptance by others. I know the price of hate, bias, and discrimination. I see how the isms of our society (racism, sexism, classism, heterosexism, ageism, and ethnocentrism) stifle our potential. As an educator, I want to believe in a world of greater tolerance, love, and hope. The writings of other contributors to this volume further my belief such things are possible. I am always encouraged by others who have had similar experiences and have emerged triumphant. I am glad I can help others find their way to self-acceptance as they unravel their emerging identities. I am not perfect. I have not figured everything out. Still, I am humbled and proud to share my odyssey to self-esteem and self-love. I hope my story will spare others from at least some of the same pain and disappointment I experienced along the way.

I have described my identities as a gay, black male who grew up poor. These factors have greatly affected my life and my identity. These elements have shaped the tapestry of my life, and this is an apt metaphor because tapestries are vivid reminders of our potential beauty. A tapestry is incomplete and its beauty diminished if one removes a color or isolates one part of the total picture. Tapestry, like the individual, is best viewed as an integrated whole, not with the different components standing alone. I recently had a dispute with a friend who said: "I don't see you as gay, as black, or as anything but a person." He was surprised when I replied, "When you fail to see me as gay or black, you fail to see me at all." The notion of colorblindness is utopian—it implies a place where everyone is judged only by the content of their character. But life is still not that way. We live in a world in which people are denied civil rights based on their ethnicity, sexual orientation, and socioeconomic status. Too often, certain individuals are simply overlooked. To fail to see that these people are triumphant, to recognize they are individuals born out of struggle, possessing a pride born of rejection, or a hope born from despair is to ignore their potential. I want everyone to know that I, as a college professor who is also a gay, black male who grew up poor, am still standing, still proud, and still boldly reflecting the light that shines on the tapestry of my life.

I close by paraphrasing my St. Mary's College colleague, Lucille Clifton, who is also the National Book Award winner and poet laureate of the State of Maryland. She writes:

"won't you celebrate with me . . ."

won't you celebrate with me
what i have shaped into
a kind of life? i had no model.
born in babylon
nonwhite, homosexual, and poor
what did i see to be except myself?
i made it up
here on this bridge between
starshine and clay,
my one hand holding tight
my other hand; come celebrate
with me that everyday
something has tried to kill me
and has failed.

REFERENCES

hooks, bell (2000). *Where We Stand: Class Matters*. New York: Routledge.
Majors, Richard G., and Janet Mancini Billison (1992). *Cool Pose: The Dilemmas of Black Manhood in America*. New York: Lexington Books.
West, Cornel (1993). *Race Matters*. Boston: Beacon Press.

THIRTEEN

Possibilities

ANGELIA R. WILSON

I learned the lessons of "class" during internal discussions of the Turkish delegation to the United Nations. In this rather impromptu meeting lubricated by alcohol and located in a Norman, Oklahoma, fraternity house, our delegation strategized, over a topic that now eludes me, for the next session of the Model UN. Sandy, a rather tall, impeccably dressed, law student casually flicked her hair, turning her head just enough for me to catch a phrase spoken to another but loosely aimed in my direction, "My father says regardless of education and potential, the lower classes will always be lower class." A rather popular young woman with the boys, and a couple of years older than I, we had not become firm friends, despite being sorority sisters and, now, Turkish ambassadors to the Model UN. I tapped her on the shoulder and, rather too politely and innocently, asked her to explain what she meant by that last statement. She lowered her eyes toward the top of my head and announced, "*You* would have to be very exceptional to make the move to the middle class." I wish now that I had retorted with a reference to Marx, or even Rawlsian liberal social justice, but I was only a sophomore when she insulted me. I had not yet read Rawls. As it turned out, nobody in McMurry University's two-man Politics Department (one middling liberal and one staunch Republican) ever required students to read Marx. Sometimes I wish I had punched her, or at least kicked her in the shin, but I suppose that would have only perpetuated my white-trash standing and grated against my Methodist preacher's daughter upbringing. Honestly, I don't recall much of anything else about that particular meeting of the Turkish minds or the subsequent Model UN political drivel. But twenty years later, I still remember clearly the first time I was "outclassed."

GO BACK TO THE FARM

In 1989, I arrived in London dragging two borrowed suitcases expectantly holding everything I assumed necessary to survive. All my belongings were tied together firmly with a rainbow belt. My journey had begun a few years before on Route 66. The only building in town big enough to host our high school graduation ceremony was the Baptist Church and, as location is key for a successful business, the sanctuary doors opened onto possibly the loneliest, most sinful highway in America. I tried in vain to convince my classmates that our graduation song should be "My Turn." Instead, they chose some 1980s pop crap about friendship. As a transient preacher's daughter with a distinctly different approach to life, a small town in the Texas Panhandle had not been the epitome of friendship. Now, it was My Turn. After completing my university degree and showing appropriate gratitude for a "lift out of the gutter" via Rotary Foundation generosity, I left for England and a one-year master's in Political Philosophy: the Idea of Toleration. It is hard to believe that was almost twenty years ago.

At the luggage carousel in Heathrow, I noticed I had the wrong bags—the highly unfashionable ones. Mine were huge family heirlooms and all other student-types had well-worn backpacks, some marked with stickers announcing exotic travels. By the time I had lugged my bags across London, along the east coast on a slow moving Sunday train, and eventually up three flights of stairs to my dorm in York, I wondered if I had brought too much stuff. Heeding warnings about the city's cold wet winters, I had packed plenty of layers. Tucked neatly together among sweaters and gifts for host Rotarians were several items that gave me a distinct identity, including Christianity, self-belief, Protestant work ethic, American pragmatism, lesbianism, and a rather thick southern drawl. Over the next few years, the value of all these attributes, as well as my brightly colored American sweaters, turned out to be variable and often culturally inappropriate.

My southern drawl, for example, was apparently a universal sign for "intellectually challenged." During my first class, where discussions centered on the English Civil War, I never spoke a word. I never understood a word either. While this particular topic had not figured prominently in my Texas education, one might have assumed my "Mensa" skills of logic would have given me a general level of comprehension. But I could not, literally, understand a word mumbled in their strange accents. Each of the eight other students came from different parts of Britain, which, although significantly smaller than Texas, is home to innumerable dialects, local phrases, and speech rhythms. Moreover, British accents are particularly indicative of one's class and most British citizens upon first meeting a stranger can place them according to region, family class, and educational status within the first few words—think Dr. Higgins meets Eliza Doolittle. One sentence reveals not just where you are from, but what your father does for a living. Given that doing a master's in political theory is generally how the overprivileged but directionless spend another year in studentland, my classmates had mumbling, stuttering voices that rarely included words of less than five syllables. While incomprehensible, I assumed the eloquently flowing sounds indicated great knowledge. Knowing I had none of the former, I began to wonder if I was capable of the latter.

A few weeks in, I realized all the other students were not only upper middle class, but also either mad British Marxists busying themselves planning the revolution until their inheritance kicked in and they took up residence in the House of Lords, or "nice" social democrats destined for a life in the academy or civil service. It was the late 1980s and they all pretended to hate Thatcher and America in equal measure. Fortunately, the combination of my accent and no-nonsense approach to philosophical ponderings kept them amused if not intellectually engaged. I recall, after a year of courses, one night in the pub when two fellow students insisted on arguing about the meaning of "toleration." My attempt to lure them into the normal Saturday frivolity was met by their efforts to engage me in philosophical discussion, "Hey, Tex, what does toleration mean?" they asked. I could see my answer, "to put up with," appeared parochial, so I added, "only if you have never felt tolerated, would you waste hours pondering the meaning of toleration."

Unbeknownst to me at the time, the theme of toleration would underpin the next three years of my academic study. Although a respectable American university had accepted me into one of its doctoral programs, I could not afford to go there. So, when the opportunity arose for me to stay in the UK and complete a doctorate within three years, with cobbled together but workable finances, I was relieved. Ideally, at a British university, one begins doctoral research with a clear plan, having already completed methodology courses, and then has challenging yet supportive, regular sessions with one's supervisor until, after thirty-six months, one produces a dissertation ready for examination. I had only a vague idea of wanting to think about "autonomy and community" and was sent away to "do a bit of reading" about these subjects for a few weeks. Before our first proper meeting, I enthusiastically sent a dozen pages to my supervisor summarizing my initial thoughts. I looked forward to our working out the research plan together. Collecting my mail that day, I wondered why my supervisor had written a letter when we had an appointment in just a few hours. I carried the letter next door to the coffee shop, ordered warmed cheese scones, which were the closest thing to my mom's southern biscuits I could find, and, having covered them with apricot jam, began reading. I can't remember every word of the letter—there is actually no need as I have it in my desk to this day—but I can at any moment recite particular phrases: "Your work will have to improve beyond recognition if there is any chance, however remote, of you completing an MPhil (research-based lesser master's degree) much less a PhD." Like many women graduate students, I began questioning my "right" to be there. Gaining my "double major" BA summa cum laude, completing master's courses with good marks, and being accepted into a PhD program became meaningless after reading this letter. In the supervision session later that day, her advice was clear: "Go back to the farm."

My supervisor and I didn't see each other much after that. There was the one time a few months later when I detailed my selected topic: "The Lesbian and Gay Agenda: Justice, Equality and Freedom." Apparently, this cemented my supervisor's belief that I was out of place. Even at my oral examination a few years later, it was only the examiners and I. My supervisor didn't bother showing up. I suppose I did okay, as the major revision to the dissertation was changing a few places where I had cited Robert Plant instead of Raymond Plant—a reasonable request given this was not a doctorate in rock legends. Professor Jeffrey Weeks, distinguished sociologist and grandfather of British gay and lesbian studies, acted as the external examiner, which, according to reference letters from my home department later, proved I was not a political theorist, just a "queer." My referees, who unbeknownst to me did not think it possible to be both a political theorist and queer, reflected the general attitude of the profession toward the emerging study of gay and lesbian politics.

VALUE ADDED

In the last two paragraphs, I used the word "unbeknownst," as this appropriately describes my rather naïve state of mind as a graduate student of political theory. Back in Smallville, Texas Panhandle, there were two alternative routes out of the city limits. One, a strong, seductive, gleaming path to a free university education, full-time employment, health insurance, and a chance to see the world, was the road chosen by many male classmates now serving in America's armed forces. The other road "less traveled," and rarely financially accessible or culturally valued, led directly to university. By the luck of the draw, I could choose the latter. Not, it is worth noting, because it was financially accessible but, since I was the first in my family interested and enabled by circumstances, it was financially *possible*. With scholarships, my parents' extra employment, my three part-time jobs, and hefty student loans, I could move beyond the population signs and find a bigger world—a world that stretched my mind, challenged my values, and gave me space to find my most intimate self. According to Hillary Clinton, "it takes a village": church members gave me an extra $10; the Lion's Club paid for my books for one year; and the

Optimist Club granted me $100 for tuition. Each contribution offered that little bit of support needed to make another year at university *possible*.

I attended McMurry University in Abilene, Texas, for one reason. My father, who had left school at sixteen to get a job and then, at thirty, decided to become a Methodist minister, had attended McMurry for two years. This was just enough for him to get his preacher's licence and his first church with a small salary to support his wife and four children. He never had enough money to return and graduate. So, I went for him. What this little liberal arts university lacks in academic depth, it makes up for in dedication to students. The work-study program gave me a part-time job to pay for accommodations and the religion department helped me find work as a youth pastor at a local rural church. I checked out groceries, short-order cooked at a bar, cleaned houses, babysat, gofered at a law firm, nannied for twin newborns, and sold health insurance, hardware, and clothes. Steadily, week by week, I made enough money for food and beer. I remember this rich lady whose house I cleaned a couple of times. She would follow me through each room assessing the quality of my work and presumably seeing whether her valuables remained in place. My neurotic Monica-from-*Friends*-like cleaning ability impressed her, but it was only after I told her I was about to leave for graduate school in England that she decided it was safe to leave "her help" alone vacuuming. The senior partner at the law firm called me "the girl" and the senior pastor called me "sinner," after I turned up with beer breath to lead Sunday night service. I became used to labels, even comfortable with other people's expectations of me. This turned out to be a transferable skill that served me well both inside and outside the academy.

My big break came during my act with the local Rotary Foundation. The account that follows is not meant to undermine the opportunities sponsored by the International Rotary Foundation, who were, at one critical moment in my life, very supportive. Instead, it is a story of expectations, fulfillment, and a salmon-colored dress. In my junior year at university, my best friend, a senior, received a Rotary fellowship to attend graduate school in England for one year. While in England, she encouraged me to apply and surprisingly the local Rotary club agreed to sponsor my application to the state-wide selection committee. However, they had a reputation for sponsoring winners and, as a matter of pride, took it upon themselves to make sure applicants were *exactly* what they thought the judges wanted. In my first meeting with the Rotarians to discuss my application, four businessmen taught me how to present information to a particular audience. For example, given the political nature of Rotarians, there was a lengthy discussion about the inappropriateness of including my presidency of the local chapter of Young Democrats. It was the only time I refused their advice. Undoubtedly, it was this that led to the detailed discussion of U.S. economic policy and welfare during the interview, in which, having learnt well, I declared my love of capitalism and free markets.

The next three meetings were mock interviews. The Rotarian advisors told me to purchase my interview outfit and attend for a full dress rehearsal. I spent my week's wages on a salmon-colored skirt and sweater combo that was just the right balance between femininity and serious business. Or so I thought. The interview, and two subsequent ones, involved my sitting in the middle of a large room surrounded by twenty Rotarians who fired questions at me, discussed and revised my answers, and, toward the end, evaluated my appearance. They didn't like the dress. So the next week I bought a suit. They liked it better, but sent me to have a complete Texas-style makeover. When I walked into the actual interview, I had perfect 1988 "helmet" hair, shoes matching my shirt and bag, conservative jewelery, talons, and Hollywood makeup—a kind of "nice preacher's daughter becomes Sue Ellen from *Dallas*." I also knew every answer to every question, as well as when to be smart, coy, articulate, and soft with a thick southern drawl. I didn't get a Grammy, but I got out of Texas.

It was worth it. I cannot thank those Rotarians enough. All their gendered power, their sexism, their conservatism stripped me of my "Everyone can grow up to be president" innocence and honed skills that still serve me well. Moreover, they were right about the dress. One of them explained to me that these scholarships, because they are unavailable to anyone directly connected to Rotarians, were one way they could give back to the community and "help young people out of the gutter." To my mind, growing up in a parsonage was a long way from the gutter, but I was in no position to argue.

In the early 1990s, the British government began publishing "League Tables" of schools detailing, among other things, how much "value added" each school provided to individual students. In other words, schools with high percentages of smart middle-class students who went on to attend Oxford were seen as adding little value. Whereas schools with a high percentage of students from less well-educated, working-class families who, upon leaving the school, attended Oxford were seen as adding considerable value. I later taught a couple of lectures on education policy and was fascinated by the concept of "valued added."

Reflecting on my journey through education, it seems there is a signifi-cant difference between my encounters with the British academy and my education in Texas. All of those, including the Rotarians, who touched my life in Texas added value. Each in a patronizing, sexist, or Christian mission way, gave me a hand. Undoubtedly, demarcations of class were tangible and informed the process. But differences in class were not, in most cases, sufficient reasons to perpetuate the distance between me and "them." Stereotypically, Americans have a "can-do" attitude, a spirit of hope that sees opportunities for change, progress, and adding value. Due to a chain of possibles, of other's visions of my future, and my own cultural programming of hope, I made the leap across the ocean and through the next few years of impossibles during graduate school.

UNIVERSALS AND ESSENTIALS

Of course, the Protestant Texan civility was extended to a straight girl. As noted, I had learned to sit comfortably while others labeled me with their expectations. I had learned to kiss, rather than bite, the feeding hand and wait, until beyond its reach, to label and feed my own hunger. I had girlfriends in Texas. I just kept them at a safe distance from McMurry, a Methodist university, and from the churches providing me a salary in exchange for my work as spiritual guide to their teenagers.

In the mid-1980s, homophobia in America had yet to reach its current level of madness and the average citizen of Abilene, Texas, simply did not see homosexuality. They knew it was there, but just not amongst *them* and *their* friends. Homosexuals lived on the other side of the tracks with drug addicts and prostitutes, not in the nice, white, suburban neighborhoods of doctors and teachers. One church where I worked as a youth minister had three queers in that job consecutively and never learned of their sexual orientation. The three of us figured it out one Saturday night when we spotted each other in the only gay club for miles and smiled knowingly the next morning at church. People see what they want to see or what they are told to see. Presenting myself as essentially what they wanted to see meant I could take advantage of possibilities, and, in turn, receive their blessings.

Outside the closet door, such possibilities and hope had limits. For my book *Below the Belt: Sexuality, Religion and the American South* (Wilson 2000), I interviewed a national director of an anti-abortion campaign group in Dallas. He was adamant that abortion was murder and must be stopped at all costs. As the interview ended and I was standing at the door, I asked if there were any circumstances (e.g., rape or incest) when abortion would be morally understandable. His reply was immediate, "Only one . . . if they find a gay gene." I made a quick exit. Even a violent anti-abortion campaigner could find one case where he could justify, in his words, "murder." Being gay, even if proven to be genetically determined, is so essentially wrong it is, according to this man of influence among Texas Republicans, morally justifiable to eradicate them. In the Bible Belt, where anyone can be saved and road signs read "God doesn't make trash," hatred of homosexuals is universal and more than occasionally leads to violence. Thank the Lord I made it to (hedonistic) Europe, where England has become a gay utopia with equal rights, civil partnerships, and protections against discrimination.

Well, kind of. As any student of public policy knows, there is usually a noticeable gap between legislation and public opinion or social norms. In 1999, a gay pub in London was bombed, killing three and injuring seventy. Now in Britain, the government keeps homophobic hate crime statistics and the national media sympathetically report individual attacks. The UK government has made policy changes that make society a safer place for gay and lesbian citizens—hate crime legislation as well as policies enforcing nondiscrimination in schools, public services and employment. Generally, in the United States, homophobic attacks are not reported to police, noted as statistically significant, or portrayed sympathetically by the national media. Successive U.S. governments do not feel obligated to protect gay and lesbian citizens.

To paraphrase Texan vice-presidential candidate Lloyd Benson debating Dan Quayle, I have known American homophobic hatred and the UK is no place of hatred. In my twenty years here, I have never seen a British heterosexual become particularly animated about homosexuality. They come alive over soccer, "foreigners," and in the pre-Thatcher years, working-class issues such as decent employment. But, usually, British heterosexuals are tantalizingly interested in "deviant sexuality" or only mildly—by Texan standards—homophobic. Because discrimination based on sexual orientation is on the UK sociopolitical agenda *as an issue of justice*, acceptable homophobia, or heterosexism, encountered on a daily basis is mildly irritating but not life threatening or soul saving. No Brit has ever tried to save my soul or openly expressed a desire for my death due to my sexual orientation. So, relatively speaking, living here is a relief.

However, knowledge of hatred/homophobia in Texas didn't equip me for British subtleties and their capacity for irony. Just when you think you know the face of prejudice, it gets a makeover. My journey from working class to "working class made good" coupled with my journey across the Atlantic placed me in unfamiliar territory where, for example, what appeared as kindness was actually patronizing, what appeared as amusement was disdain. At a retirement party for a colleague, I struck up a conversation with a professor from another discipline. She asked me politely about my research and then about my partner and our children. Then with incredible seriousness she said, "So when you go to conferences you let this other woman look after *your* children . . . how *very* interesting." I smiled as I walked away and then in the car on the way home rehearsed what I should have said, "So when you go to conferences, you let this heterosexual man, whom we know statistically to be the most likely to abuse children and probably can't cook or do ironing, look after *your* children." But that would have been so "angry dyke" of me. Over the years, I have had plenty of opportunities to let such middle-class disdain for my research turn me into a cynical old dyke. Perhaps someday it will.

Meanwhile, as I await promotion, I see their attempts to be offensive as quite ridiculous, even laughable. Since my teenage years, I have known that just because you're invited to a party, doesn't mean anyone will ask you to dance. You can find my life "interesting," love, but where I come from they drag people like me behind trucks until our bodies give up on life.

IN CLASS/OUTCLASSED

My first teaching post was at South Bank University in London where, like many inner-city universities, the students' faces were a rainbow of colors, their accents were a cacophony of rhythm and sound, and their journeys to higher education were a testament to possibilities. My second academic job was at the University of Central Lancashire, a "new" university set in the northern industrial town of Preston, the inspiration for Charles Dickens's *Hard Times*. Many UCL students were nontraditional/mature and came with vivid memories of the miners' strikes and the 1979 Winter of Discontent. They quoted Marx, chapter and verse. My current home is the "old red brick" University of Manchester, the largest university in Europe with over 35,000 students from around the world. Most British students I teach are from middle-class backgrounds and are assured of middle-class futures. A few years ago, I realized how much this country had changed when students no longer knew much about Marx or even socialist politics, regardless of their class. I used to teach an introductory level social policy course with about 350 students from across the social sciences. As I sat in a small group tutorial one morning, a very well-dressed young male economics student asked, "Why should I have to learn about poverty and unemployment when I will never be poor or unemployed?" There are two things certain in life: death and taxes. As I pondered how close he came to the former by making such a remark in my office, I launched a discussion about tax rates paid by the wealthy. Of course, the university does have a widening participation program that recruits a few mature or working-class students. What their experience is like once they arrive on campus I can only guess. A "feminist" colleague once told me how much she preferred teaching beautiful, articulate, middle-class young men over mature women, particularly single mothers.

As much as I love research, to the detriment of my career progression I also love teaching. The big introductory courses of three hundred to four hundred people are my congregation to which I get to preach politics or political theory each week. I enjoy the entertainment of using my thick southern accent and Texan vocabulary to make Rawls or Nozick accessible. I have learned the art of irony to articulate the irrationality of discrimination and the sense of feminism. The elitist language of postmodernism is a stumbling block for graduate and undergraduate students alike and I spend time with them unpacking the nonsense of word games. I too doubt that The Truth of Justice (etc.) is out there to be discovered by rational thought, but contextuality, shifting subjectivities, and performativity can be taught without mumbling five-syllable words. Learning and doing political theory are different tasks and I encourage students to develop skills and writing styles to help them feel comfortable participating in theoretical conversations. My first PhD student was a working-class young woman with a desire for possibilities to match her keen intellect. I may not have been the best supervisor ever, but I worked hard to make damn sure I was not the worst.

Conversing with my fellow Turkish delegate at the Model UN, I felt *outclassed*. She was better dressed, better educated, and better at conversational sparring in front of a male audience. In my role as youth minister/sinner, I knew beyond the closet door that I would become a member of a suspect class of homosexuals, a class kept apart, *outcast*, from normalcy, from my rural community, and from my culture. My mother was the eldest of five sisters. Her mother died of tuberculosis when she was ten and her father was an East Texas farm laborer during the depression. My mother left school to care for her younger sisters and married my father at fifteen. They were married fifty-one years before he passed away. Just after I was born, she announced that she was going to become a nurse. It was the late 1960s, she had four children between three and fifteen years of age, worked full-time as a night-shift nurses' aid, fulfilled her duties as a preacher's wife, and went to school during the day. She never read feminist theory, but she was feminism embodied. All my life she worked three jobs and still made Halloween costumes and attended basketball games. No matter what the cost in hours worked, or debt incurred, she encouraged me to get my education. "It is the one thing," she would say, "they can't take away from you." She knew poverty and debt, making do with old clothes, and stretching dinner with bread and gravy. She knew how it felt to be outclassed and outcast. She wanted to protect me from these feelings, and teach me about life's possibilities.

In the UK, gay and lesbian citizens benefit from policies that normalize our lives and our families of choice. My family is *so* normal: a civil partner of almost ten years, two kids—one boy, one girl—two full-time jobs, a mortgage, and more debts than savings. The kids bring us into contact with innumerable similar heterosexual couples. Some of them look puzzled when we explain there are two moms in our family, but they remain friendly and are never hostile. Our children are young and who knows what homophobia awaits them and us when preteen friends know the meaning of "lesbian." But we are middle class now and live in the UK, so I can't imagine this will be an impossible problem. I know now the only accoutrements I needed to have brought from Texas were parental love and desire for the possible—both of which I will give my children in abundance. With my high school diploma in hand stepping out onto Route 66, or wearing a salmon-colored sweater-skirt combo, or my PhD supervisor telling me to go back to the farm—who would have thought it possible?

REFERENCE

Wilson, Angelia R. (2000). *Below the Belt: Sexuality, Religion and the American South*. New York: Cassell.

FOURTEEN

Hate Is Not a Family Value

SUSAN E. BORREGO

No one in my family went to college. My mother finished high school when I was in ninth grade. No one ever talked to me about attending college, not at home or at school. The educational experiences in my life came mostly from the neighborhood and my grandma's "school-of-hard-knocks" wisdom. We didn't visit museums, attend concerts, go to plays, or have other such learning experiences. We did not travel or discuss things like politics and literature around the dinner table. In fact, we spent little time together at the dinner table. My mom worked various jobs, primarily at the A&P and tending bar. My dad worked at the Ford factory until he was injured. Later he was injured again and a fight with the union over medical care cost him his job. Afterward, he took a job pumping gas. College was not part of my family history.

As a kid, I liked school. The teachers were nice and it was a break from the chaos of a difficult family situation at home. I did my homework, got good grades, and was very curious, an especially helpful trait since school wasn't that challenging. I wasn't much trouble; my worst school performance transgressions were in the "creates a disturbance" column on my report card. "Ma," as my brother and I called my grandmother, taught me to read when I was four. She brought Dr. Seuss books at the market and I begged her to teach me to read. This way, I wouldn't have to wait for her to get home from work to read to me.

Ma worked full-time as a bookkeeper in a machine shop. She baked and decorated cakes in the evenings for extra money or free for family and friends who couldn't afford a special occasion cake. I remember sitting in a chair in her tiny kitchen watching her work. There were cakes on every flat surface, including card tables, in the living room, and sometimes in the garage. As she moved around baking and decorating, I would read aloud from such classics

223

as "Go Dog Go" or "One Fish, Two Fish, Red Fish, Blue Fish." I was proud I could read to Ma as she worked on cakes. I knew it helped her.

In kindergarten and first grade, they told Ma teaching me to read was a mistake. They said it made school boring for me. Ma suggested the teachers give me something to read instead of color and I wouldn't be bored.

By second grade, I was reading Nancy Drew and riding my bike to the public library to find other books. Unfortunately, at school I had to suffer through "Dick and Jane." Not only was this tedious, I didn't know anyone who lived that way—little golden-haired, stupid children, mother in an apron, home, and baking. Who called their mom "Mother" anyway? Dick was always chasing Jane. I knew Nancy Drew would have never run from Dick.

Despite those comments from my early teachers, I know Ma's teaching me to read was the best thing that ever happened to me. Eventually reading combined with my sense of curiosity would propel me to college, despite all the obstacles I faced as a youngster. Add these traits to my general tenacity and this explains why I finished my various academic degrees. Ironically, I spent my adult life trying not to let the very thing Ma made possible separate us.

I was an active and athletic kid who played as much as she read. I never understood why it surprised people I enjoyed reading so much. As a child, I was a kinesthetic learner who might have been diagnosed with ADHD, had that diagnosis been popular then. But I could spend hours hiding someplace so my brothers wouldn't bug me while I was reading.

Throughout my school years, I was lucky that my teachers and librarians liked me. Because it was a small town, I wondered if the librarians called ahead—the elementary librarian to the junior high, the junior high to the high school, to tell the next one I was coming. They all always seemed ready for me with book selections. The elementary librarian had great sports fiction picked out for me. Soon, she was adding autobiographies. The junior high librarian moved me into world history, introducing me to Babi Yar and Anne Frank. Kids in my neighborhood thought librarians weren't supposed to like us so even my friends were surprised the librarians were always so nice to me. My friends thought I was not the "library type," whatever that means. Looking back, I wasn't really known as "studious" mostly because kids on my side of the tracks weren't supposed to exhibit "bookish behavior."

Though I didn't know it, by the time high school rolled around, I had been "tracked." In my school system, your junior high math and science courses determined your high school math and science placements. Of course, nobody in my family knew about math placements, and since no one was considering college as an option for me, including me, high school placements weren't an issue.

I remember the strange experience of starting high school and seeing a bunch of my friends in a set of classes I wasn't in. They were in courses like trigonometry and advanced chemistry. I didn't know why for the first time we were taking different classes. I vaguely remember thinking it had something to do with their going to college but that was it. More puzzling was honor society. Several friends were in honor society and, despite having good grades, I was never asked to join. It was another one of those things that crossed my mind, but I didn't think much more about it, other than that it seemed strange. It would be many years before I understood the importance of weighted grades, college preparatory courses, and that the honor society was something somebody had to *nominate* you for. Given that I was not "college-track" automatically meant I didn't qualify for being nominated. I was never asked if I wanted to be "college track." I don't remember a guidance counselor asking what I wanted to do with my life or suggesting college as a possibility. When college recruiters came to my high school, I only heard about them when my friends discussed the presentations, but I wasn't on the notification or invitation list. However, every time the armed forces recruiters visited my school, I got a pass to attend their presentations. The conventional wisdom of my guidance counselors was not to create any expectations or aspirations for kids like me toward things we could never achieve. Today I often hear students speaking about how their school counselors never compared their (the counselors') low expectations against the students' real ambitions.

Many working-class people I interviewed while researching my dissertation spoke of how if you are from "the wrong side of the tracks," "uptown," or "downriver," school officials and many teachers will have low expectations of your attending college. College preparatory courses are a key indicator of how class shapes countless future opportunities. If you are not placed in the appropriate math classes by junior high school, you have little chance of qualifying for the college preparatory schedule in high school. Poor or working-class students and their families are seldom asked if they want to be in the college preparatory track. It is assumed they do not want to be there and they are put in "easier" courses. Moreover, no matter how well we did in high school, few of us were encouraged to submit college or financial aid applications, nor were we told of scholarship opportunities. Most of us were not encouraged to apply to college at all. Instead, we were coached toward less ambitious futures.

Despite all that was happening around us, we grew up not knowing we were poor or disadvantaged. Certainly, formal schooling did not fill our heads with ideas about social or cultural capital. For sure, we were not encouraged toward a social class consciousness.

If anything, formal schooling did as much to disadvantage us as our birth circumstances did. My grandma taught me the world was full of good people and while I may be more fortunate than others I should never think of myself as "better than." She taught me to believe we are obliged to care for the less fortunate. Of course, I knew we didn't have as many nice things as some friends had. For example, we didn't go on vacations and we lived "uptown," not in a nice home in a subdivision. Still, none of this translated into disadvantage and a real appreciation for how being disadvantaged affected someone's future. Absolutely nothing in my youth communicated "disadvantage" to me. It was not until college, when I began comparing my own origins and current living conditions to my classmates (what an appropriate term, when you think about it: *class*mates) for what they had, where they had traveled, and on and on, did the real meaning of "disadvantage" begin creeping into my consciousness. The academy taught me that, despite our good intentions, we categorize people with this pejorative term, without understanding that college campuses are especially effective at marginalizing students of poor and working-class origins. Instead of acknowledging how social capital prepares some far more than others to succeed, we see those who come with less social capital as having "problems." Both on campus and off, our society's norms, language, and system are weighted toward middle- and upper-class values. Everything is measured by these standards and anyone who fails to meet them is "less than."

Looking back, I realize I had teachers who loved what they were doing and liked us. Notwithstanding "tracking," some teachers saw something in me that the guidance counselors missed. I made a strong connection with two English teachers. It was the mid-1970s. I don't remember "interventions" for "at-risks" students like me. I'm not sure I would have understood to sign up if these options had been available. As hard as it is to believe today, I simply had no idea my class or the social and educational systems disadvantaged me.

Anyway, the two English teachers cared about me and took me seriously. I knew they believed in me. Years later, I would find out they had provided me with the support I needed to hang on. One course they pulled me into was "EMU English." Eastern Michigan University offered the class and, although I did not know it, it was presented as a college-level course. I must have filled out the paperwork on my high school English teachers' prompting, but it meant nothing to me then. When I got to college, I learned because I had completed EMU English with an A grade, I was waived from freshman English.

In the fall of my senior year, a newly hired chemistry teacher at the high school told me I should go to college. As a joke, my college-bound lab partner returned an information card with my name on it to a small, church-related college in Idaho. The teacher overheard me telling my lab partner the admissions people from the college had been sending me information. Because my chemistry teacher was new, she didn't know what most other folks in my small town knew—my family had fallen apart and I was living with another family until I finished high school.

Ms. Deck, the chemistry teacher, said I should go to the college in Idaho so I would be far from my hometown. She said if I stayed in town,

I would likely end up "drinking beer and dragging 'Main Street' " and she knew I could do better than that. I took her advice and applied to the small, church-related college in Idaho. I was accepted!

When I returned to town for our twentieth high school reunion, I stopped by the high school. I stood in the hall watching one of my favorite English teachers lecture about *Fahrenheit 451*. It was so strange—the same book had a huge effect on me when she taught it in 1975. I hadn't been back to my high school since graduation in 1976 and wasn't sure she would recognize me. She glanced into the hallway and saw me. She broke into a huge smile and walked out to greet me and said, "You should be teaching this section—remember, you enjoyed this so much." Of course, I remembered, and I was *stunned* she had, too. On the edge of beginning doctoral work, I was there finally to thank her; I had come to understand in many ways that she was one of the teachers who kept me alive. She said, "We always knew if you could just hang on long enough to get out of here, you would do well." "You knew?" I asked, surprised. "We all knew," she explained with a broad smile.

Today I know I made it to college despite low expectations and a family crisis. Perhaps I made it because of those low expectations. Though it would be several years before I had the language to interpret the effects of those low expectations, I recognized them intuitively and pushed against them. Proving everyone wrong was a great motivator. I especially wanted to go to college so I could send the diploma back to my high school principal and tell him to shove it.

OFF TO COLLEGE

One thing I really liked about attending the college in Idaho was that it meant I would be going far away from home—because home had disintegrated, I had no reason to stay. A very nice college admissions director sent me a handwritten note saying I had been accepted and sealed the deal for my choosing the church-related school in Idaho, or should I say it chose me? Today, as a college administrator, I shudder at how little I knew about college selections and student life.

I arrived on that Idaho campus a day early, army duffel bag in hand, not understanding the residence halls would still be closed. Thankfully, some kind soul opened the dorm and put me in an empty room. The next day students began arriving with their families. Evidently, I was the only one who didn't know the dorm would open the next day.

Most of my peers came to school accompanied by their parents. Some parents were driving a second family car they planned to leave with their son or daughter. Early in the morning, families carried box after box into the dorm rooms. I didn't have to do much carrying. I only had two items: an army duffle bag and a sleeping bag.

I thought sheets and towels came with the room. Imagine my surprise. My first night in the hall I had rolled my sleeping bag out on one of the plastic-covered mattresses. When my roommate, Cindy, and her mom arrived, they scurried about the room, planning for matching rugs, comforters, and towels. I was mortified. I hadn't eaten since the day before because I didn't have money for food, so there was *no* way I could purchase room decorations. They went shopping and by nightfall, like magic, curtains, rugs, and comforters began appearing in the room. They arranged a comforter, quite nicely I might add, over my sleeping bag.

From my earliest undergraduate days, I knew my heart beat differently on a campus. Intuitively it seemed like such a place of opportunities. Most faculty, staff, and other students were generous to each other and to me. The college was old and welcoming, and there were books everywhere. Despite often feeling out of place, at the same time I considered myself fortunate to be in college. It had not occurred to me that someone could make a living (and a life) working at a university. Back then, I didn't have the luxury of thinking about such things. I was busy trying to survive in my new setting, including taking and finishing all the right courses for my degree. Besides school, I played sports and held various jobs to cover expenses.

College was an incredible time for me. It was filled with great fun experiences, hard work, and a constant disequilibrium. More than anything, it opened my life to different choices. Most folks I grew up with lived without many options. They mostly knew they would work for Ford Motor Company, BASF Chemical Company, or another factory in the area. The college-bound kids, on the other hand, had seemingly endless career horizons. A few of the more well-to-do kids even talked of becoming doctors. Prior to college, I don't remember dreaming about the future. No one in my neighborhood talked much about what they wanted to do when they grew up.

My disequilibrium in college came from sensing that everyone knew things I didn't. It wasn't so much the coursework, it was the other stuff, such as "prerequisites," financial aid forms, and registration. My peers, even those without a major or any idea of what they were going to do after college, seemed to move easily on campus. They talked about studying abroad, summer internships, and high school trips to Europe. I, on the other hand, couldn't figure out how I could take an unpaid internship or volunteer for any academic learning opportunities involving travel. I was working forty hours per week, going to school, and playing basketball and volleyball. I can't remember if I was too embarrassed to let on I didn't understand how to make things happen or if I didn't even think to ask. So much of my focus was on moving from class to class and figuring how to live month to month. There was little time or place to consider how things could be different.

Every few years, my grandparents would drive from Detroit to Las Vegas or California to visit one of my grandma's sisters. On the way, they would visit me at college. They carried sheets of cast-off foam rubber from the BASF factory in the back of their station wagon. They slept on the foam rubber in the back of their car while it was parked in the dorm lot. In the morning, after the other girls had gone to class, Ma would take a shower in the dorm bathroom. After she finished I would stand guard so my grandpa could follow her to shower and shave. It didn't occur to me until years later that no one else's family I knew slept in the back of a car in the parking lot while visiting their kids at college. It all makes sense to me now, but then I had no language, no appreciation of how the differences in my life related to class origin, and there were few places for me to develop this understanding—this social class consciousness—while at college. The majority of systems and structures in higher education are embedded with middle- and upper-class norms and there is little opportunity for students to explore the implications of class-based social arrangements.

I recall a missed opportunity to examine class heritage. It was one of the most embarrassing experiences in my life. One day a visiting sociologist, a white woman, was describing black, urban culture. As she explained the descriptors, I realized how many of these traits matched my own (white) family background and circumstances. I had not spoken much in my classes for the year I had been there. I managed to gather my courage and ask whether she was describing "urban" or "black." She responded with a scathing blast about white privilege. She said because I was white I should never compare my experience to what blacks face in this culture. I was humiliated. I had not been saying my experiences were the same as that of the black, urban culture. Instead, I was trying to figure out why her descriptors were so familiar. I don't think I ask another question in class for the next decade. Not until I was a doctoral student did I fully understand what the sociologist was defining as "urban" encompassed working and poor classes. Intuitively I had known there was something familiar about what the sociologist was saying, but it would be years before I learned about "cultural capital" and how it had shaped my life.

I continued working my way though college, unsure of what I would do for a job when I finished. I changed my major six or seven times. I worked in the cafeteria, applied for a job as a resident assistant (which I didn't get because, according to friends, I was not Nazarene), worked off campus at an arcade, and served as a "Gal Friday" for one of my professors. I made my way through classes, some terms buying books and other terms not being able to afford them. As my senior year began, I was a student government officer in charge of campus events and activities. I don't remember if it was an appointed or elected position, but it was fun. Now and then Ms. Wilson would suggest I become a Dean of Women. I had no idea what that meant and I couldn't find many Dean of Women positions listed in my infrequent trips to the career center.

The first week of school my senior year I met a guy who was two years younger. He asked if I was going to some event, which, in fact, I was in charge of. When I said "Yes," he invited me to go with him. As my senior year unfolded, he asked me to marry him. In trying to decide what to say to him, I talked to several people, including my coach, a friend, and the dean of upper division students. In the end, I could see no reason not to marry him. He was nice, his parents were nice to me, and I had no real plans that conflicted with being married.

In May, I was offered a job as an admissions counselor for the college. They had never had a woman travel as a recruiter and explained they needed to see if there would be any negative reaction to my doing so. I started working in June, the week after graduation. In September, I got married.

In retrospect, I can observe numerous class-related events about my job with the college. Some were funny and some not. For one, when they sent me on the road to recruit prospective students, we were to visit high schools in the day and call other possible applicants in the evening. The college provided me with an institutional credit card and a car. Instead of giving me a budget, they said to stay in bargain hotels and eat at "cheap" places. On my first trip, I stayed in a Motel 6. After visiting some high schools, I went to Wendy's for dinner. When I tried to pay at the counter, they would not take my credit card. Next, I went to McDonald's. They also rejected my credit card. It was the same at Burger King. Finally I went to a market, got fruit, and went back to my room to call potential students before it got too late. Imagine my surprise when I realized there were no phones in the rooms of Motel 6. In 1980, Motel 6 only had phones in the lobby.

Next morning I called the secretary in my college's admissions office. She was one of my behind-the-scene coaches. After she quit laughing at my description of looking for "cheap" lodging and trouble buying meals, she said to check out of Motel 6 and look for a Best Western or Red Lion Inn. She told me to go to restaurants with sit-down service because they take credit cards. I was starting to understand that "cheap" is a relative term.

I spent about two years working in admissions and recruitment before I got pregnant. About that time, my husband finished his education degree and we began looking for teaching positions for him and graduate school opportunities for me. My boss said it would be in my husband's best interest if I resigned and went wherever he got a teaching job, which I did.

The teaching job we moved to in Portland, Oregon fell through so we returned to Idaho. I took a job with my alma mater working in public information. It was a great opportunity to expand my experience and I started scoping out graduate schools. I was working for a talented vice president and learning a lot about "institutional advancement." One day at work, my boss said I needed to go back to school if I wanted to stay in education administration. I was taken aback, not sure whether to be hurt or mad. A few days later, I gathered enough courage to ask him why he said I should get a graduate degree. He said no one did what I did as well as I did it. But, he cautioned, I needed to know why I was so good at what I did; if I wanted to remain in higher education, I needed to understand why I was successful. He then cautioned, quite insightfully, there would be times in graduate school when my professors would frustrate me, but I should put my "street smarts" on the back burner and focus on learning the system. My boss concluded by insisting graduate school would be a lesson in persistence for me. It was the best advice he could have given. In moments when graduate school seemed amazingly disconnected from anything real, I focused on persisting.

Leaving this small closely knit community to prepare for a future as a Dean of Students or Director of Alumni at another institution was a huge risk. In trying to decide what to say to my boss, I talked to several people, including my coach, a friend, and the dean of upper division students. I was starting a master's degree with no idea that ultimately I would need a doctorate to succeed in higher education. There was no one I could turn to for advice, which made my life even more complex. Most folks thought it was crazy to leave a good job to go back for more formal schooling. Nevertheless, I set off to earn a graduate degree.

FINDING A GRADUATE PROGRAM

When I think of my graduate applications, I am chagrined. I had no idea how to use the language of the field to write a convincing cover letter. I didn't have any real "connections" and, even if I did, I wouldn't have known how to use them. Someone did recommend I apply for head resident positions, as they would pay for housing and, in some places, tuition. Although I tried, I could not land a head resident job.

One day, walking across campus on my way to work, I ran into another colleague who described a master's program that had fellowships covering tuition. He encouraged me to check it out, so I made a call and the school sent me the materials. I didn't learn till later than *lots* of programs offered stipends and tuition waivers. I only knew I couldn't quit work to attend school full time. When the college accepted me, I negotiated for a double internship, meaning I would get $16,000 and a tuition waiver as a graduate student. Three months after starting my graduate program, I was appointed Director of Student Activities. I continued with my graduate studies while working full time. Although I lost my internship monies, as a full-time university employee, I qualified for tuition remission. I finished my master's degree three years later.

The first year went so fast I hardly remember it. At the end of my second year, I became an associate dean and my responsibilities increased accordingly. In the fall of my third year, the dean of students said that after the start of that year, he would become vice president and I would be named to his job. In January, he took me to breakfast, talked me through the scope of the job, and offered me the position. I was about to turn thirty.

I loved the small campus and that spring I was voted outstanding administrator. I was enjoying my classes and the students I was working with. There were many opportunities to do new things with few bureaucratic obstacles. I was having a ball. It was a great place for my family; my two young children hung out in the residence halls and attended various activities. I had a host of babysitters, and a grand group of college students was spoiling my kids. I was working with students to develop programs to benefit them. I couldn't have imagined a better life. Then, unexpectedly, I fell in love with a woman.

This had not been in the cards and I worked hard to deny it. While I was completely terrified, at some level I was relieved. So many pieces of my emotional life were finally making sense. The years of being just a step out of sync with my girlfriends and yet having no words, no impressions, no way to understand what was missing, were over. I wanted to pop open some champagne and celebrate, yet I knew my life would come unglued if I committed to a lesbian relationship. I was married to a man, we had two young children, and I was working at a Christian college. I was sure my life as I knew it would end.

I was living a life that was more fun and fulfilling than anything I could have imagined. I could not picture the ruin that would accompany my "fall from grace." I would probably lose my kids and my job. I spent a lot of time trying to find a way out. The options I considered ranged from driving off a cliff to denying and ignoring my feelings. There was no easy resolution. Initially, I thought I could brush aside my sexuality. I had done that most of my life.

One night in the midst of team-teaching a graduate class I realized my life had shifted. My teaching partner was demonstrating how to create goals/objectives/strategies. He wrote three questions on the board. These were: (1) "What is important?," (2) "What are we going to do about it?," and (3) "How will we do it?"

As he described the process of choosing what to do, it became clear to me in an instant what I had to do. I realized my daily routine and the structure of my life were incongruent with my internal reality. I am a lesbian. The realization astounded me. For the first time, the picture was clear and simple. Over the years I had become tangled in a web of fear and loss. I had been telling myself I was just confused—it was nothing that required rethinking my entire identity. Now **I knew I was a lesbian.** I was in love and feeling complete in ways I had never experienced. I also knew it would unravel my life in far too many ways to count.

I spent the next several days swinging emotionally between the relief and joy of "getting it," of feeling at home emotionally, and despair about what it would mean to my family and especially the fear of losing my kids. I did not tell my husband I was gay, but I told him I was leaving. I feared if I told him I was a lesbian, he would take our children away from me. When he asked if there was anything he could do to "fix" our relationship, I said no. He moved down the street, I remained in our house, and we shared custody of the children. A year later, after we had been divorced, he came out.

During those early days of realizing I was gay, there was no one to talk with about my options or how I could protect myself. I was extremely sad knowing I couldn't accept a Dean of Students job at a religious college because of my sexual orientation. Though I was still not "out," I knew my life would soon change, and dramatically. Even if I postponed coming out, my present life could not go on as it was. I have always had a high need for congruence and only by changing my life radically could I resolve my cognitive dissonance.

The university's doctrinal statement had no place for gay staff members. I wanted to leave on my own terms and not be fired because of my sexual orientation. I spent the two-week Christmas break preparing myself for the dean's offer. The dean took me to breakfast on January 4 and offered me the job. With a broken heart, I said I couldn't accept the position. All I said was that I no longer supported some of the university's doctrinal tenets. It was a very difficult conversation for both of us. He asked good questions and pushed a bit about wanting me to be sure of my decision. At the end, he gave me extra time to consider whether I wanted the job. I thanked him and explained I had been thinking a lot about it and my answer was "No." We both got teary. We left the restaurant and walked in silence back to campus.

The next six weeks were a blur. I was fighting the emotions of leaving a "dream job" and, at the same time, looking for a new employer. I lined up a job at an AIDS organization in Orange County and began handing off my university projects to others. Every day I questioned my decision, not because I was unclear about being gay, but because I knew I would really miss this job; I loved what I was doing. There were a few folks I trusted so I talked with them about why I was leaving. Mostly, they encouraged me to stay at the university so gay students would have someone to talk to. The problem was being gay at this university was against the rules—unless, of course, you didn't "act on" being gay. I shuddered at the idea of living a closeted life while serving as a confidante for gay students. I realized that the church would rather I live without integrity than in truth. The irony was that if I chose a lie, I could have stayed in my job. The logic was clear. I had to leave. It all seemed so unchristian.

I cried every time I drove by the campus sign on the freeway for the first six months after I resigned. It would be fifteen years before I would have another chance to become a Dean of Students.

After nearly two years of working for the AIDS organization, I returned to a college campus. Caltech was looking for an executive director for its Caltech Y, a nonprofit organization founded to provide out-of-class activities for California Institute of Technology students. Caltech Y started as a YMCA, but split with the parent organization some forty some years ago. I applied for the job and was hired. My class background and sexual orientation had huge implications for this period of my professional life. The Y job was perfect for combining nonprofit work and higher education in an organization describing itself as the social consciousness of the campus. Not a traditional Y, the organization had been on campus over eighty years providing cocurricular opportunities for students, including multicultural speakers, volunteer projects, events, and activities offering an outlet from a demanding academic life. I had no idea Caltech was as conservative as it was, and the Y board of directors even more so. As executive director, I reported directly to the board. I learned from my experiences never to put myself in that position again. Lacking both a financial safety net and being a lesbian, I find that the risk of reporting to a board without a contract and with little professional protection is too large for me.

The board was composed of about twenty-five to thirty couples, nearly all senior adults. There were about eighteen student members. Many of the adult couples interacted socially and had known each other for years. They were mostly nice people who cared about students and they gave me a great deal of support, at least a majority did. However, I also came to see the differentiating implications of class relations with the board.

After accepting the executive director position, I asked the board chair about the other finalist. The chair said I was hands-down the first pick. The only issue they discussed in the committee was how I had held my silverware improperly at the dinner interview. I didn't know whether to laugh out loud or crawl under the rug or both. Initially I thought she was joking, except that to my embarrassment she began explaining the difference between the "continental" and "American" way of grasping silverware. Apparently, I held my silverware "continental" style, except I had not bent my finger at the correct angle and I committed the egregious error of gesturing with silverware in my hand. The hiring committee decided this was a small and correctable issue and hired me despite my faux pas. She finished explaining the proper way to grip silverware and the reasons it was important. What an inauspicious beginning.

A large part of my job was interacting with the board and, when I think back, there were some funny things that happened, mostly related to social class. I decided about four months after being at the Y to stop serving wine at board meetings. It seemed a waste of money and some students present were drinking underage. My policy lasted one month. The board members were upset when they arrived for a meeting and no wine was being served. Following that, a board couple volunteered to be in charge of purchasing wine. I had no idea I had violated a fundamental rule of hospitality.

After about five years of working at the Y, two long-time board members began showing up at my office when I wasn't there. The staff reported feeling uncomfortable because the two women asked odd questions about me and had once or twice gone into my office looking through artwork, books, and items on my desk. I talked to the board chair about the two women's actions. He was supportive and assured me he would handle the problem. Just before the holidays, the board chair called to inform me there would be a financial audit of operations. He apologized and explained that, although it did not make sense to him, there had been some "fiscal allegations" and there was need for an audit. When I began as executive director, I had arranged for an outside accountant to review the books regularly and make quarterly reports to the board. I was confused.

We were a small organization with a small budget, but the audit took about ten days. It involved reviewing $20,000 of expenditures. It cost the Y $7,000 to conduct the audit. The findings confirmed that there were no questionable business practices in use and no improprieties anywhere else. The audit did report that the Y owed me $2.32. The audit conclusions were announced at an executive committee meeting in the richly paneled library in a board member's home. One of the women bringing the complaint was allowed to attend, although she was not a member of the executive or personnel committees. When the accountant reported the clean audit, I could feel tears stinging my eyes.

I was furious at myself for being naive enough to believe integrity matters most and I was angry with the board for indulging these two women. I was the outsider. The board members were all in the same social circle and they didn't want to offend their colleagues. As I fought back tears, the board chair asked the accuser if she was satisfied. The accuser sat quietly for a minute and then said, "Did you subscribe to gay magazines? Did you join a gay organization?" The room was quiet, with no one making eye contact. My partner and I had been at many events, including being in the homes of people in the room. They knew us. No one stopped the discussion by declaring the questioning inappropriate.

I took a breath and replied we had subscriptions to over twenty-five magazines at the Y. And, yes, one subscription was to the *Advocate*, and, yes, we had a membership at the Gay and Lesbian Center as well as the African American museum, the Los Angeles Museum of Art, the Huntington Library, a couple of local video stores, and assorted others. Our students took advantage of the benefits and arranged trips for groups and we rotated memberships depending on the student program recommendations. I was struck by the absurdity of the moment. Here I was surrounded by a group of people who had hired me for diversity purposes. We were all sitting in the room of a house I would never have otherwise been inside and here was this woman making accusations about my integrity, sexuality, and use of organizational resources. She deserved to be busted (that's how things like this would have been settled in my working-class neighborhood in Detroit) in the chops instead of indulged at my expense. Emboldened by the moment, I looked her in the eye and asked, "Is that what all this is about? About me being a lesbian?" Just then, the board chair called the meeting to an end. They thanked me, apologized for the fact that they felt they had to conduct the financial review, and offered me a drink. I excused myself and got into the car. As I drove home, I could feel the fury building as I weighed the injustice of it all and the fact that there was nothing I could do. The following day I started a job search.

The next time the board chair and I had lunch I said I was leaving; the auditing episode had broken my heart. He tried to explain the obligation to investigate fiscal allegations and that having the books reviewed regularly by an outside accountant didn't satisfy the particular board member who raised the issue. We never discussed that the fiscal complaint was a ruse for a challenge based on my sexuality and brought by a board colleague he couldn't confront. I realized he couldn't support me in the ways he thought he could, and that I needed for my own protection. Sadly, this helped me see that working for a board left me vulnerable to a homphobic backlash that could cost me my job.

Some colleagues have said I spent seven of the ten years underemployed as Y executive director. Technically, they are correct, but during these years, I was busy with my family. I was a single parent part of the time, became partnered with a woman, coached my kids' athletic teams, worked full time, bought a house, hosted junior and senior high parties, was "mom on call," completed my PhD, and took care of my grandparents as they died.

As I moved through my professional life, I felt good about finding ways to get my master's and PhD without accruing debt. It *never* occurred to me to quit work and attend school full time. I looked for graduate programs with internships or tuition stipends. I received no advice about types of degrees, kinds of institutions, social and professional networks, and so forth. Only now, after watching people with more social capital successfully navigate the educational system, do I fully appreciate the importance of all this informa-tion, all this knowledge. What are some things that matter? Among others, they include knowing the value of getting good recommendations from the "right" people, making informal contacts to get good jobs, and doing much the same to get promoted. In my work as an advisor to graduate students, I saw that upper-class students were nearly always connected to the resources necessary for moving along smoothly.

As a graduate student, I read books and articles about women who returned to college later in life. I was glad I wasn't one of them, one of the nontraditional women. I realize now I always saw myself as an exception to the rule and perhaps, therefore, not as limited as others might be. I had gone for my bachelor's degree directly from high school, and even though it took longer than I wanted to start a master's degree and then a PhD program, I was still young when I began graduate school. The reality is I was one of them—one of those who worked full time, took care of a family, found a way to survive, and finish school. I completed my PhD at age forty-two.

In sum, I now understand how much my class background shaped my graduate school choices and experiences. My professional options were constrained in ways I never anticipated, ranging from where I got my degree, to my chosen field of study, to meager research opportunities, to the professional network I didn't have.

THE FIRST STIRRINGS OF CLASS CONSCIOUSNESS

I was in my thirties—starting a doctoral program—before I recognized the social class aspects of higher education and how I had always reacted to these middle- and upper-class assumptions. In my first doctoral course, a professor began describing the working class. She listed a series of common working-class experiences. That night, for the first time in eighteen years of being in classrooms, I heard someone objectively acknowledge the separate existence of people like me.

The discussion was more descriptive than critical. She was not accusatory. She did not describe these lives as less than or lacking. She did not criticize working-class people. Despite this absence of negative comments from the professor, I became very self-conscious. I thought everyone sitting around me knew the professor was describing my family and me. My own classist assumptions were critical. Would people pigeonhole me according to all the stereotypical shortcomings held about the working class? I was simultaneously relieved, curious, and embarrassed. This professor had always encouraged dialogue in class, but I simply couldn't find the words to speak after hearing her describe my social class. I could only sit in silence amazed at this new knowledge.

I was relieved to finally hear a noncritical description of life as I knew it, life in my neighborhood, in my family, as part of an in-class experience. Nevertheless, I was embarrassed that I didn't know anything about class—at least, not intellectually. I had never thought of my life in "working-class" terms. It seemed so simple and so fundamental I couldn't believe I had never heard a class-based analysis. That night was an "ah-ha!" moment, an experience that shook me to my core. It was learning in a way I had never encountered. That discussion was like the slightest twist of a kaleidoscope lens, a rotation that results in a new and breathtaking collection of colors and shapes.

I left class and walked for hours, my heart beating rapidly, inexplicably emotional, ideas swirling. I was relieved, stunned, mad, and sad all at once. How could I have spent so long learning and not *know and appreciate* my own class heritage? This was my first step toward my own social class consciousness. I kept asking myself, "How could I have been working so hard to learn (get my degree) and remain clueless about how my higher education success would only be partly about degrees? I understood how much effort I had invested in trying to hide my "rough edges," assuming that if I acted appropriately, no one would know how different my life had been from the lives of most of my peers. Later, I would wonder who had defined my edges as "rough" and why I had accepted that description. I was starting to realize higher education is a gradual but relentless process. One slowly assumes upper-middle-class values in exchange for losing connections with one's working-class roots.

That night, in only a few hours, the pieces of the puzzle of my experience had a border, a context. Although there was no concrete portrait like those on the front of puzzle boxes we looked at as kids, I had the border pieces in place. Now I would start assembling the picture, or so I thought.

For the next several months, my world spun in a tangle of emotions. I was confused by a sense of loss, but I could not decide what was lost. It was clear I had unconsciously devised ways to hide and adapt to the behaviors and language of those around me, all the while becoming more distant from how I grew up.

Since leaving for college fifteen years earlier, I had been gradually and unconsciously distancing myself from my friends, grandparents, and neighborhood. I seldom returned to my downriver hometown, south of Detroit. It was more convenient to stay out west. I couldn't afford plane fare. The weather out here was much better—I devised a million reasons not to go home. While I stayed away, I missed countless significant events in my family's and friends' lives, including the wedding of my best high school buddy, the funeral of my great grandma, and the death of a close childhood friend. I could not resolve the ambivalence I felt toward my roots and I have no way of knowing all the things I missed during those years. I ignored the discomfort by rarely going home.

Two experiences exemplify my profound ambivalence about going back. I had decided to go home for Christmas break after my first semester at college. After having been away at school for four months, I drove into town late one night. A good friend was working as a cook at the diner on the city's edge. It was near midnight and I knew she would be working the graveyard shift so I stopped to see her. Four other high school friends were hanging out at the diner having coffee. It was great seeing everyone. I joined them and we began laughing and catching up. Then the conversation turned and they started talking about how they hated their jobs, how they had all these bills, and how life was a drag. I, on the other hand, was away at college, which, by comparison to the descriptions they had just offered, was fun. As we talked, it was as if the gulf between us quietly grew.

They teased me some about leaving. They meant no harm. But, as I sat there, I felt increasingly like a visitor, an outsider. I had known these people since elementary school. We had snowmobiled, fished, gone to dances, delivered newspapers, spent nights at each others' houses, and pranked our friends' homes. But somehow, by leaving for college, a distance opened between us. I felt I no longer shared their experiences.

I left the diner that night and continued driving into town. I noticed little had changed along the highway, but it seemed I was seeing everything for the first time. I had seldom been outside the greater Detroit area until I left for college. For the first time, I noticed how the buildings were worn, almost sad looking. I also saw for the first time how hard my friends' lives were. I felt as gray as the dirty Michigan snow. I still felt out of place at college and now I felt out of place in my hometown as well. I was happy to be at college, but didn't want to lose my place at home with my friends. The conversation in the diner was confusing. I liked being away. I had high hopes for myself, yet felt guilty. I had no way of understanding my feelings.

The second disconcerting experience that Christmas involved Ma. Ma had always been the smartest person I knew. She did crossword puzzles every night while watching Johnny Carson. Even in college, I couldn't work crossword puzzles. When I was a child and asked her how to spell a word, she would say, "Look it up." This frustrated me. "How can I look it up if I don't know how to spell it?" I would ask her impatiently. She would reply, "What letter does the word start with?" After I told her the first letter, she would say I should now be able to find the word in the dictionary. Navigating the dictionary was only one of many things she taught me.

Now back from college, when I heard Ma use the wrong words or make inaccurate statements, I felt bad. I hated knowing she was incorrect and realizing she didn't know. I didn't correct her. All these years later, I still get a sick feeling in my stomach when I recall discovering Ma did not know everything. She was a tough-assed broad with a heart as big as the world. She both told you exactly what she thought and made sure anyone in need got help.

For a time, I worried Ma would be embarrassed around my college friends. I worried as much about whether *I* would be embarrassed when she was around my college friends. In retrospect, I understand these mixed emotions. My guilt, relief, shame, and ambivalence flowed from trying to navigate two very different worlds. All this had less to do with her than with my own loss and confusion. The more I learned, the more I realized Ma had taught me everything I *really* needed to know. In between, there were years I relinquished too much of home, too much of her.

No one ever directly said I had to abandon my neighborhood, my friends, or my past because of what would happen to me in college. Intuitively, I knew my neighborhood and the college atmosphere didn't mix well. The absence of anything mirroring my growing-up experiences, the lack of value for anything I knew or brought with me as a working-class student was a profound, if silent, message. The absence made it unnecessary for anyone to tell me directly to forsake my roots. The past didn't fit the world I had moved into.

Sometimes professors or students would talk about "city people." By implication, they really meant less educated factory workers. There would be some example, some story, told with an air of superiority about how much better we are if we are college educated. Sometimes I would stare at my desk and wonder if anyone noticed or knew that the people and experiences they were describing were mine. I was silently complicit in these acts of classism. I *knew* many people I grew up with were smart and had jobs. Even if they hadn't gone to college, they were smart in other ways. I was ashamed I couldn't defend my community; few colleges offer working-class students the tools and insights to value social class origins and heritage. I wasn't even sure what the defense should be, I just knew in those conversations people like me were considered inferior. We were undereducated, somehow "less than." I didn't understand all this until I was a doctoral student. As an undergraduate and MA student, I couldn't have explained what I was feeling.

PUTTING CLASS IN PERSPECTIVE

As I struggle today to understand those experiences, I worry about dwelling too much on the absence of something rather than on advantages I had. An orientation to seeing life by counting shortcomings is common. For instance, many college faculty and administrators talk about what is missing from the lives of students from poor or working-class homes, instead of acknowledging the incredible survival skills these same students bring to higher education. The focus is frequently on disadvantage instead of different perspectives—alternative interpretations of events and reality—that such students bring to campus.

I worry about attributing too much meaning to the past when telling about how my life unfolded, but the lives of first-generation college students have many common themes and experiences. As I began talking to my working-class peers, I frequently heard them mention how they, too, felt like outsiders, not understanding academic culture. They talked of speaking or dressing inappropriately. Over the years, I have come to see shared commonalities among working-class folks at all levels within academics, ranging from students, to faculty, to staffers.

University communities suggest, in subtle and not so subtle ways, that working-class and first-generation people succeed by leaving all their old lives behind and replacing them with a new and improved way of living gained via a college education. Sharing particular values and norms about achievement, accomplishment, independence, and individuality is assumed and these values are reinforced at every stage. Few colleges engage students in developing a bicultural response to the two worlds. Students come to believe they have to surrender the values and views of home if they want to "make it." "You can't go home again," is quoted as if it were a fait accompli. Even as the higher education community has developed a better understanding of the important role of pluralism on campus, class culture remains a mostly unexamined topic. College students from working and poor backgrounds have little opportunity to see their skills, music, language, and experiences validated in curricular or extracurricular life.

Lacking a sophisticated appreciation of all cultures, colleges advocate education as a way to build a life, as if the student had no life before college just because it was based on working-class values. It doesn't make sense to ask people to abandon who they are at their core in exchange for advancement. Providing educational opportunities so individuals can have more choices, or helping them learn empowering skills, is very different from suggesting they are incomplete or somehow "less" because of where they started. In becoming bicultural, these students have so much to offer friends, family, community, and their respective professions.

SOCIAL CAPITAL, SOCIAL MOBILITY, AND COLLEGE ADMINISTRATION

I have spent most of my twenty-year career in higher education. Only during the last few years have I begun understanding a particularly important aspect of the culture of higher education. That is, knowing how to "network" so you can move up the hierarchy. This view contrasts starkly with what I was taught growing up, about the importance of working hard and well and succeeding by *merit* alone. I'm not saying merit is always irrelevant—it counts for something—but I have learned there are other, far more important characteristics that affect how you advance in higher education administration.

As I began my career, I quickly became a successful administrator and educator. I worked well with staff and presented papers at national meetings.

Still, I never fully understood the value of professional networking. I assumed one's good work would speak for itself in terms of professional advancement. In the past three to four years, I have begun acknowledging to myself the critical role social capital, in the form of peer networking, plays in someone's professional appointments and advancements. Many top positions are filled based on recommendations from leaders in the field. If you haven't developed an extensive professional network, it is very difficult to move higher.

Today, as a college administrator and adjunct faculty member, I think more and more about how my class background has affected my own professional path, as well as that of others. I don't believe the threads of race, class, gender, and sexual orientation can be separated, but I know they have tremendous implications for one's career. You only have to look at who is promoted, who is tapped for leadership within professional organizations, and who is nominated for senior-level openings to appreciate this point. While it is hard to distinguish the significance of class, the critical role of social capital is clear. The better your connections, the more likely you are to advance.

I know from stories that other working-class professionals tell me that understanding the intricacies of positioning yourself for strategic career moves is complicated, for various reasons. Sometimes it relates to having little geographic flexibility due to family care obligations. Other times, the hurdle is not knowing or understanding there is a "track," so to speak, for moving into senior positions. There is also a nuance to mentoring and using professional organizations to make the right connections. As strange as it might sound, aspiring to senior leadership may come late to working-class professionals because we couldn't imagine ourselves in the roles, plus no one expected us to rise to these levels. Unpacking the specific implications of these issues is not easy. However, it isn't difficult to notice the absence of working-class people, especially lesbians, in leadership positions in higher education.

MOVING CROSS COUNTRY: TAKING ANOTHER STEP UP THE
ADMINISTRATIVE LADDER

Before taking the post I now have with California State University at Monterey Bay, I left my family in California and moved cross-country to take a position that allowed me to work with a great supervisor. The new situation would position me for a college vice presidency. It was a difficult decision because it meant living apart from my partner, but we agreed the move to Arkansas was imperative for my next professional appointment. At some level, the move contradicted who I am. I was torn between feelings of great opportunity and a longing to be home, with my partner, in my neighborhood, and in a familiar community.

After some reflection, I realized the family pattern I was most familiar and comfortable with was everyone living close together even as they grew up. Most families I know live no more than an hour apart, their kids grow up and have kids, and the grandparents are close. Something about moving across country for a job opportunity didn't feel quite right.

When my grandparents became ill at home in Detroit, I was living in California. I traveled back and forth every two to three weeks to take care of medical concerns until each of them passed away. The distance did not relieve me of my provider responsibilities. It would have never occurred to me to let someone else care for them. I don't know how much of what I feel about my current situation is related to class, but I suspect it is deeply so. People from working-class backgrounds have been taught to live close and take care of each other. Leaving home and living apart seems like an odd choice for me—it feels incongruent.

CONCLUSION: THE INTERSECTIONS OF SEXUAL ORIENTATION AND SOCIAL CLASS

It is impossible to distinguish precisely how multiple identities affect one's life. I have seen how much social capital affects one's academic trajectory and, in turn, I understand how different my options and choices would have been had I known more about the politics of higher education if only I had had more social capital. One's social class heritage profoundly shapes one's life, leading people to make intended and unintended choices about schooling and careers.

The idea of having educational choices didn't really enter my mind until I was a graduate student. A professor who was listening as I described how lucky I was to be in college acknowledged my exuberance and then asked what I wanted from my education. I was dumbfounded. I had never thought of this. I sat looking at her, amused by the question. I responded by asking her what difference would that make, what I wanted? I would encounter this situation in various forms over the next few years. Even today, it requires a conscious effort on my part to realize I have options, educational and professional, and they matter, greatly.

Had I had all the social capital I needed, such as having the right connections, getting appropriate advising and mentoring, knowing which college to attend, and various other forms of knowledge, almost certainly I would have never selected the undergraduate school I attended and perhaps not the graduate school where I got my master's degree either. Of course, the same holds true for the various jobs I have taken during and after I finished college. Had I understood the importance of networking, it is unlikely I would have spent so much time being an "outsider" in environments that "tolerated" my "diversity," but were not good career and personal matches. Probably, I would have worked in places more conducive to my coming out about my sexuality, and, perhaps, I would not have had to choose between keeping my job and staying closeted.

That particular job allowed me some trade-offs that made my life more comfortable in a larger sense. My path was similar to that of other working-class women I have met during my years in higher education.

In the middle of my career, I started gaining more senior-level administrative positions. As I have climbed the bureaucratic ladder, I have thought more and more about the implications of both class and sexual orientation for my career. Today, the bottleneck for senior-level positions makes the job market for upper-level academic jobs *very* competitive. At these highest levels, search committees look more intently for prestigious academic credentials, broader life experiences, and travel. At this point, professional networks are more critical than ever. Many working-class individuals lack the prestigious university credentials, research records, and professional networks needed to ascend the career ladder. Many LGBTQ professionals feel they are overlooked because of their sexual orientation. The unwritten rule is to favor institutional heterosexism.

As with most forms of institutional or organizational oppression, it is hard to measure precisely the impact of heterosexism and classism. People usually insist their personnel decisions derive from merit alone. They say there is no way of knowing someone's social class or sexual orientation unless the person is "out" about one or both, so it simply doesn't factor in. Yet, working-class or LGBTQ professionals can describe countless instances of day-to-day marginalization because of embedded class and heterosexist norms.

Today, I mostly avoid conversations about the limiting implications of sexual and social class prejudices. I have grown tired of people trying to explain away the impact of social capital or heterosexism. I don't imagine it would change my life much even if they did understand. I don't need to argue about what my experiences have been. On those few occasions when I am wondering aloud to my colleagues about how my professional and personal life might have been different today had I been born to wealthy and well-educated parents and was heterosexual, they assure me neither condition has affected my career trajectory *that* much.

I wish I could believe this, but every day I recognize the subtle and obvious ways class and sexual orientation affect one's professional life. My professional work is deeply influenced and shaped by who I am. I have the power to develop or change policies so they are more inclusive. I can alter business practices to make them more class or LGBTQ friendly. I am at the table when decisions are made and I have the power to effect a more equitable distribution of resources. I hope over the years I can help wear down prejudices so in the future there will be more space for people like me. Someday, if things go well, we will value each person's background and perspective, recognizing that each element affects what values an individual might contribute to the organization.

While I understand the limitations social class origins and sexual orientation can impose on one's professional life, I have lived in circumstances where being out about both class and sexual orientation has given me a remarkable freedom. Additionally, my grandmother gave me the profound gift of unconditional love. That was my social capital, and still is.

Ma called me not long before she died. Emboldened by a couple of Manhattans, she asked, "Are you gay?" At first, I tried to evade her question, but then I stopped and said, "Yes." She was silent for a few seconds and I realized she was crying. "I was so afraid you would never let me visit you again," she explained. I knew this meant she felt I had been pulling away and although it wasn't true, she feared I would lose all contact with her. Still, I was glad I had come out to her.

Not long after that telephone call, my grandmother began wearing a "HATE IS NOT A FAMILY VALUE" pin on the lapel of her coat. When she died, I buried the pin with her. Ma was the smartest person I have ever known.

NOTE

This chapter is dedicated in loving memory of "Ma" (Margaret E. Moll), 1919–1997.

Contributors

Donald C. Barrett is associate professor of sociology at California State University, San Marcos (CSUSM) and co-editor of *Sociological Perspectives* (2003–2007). His teaching and scholarship focus on social class, sexuality, and health, particularly on the experiences of working-class gay and homosexually active men.

Susan E. Borrego is an educator, administrator, and student advocate with twenty-five years of experience in student affairs and higher education. As a scholar/practitioner, she has spent her career grappling with the research and practice of creating inclusive campus environments. She is known for her abilities to motivate and foster a collaborative problem-solving climate and to quickly establish rapport with various campus constituencies. Additionally, she has served as a national consultant in higher education settings. She is currently Vice President of Student Affairs at California State University, Monterey Bay. She and her partner have two children.

Renny Christopher is Interim Associate Vice President for Faculty Affairs at CSU Channel Islands. She was formerly a professor of English. The Gustavas Myers Center for the Study of Human Rights in North America named her *The Viet Nam War/The American War: Images and Representations in Euro-American and Vietnamese Exile Narratives* (University of Massachusetts Press, 1995) as its outstanding book on human rights. Before she earned her PhD, she worked as a printing press operator, typesetter, carpenter, and horse wrangler. A poet as well as a teacher and scholar, she has published in a number of venues. *My Name is Medea* won the New Spirit Press chapbook award in 1996; *Longing Fervently for Revolution* won the Slipstream Press chapbook competition in 1998; and *Viet Nam and California*, a full-length collection, was published by Viet Nam Generation/Burning Cities Press in 1998.

Richard Greggory Johnson III is an assistant professor of educational leadership and policy studies in the College of Education and Social Services at the University of Vermont. He teaches classes in human resources management, and public policy and race in the United States. He has published articles in the *Journal of Public Affairs Education* and the *American Review of Public Administration*. His research addresses issues of social justice, including race, class, gender, and sexual orientation. He holds a doctorate in public administration and policy from Golden Gate University, MPS from DePaul University, and MA in Social and Public Policy from Georgetown University. Professor Johnson is a native of the Bronx, New York, and currently resides in Shelburne, Vermont.

Terell P. Lasane is a professor of psychology and faculty liaison for diversity and academic engagement at St. Mary's College of Maryland, the state's public honors college. He has taught at St. Mary's since 1994. He received his BS degree from Howard University in 1990, his MA and PhD degrees from the University of Delaware in 1993 and 1995, respectively. He conducts research on the academic self-concept of college students, with a special emphasis on racial identity development, sexual orientation identity development, and how the quality of intimate relationships correlates with individual self-esteem and emotional self-regulation. He has done extensive work in state and local governments, conducting needs assessments and program evaluations for community-based social service programs.

Andrea R. Lehrermeier is associate professor of geology at a large urban university. Her current scholarship focuses on effective science pedagogies for diverse student populations.

Michallene McDaniel is an assistant professor of sociology at Gainesville State College in Georgia. A native of Florida, she is finishing her PhD at the University of Georgia. She lives outside Atlanta with her partner and too many pets.

Kenneth Oldfield is an award-winning author and emeritus professor of public administration at the University of Illinois at Springfield. He has published articles on various topics, including property tax administration, Graduate Record Examination predictive validity, the Office of Economic Opportunity, personnel selection and orientation, community college funding disparities, property-assessment uniformity, tax increment financing, the human genome project, graduate internships, the philosophy of science, and the sociology of knowledge. His most recent research, conference presentations, and publications have focused on democratizing higher education through use of class-based affirmative action to recruit and place more college students and professors of poverty and working-class origins.

Denis M. Provencher is assistant professor of French and intercultural studies at the University of Maryland, Baltimore County. He has written on Jean Genet, the French gay press, French sexual citizenship and same-sex spaces, and the NBC sitcom *Will and Grace*. His work has appeared in *French Cultural Studies*, *Contemporary French Civilization*, *Contemporary French and Francophone Studies (SITES)*, *Speaking in Queer Tongues* (Illinois, 2004), and *The Sitcom Reader* (SUNY, 2005). His most recent book is *Queer French: Globalization, Language and Sexual Citizenship in France* (Ashgate Publishing, 2007).

Timothy J. Quain was born in 1951 to a St. Louis working-class family. He, his three brothers, and two sisters grew up in the Village of Cahokia, Illinois, on the east side of the Mississippi River. He attended Catholic schools through college and received his undergraduate degree from Quincy College in Quincy, Illinois, his master's degree from Southern Illinois University, and his doctorate from Middle Tennessee State University. He taught both elementary school and high school at inner-city Catholic schools in East St. Louis, Illinois. Since 1977, he has taught at a historically black college in Nashville, Tennessee. He spent twenty-six years with a life partner who died after a prolonged illness. Currently, he resides in suburban Nashville with his life partner of two years.

Nancy Ciucevich Story is assistant professor of English and coordinator of the Developmental English Program and the Writing Center at Community College of Denver, Colorado. She has worked at the college since 1999. Earlier, she taught at community colleges in Texas, Georgia, and Pennsylvania. She earned an MA in English at the University of North Carolina at Chapel Hill. Story has authored articles on the poetry, fiction, and literary criticism of Conrad Aiken. Her poetry has appeared in journals such as the *Black Fly Review*, *Kentucky Poetry Review*, and *The Old Red Kimono*. She has contributed photography, essays, and poetry to *Weird Sisters West*, a periodical published in Ft. Collins, Colorado. Nancy resides with her daughter, their golden retriever, and their tabby cat in Boulder, Colorado.

Bonnie R. Strickland is a lifetime academic. She was born and raised in the South where she attended public schools. She received her PhD in 1962 and took a position at Emory University. In 1973, she moved to the University of Massachusetts where she is professor emeritus and continues to teach. Her professional career in clinical psychology includes research, practice, and public advocacy.

Angelia R. Wilson teaches gender and political theory at the University of Manchester. Her research explores the intersection among feminist political theory, queer theory, and policies regulating sexuality (see, for example, "Practically between Post-Menopause and Post-Modern" in *Intersections between Feminism and Queer Theory* (Palgrave, 2006). Her book, *Below the Belt: Sexuality, Religion and the American South* (Wilson, 2000) articulates the tensions of U.S. sexual politics around constructions of femininity, masculinity, and such issues as abortion and homosexuality. Other publications consider the deconstruction of heteronormative family values and UK, EU, and U.S. policy debates.

Felice Yeskel is director of Class Action, a national, nonprofit organization focusing on issues of social class. Felice is a founder of United for a Fair Economy. She co-authored *Economic Apartheid in America* (New Press, 2000, 2005). She comes from a Jewish, working-class family from New York City's Lower East Side. Felice has led hundreds of workshops and given talks across the country about economic inequality and healing divisions among people of different class backgrounds, races, genders, and sexual orientations. She has frequently appeared as a guest on various radio shows discussing issues of economic justice and social change.

Index